REMAINS OF SOCIALISM

REMAINS OF SOCIALISM

Memory and the Futures of the Past in Postsocialist Hungary

Maya Nadkarni

CORNELL UNIVERSITY PRESS   ITHACA AND LONDON

First published 2020 by Cornell University Press

Library of Congress Cataloging-in-Publication Data

Names: Nadkarni, Maya, author.
Title: Remains of socialism : memory and the futures of the past in postsocialist Hungary / Maya Nadkarni.
Description: Ithaca : Cornell University Press, 2020. | Includes bibliographical references and index.
Identifiers: LCCN 2019039189 (print) | LCCN 2019039190 (ebook) | ISBN 9781501750175 (hardcover) | ISBN 9781501750182 (paperback) | ISBN 9781501750205 (pdf) | ISBN 9781501750199 (ebook)
Subjects: LCSH: Post-communism—Hungary. | Collective memory—Hungary. | Hungary—Civilization. | Hungary—Politics and government—1989–
Classification: LCC DB958.2 .N33 2020 (print) | LCC DB958.2 (ebook) | DDC 943.905/4—dc23
LC record available at https://lccn.loc.gov/2019039189
LC ebook record available at https://lccn.loc.gov/2019039190

To my parents, Ravindra and Sara Nadkarni
And my sisters, Neela and Asha Nadkarni

Contents

Figures

Acknowledgments

I have amassed countless personal and intellectual debts over the years of researching and writing this book. At Columbia University, I benefited from the intellectual inspiration and professional guidance of Marilyn Ivy, Claudio Lomnitz, John Pemberton, Carol Rounds, and Michael Taussig. I am particularly grateful to my dissertation advisor Rosalind C. Morris, whose scholarship, mentorship, and warm and incisive feedback set a very high standard for me to follow. And while my undergraduate mentors at Harvard University—the late Mary Steedly, Richard Rogers, and Robert Gardner—could not have anticipated the directions my research would take, I nonetheless am thankful to them for starting me on this path.

I have been very fortunate to find such a vibrant and congenial academic home in the Department of Sociology and Anthropology at Swarthmore College. I am grateful to all the past and present members of the department with whom I have had the honor to work over the years, particularly those who as chairs or colleagues helped to nurture this project or offered astute readings of portions of my manuscript: Farha Ghannam, Sarah Willie-LeBreton, Lee Smithey, Braulio Muñoz, and Christy Schuetze. Outside the department, more colleagues than I can list have offered insight and encouragement, but I am particularly grateful for conversations with the Mellon Tri-Co Brainstorming group on nostalgia (Farid Azfar, Sibelan Forrester, Tamsin Lorraine, Sangina Patnaik, and Zainab Saleh). I also thank Osman Balkan, Stacey Hogge, Rose Maio, Robert Rehak, Robert Weinberg, Patricia White, my colleagues in the Interpretation Theory program, and any others whose names I may have inadvertently omitted. Finally, the energy and intelligence of Swarthmore students are an endless source of inspiration to me. The lessons I have learned from teaching and mentoring undergraduates have made me a better scholar and writer, and I especially thank all those whose questions and enthusiasm in various iterations of my course "Memory, History, Nation" inspired me to reformulate some of the arguments in this book.

For reasons of privacy, I cannot name everyone in Hungary whose assistance is visible on these pages. But I extend my deepest appreciation to all those who opened up their lives and thoughts to me, or who otherwise helped me over the years: whether by sharing contacts, offering insight into the intricacies of Hungarian, securing access to archives and helping me locate documents, or providing perspective, criticism, and advice on my ever-evolving project. I am especially indebted to those interview subjects who agreed to speak on the record with me: Balázs Bodó, Ákos Eleőd, Sándor Holbok, Edit Kiss, Ákos Réthly, András Szilágyi, Gyula Thürmer, and Attila Vajnai. I also wish to express my gratitude to the staffs of the Fulbright Commission in Budapest, the former Magyar Millennium Commission, the former Country Image Center, the library at Parliament, the Open Society Archives, and the archives of the Budapest General Assembly for their assistance, as well as the Hungarian Film Union for loaning me copies of recent Hungarian films and ensuring me free access to Hungary's yearly film festival during the initial years of my fieldwork. And I am thankful for the support and insight of many friends and colleagues during my years of fieldwork, including Kristin Faurest, Kriszta Fenyő, György Horváth, John Nadler, Pál Nyíri, and Veronika Rónai. I am especially grateful to Ádám Tolnay, his Learning Enterprises project that brought me to Hungary as an English teacher in 1993 and 1999, and the friendship and hospitality of my host families.

In addition, I would like to thank a number of senior scholars of the region who kindly offered their feedback or advice at various points during the long trajectory of this project, including Csaba Békés, András Bozóki, István Deák, Bruce Grant, Péter György, Gail Kligman, László Kürti, Katalin Miklóssy, István Rév, Katherine Verdery, and Alexei Yurchak. Special thanks to several Hungarianist colleagues—Krisztina Fehérváry, Zsuzsa Gille, and Martha Lampland—who have been both scholarly inspiration and cherished interlocutors over the years. This book has also benefited greatly from conversations with Paulina Bren, Richard Esbenshade, Kristen Ghodsee, Jessica Greenberg, Krista Harper, Jason James, Csilla Kalocsai, Larisa Kurtović, Jessie Labov, Marikay McCabe, András Mink, Jason Moralee, Serguei Oushakine, Michael Reay, Zsófia Réti, Olga Shevchenko, Stefan Siegel, Aniko Szucs, and Marko Živković. My friend József Litkei in particular has been unfailingly generous with his scholarly and editorial expertise. Thank you all for your feedback and support; any errors are of course mine alone.

Initial research for this project was funded by a Foreign Language and Area Studies language training grant, a Faculty Fellowship from Columbia University, a Fulbright IIE fellowship, a National Science Foundation Graduate Fellowship, a fellowship from the International Dissertation Field Research Fellowship Program of the Social Science Research Council with funds provided by the Andrew W. Mellon Foundation, and an East European Studies Dissertation Fellowship from the American Council of Learned Societies. In the early years of my research, I appreciated the opportunity to develop my arguments at the Woodrow Wilson International Center's Junior Scholars' Training Seminar. I was also very grateful for the unofficial yet no less crucial support I found in the intellectual community at the yearly Soyuz Symposium of Postsocialist Cultural Studies and in the library, courses, and summer research seminars I audited at Central European University in Budapest.

More recently, I am grateful to Swarthmore College for providing me Faculty Research Grants to make trips to Hungary each summer, as well as a James A. Michener Faculty Fellowship that enabled me to take a year-long sabbatical to complete the manuscript. I have also had the good fortune to further develop this manuscript during fellowships within two communities of outstanding scholars: the Harriman Institute for Russian, Eurasian, and East European Studies at Columbia University and the Aleksanteri Institute-Finnish Centre for Russian and East European Studies at the University of Helsinki. Finally, I gratefully acknowledge the opportunity to work with Peter Dimock during my SSRC-IDRF Book Development Fellowship from the Social Science Research Council.

At Cornell University Press, I am very indebted to James Lance for his enthusiasm and support of the project, and to Ellen Labbate, Stephanie Munson, Brock Schnoke, and Kristen Bettcher and the staff at Westchester Publishing Services for their editorial and logistical assistance. My two reviewers helped me to clarify and extend the reach of my arguments and I am grateful for their thoughtful and generous engagement.

I regret that such a long list of people and institutions—not to mention the inevitable accidental omissions—cannot fully convey my appreciation of all the support and effort exerted on my behalf. But my most heartfelt thanks go to my family, almost all of whom I lost in the long years between the first glimmers of inspiration for this project and its ultimate completion: my sister Neela, my mother Sara, and my father Ravindra. The joy of having known them and the pain of their absence have shaped me and my scholarship profoundly. I also thank my sister and academic comrade-in-arms, Asha, for her friendship, wisdom, and generosity of spirit. However inadequate a tribute, I dedicate this project to them all, with love and gratitude.

Portions of the following chapters were previously published, although they appear here in substantially revised form: chapter 1, as "The Death of Socialism and the Afterlife of Its Monuments: Making and Marketing the Past in Budapest's Statue Park Museum," in *Contested Pasts (Memory and Narrative)*, ed. Kate Hodgkin, Steve Sturdy, and Susannah Radstone, 193–207 (London: Routledge, 2003). Chapter 3, as "'But It's Ours': Nostalgia and the Politics of Cultural Identity in Postsocialist Hungary," in *Postcommunist Nostalgia*, ed. Maria Todorova and Zsuzsa Gille, 190–214 (New York: Berghahn Books, 2010).

Unless otherwise indicated, all translations and photographs are my own.

Names and Abbreviations of Hungary's Main Political Parties (1990–2010)

Fidesz	Fidesz—Hungarian Civic Union (Fidesz—Magyar Polgári Szövetség)
FKGP	Independent Smallholders, Agrarian Workers, and Civic Party (Független Kisgazda-, Földmunkás- és Polgári Párt), usually shortened to Independent Smallholders' Party (Független Kisgazdapárt)
KDNP	Christian Democratic People's Party (Kereszténydemokrata Néppárt)
Jobbik	Jobbik Movement for a Better Hungary (Jobbik Magyarországért Mozgalom)
MDF	Hungarian Democratic Forum (Magyar Demokrata Fórum)
MIÉP	Hungarian Justice and Life Party (Magyar Igazság és Élet Pártja)
MSZP	Hungarian Socialist Party (Magyar Szocialista Párt)
SZDSZ	Alliance of Free Democrats—Hungarian Liberal Party (Szabad Demokraták Szövetsége—a Magyar Liberális Párt), usually shortened to Alliance of Free Democrats (Szabad Demokraták Szövetsége)
Workers' Party	Workers' Party (Munkáspárt)

REMAINS OF SOCIALISM

Introduction

With the end of communism in Hungary, many people eagerly assumed that the physical and symbolic remnants of the past era would similarly vanish from public life and everyday activity. All that remained was to sweep away the detritus of the recent past: a process wittily depicted by one of the campaign posters for the Hungarian Democratic Forum (Magyar Demokrata Fórum, MDF), the winning party of Hungary's first postsocialist democratic elections in 1990. "National spring cleaning!" (*Országos tavaszi nagytakarítást*) the poster announced, with a photograph of a garbage can overflowing with a statue of Stalin, Mao's Little Red Book, and other party memorabilia. This vivid visual argument jokingly played on Trotsky's famous phrase by tossing the formerly venerated objects of official state culture into a literal dustbin of history.

Meanwhile, in everyday life, Hungarians celebrated the end of the regime with ironic "retro" parties and new entrepreneurial ventures that marketed the relics of official state culture as kitsch to both locals and foreign tourists. For example, just a few blocks from Moscow Square (a central transportation hub in Budapest), young entrepreneurs opened a communist-themed pizzeria under the name of "Marxim"—a play on both the famous Parisian restaurant "Maxim" and Marxism. With a red star over its door and an interior decorated with images of Lenin and other state socialist kitsch, the restaurant was the subject of local and international news articles gleefully reporting that the newly capitalist Hungary was now making a profit out of socialism's remains. The pizzeria's humorous but triumphant display of mastery over the recent past made it a popular

FIGURE 0.1   "National spring cleaning!" MDF campaign poster. Artwork by Béla Aba, 1990.

hangout in the early years of postsocialism. As the owners declared on Marxim's menu, "The outside may be communist but we are capitalist to the very marrow of our bones."

Such images and stories from the time of Hungary's political transition sought to portray the disorienting transformation of everyday life into history as a process that was both natural and inevitable: a return to national authenticity by eliminating the debris of foreign occupation. Although similar examples can be found across the region, in Hungary the stakes of this transformation from Soviet satellite to member of democratic Europe were particularly high. Beginning in the early 1960s, under the leadership of General Secretary János Kádár, Hungarians had enjoyed greater liberties and a higher standard of living than many of their Soviet bloc neighbors. This experience of "goulash communism," as well as participation in the thriving second economy of late socialism, now inspired many Hungarians to consider themselves well-poised to lead the region in joining the West as political and economic equals, ready to take their place in the new global order. Even the peaceful demise of the regime itself—a bloodless and largely bureaucratic affair—offered a welcome contrast to the violent political upheavals that had punctuated Hungary's tumultuous twentieth century. Demonstrating mastery over socialism's material and metaphorical remains thus appeared to be one of the final steps to transform socialist citizens into new postsocialist subjects—and to enter the democratic and prosperous future that awaited them.

Nearly twenty years later, in 2009, a different mood prevailed as I sat in Marxim with my good friend Levente, then in his early forties. Levente had mentioned that he had met some friends there a few weeks before, and when I expressed my surprise that Marxim was still in business, he suggested that I join him there for lunch. Like many others, Levente had come to regard his initial expectations of the political transformation as painfully optimistic and naive. Such disappointment has become endemic to the region (Ghodsee 2011), but thanks to the 2008 global economic crisis that hit Hungary with disproportionate force, the disenchantment in Hungary was particularly acute. That year, a Pew Research study announced that 72 percent of the Hungarians they surveyed believed that they were currently worse off economically than they had been under communism (Pew Global Attitudes Project 2009, 5). No other postsocialist country in the survey expressed such widespread dissatisfaction. Indeed, the relative lack of interest in celebrating the twentieth anniversary of 1989 suggested that the end of state socialist rule no longer represented a chronological break, but instead a failed point of origin—a lost opportunity for cultural, political, and economic transformation.

Surprisingly, this disillusionment did not fuel a nostalgic desire to return to the communist past. Rather, it reflected a frustrated orientation toward the future: the disappointment that the bright future promised by the end of communism had still not materialized. This logic—one that mourned not "what I once had," but "what I should *already* have"—became clear to me as my friend and I waited for our pizza and discussed the effects of the financial crisis on his parents' finances and his own opportunities for freelance work as an editor and translator. In the midst of our conversation, he paused to look at Marxim's empty tables and its faded, dusty furnishings with a rueful smile. "Even this place is over its prime," he told me, gesturing at a propaganda poster. "Making fun of this stuff feels odd now, because no one says things like that anymore." Marxim no longer inspired laughter at the former era. Instead, Levente told me, it made him feel wistful for the optimism of the early years of postsocialism, when as a young university student entering adulthood, it seemed as if one could indeed remember the past only to laugh at it. "It's not a place to ironically remember the communist past anymore," he concluded. "It's become a memory to itself, to how it used to be fifteen years ago." Once a triumphant display of mastery over the remainders of the communist era, Marxim was now itself a relic of the failed hopes of transition.

Yet the obsolescence of Marxim's memory work does not mean that other attempts to banish or domesticate Hungary's remains of socialism were outdated. Instead, Hungary's recent experiences of crisis and disappointment only inspired renewed complaints that transition had failed because the past had not been dealt with *correctly*. A few months after my lunch at Marxim, in the spring of 2010, the Hungarian electorate voted into power the right-wing political party Fidesz,[1]

FIGURE 0.2   Interior of Marxim restaurant. Personal photograph, 2017.

which pledged to repair the missed opportunities of two decades earlier by finally accomplishing a "revolution" that would leave the socialist past behind. As part of this work of completing Hungary's transition from socialism, the local government in Budapest returned "Moscow Square" to its pre-1951 name of "Kálmán Széll Square" in 2011.

Unlike a generation earlier, however, Fidesz did not remove such remains of socialism simply to break from the socialist era. Instead, by declaring it urgent to eradicate the name "Moscow" from the cityscape two decades after the departure of Soviet troops, Fidesz revived the past as an ongoing danger that was necessary to fight. Over its first term in power (2010–2014), Fidesz would use the claim that it was finally eliminating Hungary's remains of socialism as one of its justifications for enacting sweeping legal and constitutional changes that threatened much of the past decades' democratic progress. Remains of socialism now enabled these political actors not to bury the socialist era, but to keep it alive as a problem that only they could solve.

This book is about the shifting fates of the memory of the socialist past in post-socialist Hungary. Beginning in the early 1990s, it spans more than two decades of political and social transformation to examine attempts at "spring cleaning" the remains of the past era from both private life and public culture—and to analyze the obstacles that would emerge to frustrate this fantasy of historical mastery. To do so, I introduce the concept of "remains"—both physical objects and cultural remainders—to symbolize all that Hungarians sought to leave behind as they struggled to remake themselves as new postsocialist subjects. Their heated attempts to master the obstinate remainders of an ambivalent past also became struggles to determine the future, as well as to mourn the futures that were never realized.

Like every postsocialist country, Hungary's physical and cultural landscapes are permeated by residues and legacies of four decades of state socialist rule. Indeed, the condition of subsisting among remnants of discredited pasts and failed historical trajectories may not be the exception but the norm in this age of "post"s. But in my formulation, "remains" are far more than simply the obvious material leftovers and legacies of Soviet occupation (what would be called *maradvány* in Hungarian). Instead, I argue for conceptualizing remains as produced by a modern historical optics that anxiously scans the present for threatening signs of an unwanted past and thus undesired future. Particular remains only intrude and demand attention at certain moments, by certain people, and to certain ends—as the impermanence of Marxim's memory work in the early years of postsocialism demonstrates. The battles to define what constitutes a remain of socialism, and how best to banish or master it, thus represent an active, contested, and shifting process through which people in Hungary—from politicians and activists to artists and entrepreneurs—struggled both to distance the recent past and to express fantasies and fears about the future yet to come.

In the chapters that follow, I track the changing fortunes of socialism's remains in order to perform an archaeology of postsocialism's future hopes and present-day frustrations, beginning with the optimism of the early years of transition and ending with the political and economic crises that inspired Hungary's recent turn toward illiberal democracy and what critics view as right-wing authoritarianism. The heterogeneity of the cultural objects, sites, and sentiments that emerged in Hungary's public culture as remains of state socialism—as well as the communities of memory that produced and were produced by these relics—demands a methodology that follows a similarly varied and restless path. My analysis thus moves in roughly chronological order to travel among museums and monuments, public protests and celebrations, and private stories, jokes, and conversations. Each chapter investigates a cultural object that exemplifies the logic of remains: from exiled statues of Lenin and commodified relics of state socialist mass culture to discredited official histories and the scandalous secrets of the communist regime's informers. My examination of the different tensions and contradictions embodied by each set of remains enables me to illuminate some of the key moments in

Hungary's postsocialist political and social transformations and to demonstrate that the debates and controversies these remains inspired did not merely reflect but actively produced far-ranging shifts in Hungary's politics of memory.

Over time, as the joyful optimism of "spring cleaning" gave way to the unexpected challenges of democratic politics and participation in the market economy, each attempt to dispose of the remnants of an unwanted past would fail to produce the desired present, thus leaving the search for remains to begin anew. Ultimately, the battle over remains would symbolize not the promise of mastering the past, but rather the perceived impossibility of doing so. The problem of remains would come to represent the frustrated ambitions of transition itself, by offering a way to explain the disappointments of the present as the failure to leave the past behind.

Why Remains?

The stories told about memory at the margins of the West tend to be narratives of loss and ruination, macabre relics and spectral hauntings.[2] These studies offer important insights into how the traumas and injustices of the past continue to affect present-day politics and society. Their focus on unwelcome legacies of troubled pasts has also provided a crucial corrective to presentist models of memory that, as Richard Werbner argues, "reduce memory to an artefact of the here and now, as if it were merely a backwards construction after the fact" (1998, 2). Instead, he maintains, "intractable traces of the past are felt on people's bodies, known in their landscapes, landmarks and souvenirs, and perceived as the tough moral fabric of their social relations" (2–3).

Although the conceptual vocabulary of ghosts, ruins, and similar metaphors of an unmastered past is valuable, it nevertheless risks limiting our attention to only the negative experiences of the past's remainders. This tendency is common in the interdisciplinary field of memory studies, due to the centrality of the Holocaust and psychoanalytic theories of trauma in some of its initial formulations.[3] Scholars have recently called for expanding the range of the affects we study: to move beyond the dysphoria of trauma, mourning, and melancholia to also consider pleasure and laughter, and to ask how such varied responses interact with nonmemorial affects to produce "affective ecologies" that ground dispositions toward past history as well as contemporary politics (Vermeulen 2012, 232; Hamilton 2010). This approach is particularly crucial in the postsocialist context where, as Alexei Yurchak reminds us, we cannot understand the socialist past without appreciating "the creative and positive meanings with which [citizens] endowed their socialist lives—sometimes in line with the announced goals of the state, sometimes in spite of them, and sometimes relating to them in ways that did not fit either-or dichotomies" (2005, 9).

I thus use the more flexible language of remains, which we can consider most simply as "matter out of time" (to borrow from Mary Douglas's famous formulation of dirt as "matter out of place" [2002, 36]), to emphasize the ambiguities of the recent past and the ambivalent emotions it continues to evoke: whether anger, sadness, humor, boredom, veneration, disgust—or affection. Even painful remembrances of guilt or persecution can inspire creative acts of cultural imagination.[4] Whether socialist remains arouse embittered laments, nostalgic longing, or mocking laughter, they nonetheless offer ways to articulate new forms of value, identity, and aspiration vis-à-vis both the problematic past and an uncertain future.

Moreover, many of the established tropes of an unpalatable past also embed temporal assumptions about the fate of that past, whether the ghost's threatened return or the ruin's failure to materialize the anticipated future.[5] In contrast, my conceptual framework of "remains" avoids assuming in advance the trajectories that the past's afterlives may take. By tracing the evolution of postsocialist memory practices over more than two decades, my analysis emphasizes the impermanence and contingency of each attempt at historical mastery, and how once-settled questions and battles would repeatedly reemerge in public life.[6] This longitudinal approach thus focuses attention on the ways in which different remains at different moments enter or fade out of cultural focus. It demonstrates that the process of identifying and grappling with socialist remains is contested and dynamic, formulated and reformulated in response to a changing present.

In other words, although my study shares the critique of approaches whose "tendency toward voluntarism" (Olick 2003, 7) reduces the burden of the past to merely a projection of the present, I do not view these historical traces as entirely predetermined or intractable. Instead, I insist on the agency of the various social and political actors who battled to define the future by eliminating signs of the past's unwanted presence. Although they each viewed the past as a problem to be solved, the nature and location of this burden, the meanings assigned to it, and who felt it most acutely varied across communities and over time. Moreover, I build on Jeffrey Olick's insight that "memorymakers don't always succeed in creating the images they want and in having them understood in the ways they intended" (2003, 7) to show how each attempt to determine and master the past via a specific set of remains only sparked further debate and controversy. The emphases and elisions to be found in any given form of remains would lay the groundwork for the ways people would define and encounter future ones.

To support these arguments, I draw inspiration from several critical trajectories. The first is the anthropological critique of postsocialist transitology. Much as Katherine Verdery anticipated in her 1996 study, *What Was Socialism, and What Comes Next?*, the past decades have demonstrated the failure of early models of "transition" that predicted a unilinear transformation from the socialist era into a future predetermined by Western ideal types of the free market and liberal democracy (15–16).[7] I extend this critique of teleological narratives of economic progress and the victory of consumer capitalism to the politics of memory, arguing against the assumption that the demise of state socialism entailed the fracturing of one historical narrative and its replacement by another: the unproblematic return of "authentic" history out of the deep freeze of state amnesia.[8] Instead, remains are emblematic of the uneven and conflicting trajectories of historical and cultural transformation: at once out of time and yet all too present.

My second inspiration is Walter Benjamin's unfinished work on the nineteenth-century proto-shopping malls, the Paris arcades. Faded and unfashionable by the time of his research in the 1920s and 1930s, the obsolete architecture and outdated commodities of the arcades were relics of an earlier, more optimistic era of consumer culture—and thus, in Benjamin's view, a crucial site to excavate capitalist modernity's past fantasies and aspirations (Benjamin 2002). His analysis of the forgotten dreams and utopian hopes that lay petrified in the now-worthless detritus of a past era guides my own investigation of Hungary's politics of memory. My emphasis on remains as sites to imagine better tomorrows and to mourn the futures that never came to pass treats hope and aspiration as ethnographic categories, by studying not merely what is and what was, but also what my subjects imagined might be. Remains thus both fracture triumphalist narratives of historical progress and offer new possibilities of disrupting the present by reminding us of its unrealized futures—whether the fantasy of Western consumerist abundance, the hopes that democracy would bring historical justice and restitution, or the utopian impulses of the state socialist project itself (Benjamin 2002; Buck-Morss 1989, 2000). Rather than view the past and future in opposition, I thus join recent work in anthropology that emphasizes the coconstruction of past and future, in which "memory practices form an explicit part of future-making" (Shaw 2013).[9]

This focus on the cultural productivity of an outdated and unwanted past resonates with the third and final body of literature that inspired this study: psychoanalytic theories of subject formation, which understand identity as constituted through not only positive identifications but also negative disavowals. Specifically, my use of "remains" parallels Jacques Lacan's concept of the remainder (as *objet petit a*): that element of the subject that is split from itself in order to produce itself as unitary and coherent.[10] That is, I argue that the crises of contemporaneity embodied by remains (what constitutes the present? what is rejected as merely past?) were ultimately crises of subjectivity: how to define who "we" are and what is "ours." Such questions are of course endemic to modernity, but they had particular inflection for the citizens of the Soviet bloc, who viewed the communist system as inhumane and unnatural and who used the regime's suppression of "true history" as a powerful means of political mobilization. After the end of the regime, they thus battled to produce themselves as new postsocialist subjects by renarrating long-familiar elements of public and everyday life as mere Soviet anachronism, and thus a divergence from the authentic course of national history.

Such memory work could not entirely efface the contradiction at the heart of the experience of late state socialism,[11] which many Hungarians experienced as injustice and oppression *and* a relatively peaceful and materially secure existence: that is, both the violence of repression and the modest luxuries of "refrigerator socialism" and the campfire songs of the Young Pioneers.[12] These dichotomized visions of the socialist past did not stand in simple opposition (a logic that Yurchak has critiqued as "binary socialism" [2005, 4]).[13] Rather, they reflected the paradoxical nature of political citizenship during late socialism. After Hungary's failed revolution against Soviet rule in 1956 and the harsh years of retaliation that followed, the regime sought to normalize relations with its citizenry by rewarding those who withdrew from political protest into a relatively comfortable and seemingly depoliticized private sphere. Over the decades, as the regime steadily increased the population's living standards and access to consumer goods, many of its citizens became accustomed to seeking meaning and fulfillment in their domestic activity (whether family life or working in the second economy) and were encouraged to regard the public world of politics as mostly irrelevant to their personal concerns. But this perception of being able to pursue private endeavors relatively independently from politics did not represent autonomy from the regime. Rather, it was one of the very ways that the regime secured its legitimation. In fact, as Martha Lampland argues, the stark public/private divide helped to reproduce the system by convincing people that they were powerless to change it, as well as encouraging them to overlook commonalities among the values, practices, and beliefs in both realms (1995, 245–247).

In the early years after the end of state socialism, the coziness and familiarity of socialist remains, as much as the painful memories of foreign occupation they also embodied, would present a challenge for a new Hungary now defined as the very negation of the past era. In everyday conversation, many people readily discussed pleasant memories of the recent past or drew negative comparisons between then and now, whether that concerned economic hardship and the loss of social welfare measures, new scandals of greed and corruption by Hungary's emerging political and economic elites, or the growing disappointment with a Western consumer culture that stigmatized Hungarian goods and consumers as inferior. But most people were also aware that such positive evaluations of the past could not be widely expressed in public or political forums without seeming to endorse the oppressive politics of the previous regime and to confirm a Western hierarchy that condemned such sentiments as evidence of Hungary's failed modernity.

In postsocialist media discourse, political rhetoric, and symbolic and actual encounters with the "West,"[14] many Hungarians thus learned to regard the recent past with discomfort and to treat these two sets of memories as incommensurable. Lacan's formulation of the remainder as that part of self that is outside the self—both an alien presence and uncomfortably familiar—helps to illuminate the ways that remains of socialism would unsettle the fantasy of a clean break with a foreign past.[15] Remains seemed to offer the possibility of historical mastery, but they also troubled the fiction of a unified national subjectivity by threatening to make visible those intimate aspects of collective historical experience that people now felt compelled to reject.

Unmastering the Past

My analysis of remains as both symbolizing and frustrating the desire for a mastered past is thus not another story of the "crisis" of historical memory and national identity in Eastern Europe. This is a familiar narrative of journalists and scholars who have treated the status of memory in the former Soviet bloc as a crucial diagnostic of national health: viewing a lack of historical consensus as pathological and analyzing the literal content of memorial practices for signs of danger—whether "too much," "not enough," or the "wrong" kinds of memory altogether.[16] In the first decade of postsocialism, for example, any sign of positive remembrance of the socialist past in the region—whether expressed as nostalgia for its mass culture or the success of communist successor parties in democratic elections—sparked a flurry of media and scholarly concern that the country's democratic transformation was in danger. And observers not only pathologized the communist past: while they hailed Eastern Europe's "return to history" in the form of revived cultural identities and the rectification of communism's historical distortions, they also feared that the renewal of national identification would lead to violence (as in the war in Yugoslavia) or the persecution of ethnic minorities.

Such moral panics, whether originating locally or abroad, were often driven by the desire to establish democratic political norms, to pay justice to history's victims, and to forestall the repetition of violence in the future. But the language of pathology their rhetoric deployed also embedded normative assumptions about what proper "mourning," "remembrance," and "coming to terms" with the past might look like—and often presumed that memory practices in the West represent the standard to which all others should aspire. Indeed, if the end of communism in Eastern Europe represented a "return to history," many in the West hailed the demise of its Cold War enemy as signaling the "end of history" (Fukuyama 1992) that proved conclusively the triumph of liberal democracy and obviated the need for any critical examination of the West's own mnemonic habits, distortions, and amnesias. This triumphalism has now begun to fade, as neoliberalism has fallen into crisis across the globe and the West's monopoly of the future seems less certain. And yet the fascination with how the countries of the former Soviet bloc remember has only become more acute, as a way for the West to buttress its shaky legitimacy by continuing to "fix Eastern Europe in the past" (Boyer 2010, 23).

Anthropologists have long critiqued such temporal disjunctions between the "normal" West and its "backward" Others, burdened by inassimilable, pathological pasts they are unwilling or unable to cast aside. This logic is perhaps exemplified by the very use of the term "postsocialism" to describe a limited region of the globe—as if the United States were not also affected by the legacies and remainders of the end of the Cold War. "Post" risks positioning its subjects—whether postauthoritarian, postcolonial, or postsocialist—as inhabiting the present in a perpetual state of belatedness:, what Marianne Hirsch, in her study of "postmemory," calls "a location in an aftermath" (2012, 5).[17]

This denial of coevalness (Fabian 1983) is familiar from developmentalism, which similarly temporalizes spatial difference and subscribes to a notion of a single modernity as an endpoint (Ferguson 2006; Gupta 1998). The violence of this subjectification enables two key political and historical elisions. First, the discourse of backwardness obscures commonalities and continuities across temporal and spatial divides: the way fantasies of being "new and modern . . . [rely] on the survival of Soviet modes of existence" (Flatley 2001, 86), and how "the socialist project, particularly its investment in heavy industry, was not restricted to the 'other' Europe, nor did its lifeline terminate abruptly in 1989" (Scribner 2003, 15, quoted in Petrović 2014, 100).

Second, this unilinear narrative of progress assumes that knowledge and value flow only from West to East (or Global North to Global South), and developmental time itself moves only in one direction. Yet, as scholars of both postsocialism and postcolonialism have argued, the fantasy of European modernity is not always a fantasy of futurity. For factory workers in the former Yugoslavia, their loss of prestige and declining production standards after the end of state socialism only distanced them farther from Europe; in the words of one worker, "We were much more a part of Europe in socialism than we are now" (Petrović 2010, 141). And even the temporality of progress itself has become increasingly anachronistic. James Ferguson argues that Western discourse about Africa has become increasingly de-developmentalized and detemporalized. That is, this logic no longer considers the continent's poorest countries to be temporally *behind* the West, but permanently *beneath* it (2006, 189–190). For the Zambian mineworkers Ferguson interviewed, modernity thus "was not an anticipated future but a dream to be remembered from the past" (186).

My analysis extends these scholars' line of critique into the realm of memory, examining how the conditions for "entering Europe" and becoming fully "modern" included the demand that Eastern Europe sacrifice previous historical narratives (whether communist or nationalist) and disavow the meaningfulness of earlier lifeways. This imperative to transform both what and how the East remembers also included the expectation that these nation-states conform to Western European memory regimes, through which claims to national suffering or cultural value are legible only insofar as they support preexisting conceptual frameworks, such as the transcendent value of European liberalism, the centrality of the Holocaust for European memory, and the battle against totalitarianism as the cornerstone of modern European identity (Kraenzle and Mayr 2017, Pakier and Wawrzyniak 2015). Many of the remains that I examine in this book thus emerge in tension with, or in response or resistance to, such transnational memory practices. For example, consumers of socialist nostalgia ironically refer to global discourses of cultural heritage to justify their enjoyment, and the local commemoration of victims of communism borrows from (and competes with) forms and practices of Holocaust commemoration established in Western Europe and North America.

Like other countries of the former Soviet bloc, Hungary is famously concerned with questions of its past. The contemporary desire to identify usable national pasts and eliminate "inauthentic" ones is deeply rooted, particularly given the political disruptions and historical discontinuities of Hungary's twentieth century. But the production of remains—signs of an unwanted past that impedes entering the future—reflects not only these local processes of memory. Instead, remains also exemplify the condition of being "post" in a temporalized global hierarchy. Remains represent local responses to the global production of both futurity and obsolescence, advancement and backwardness; they are symptoms of a global politics of the present that is always in danger of excluding certain peoples, landscapes, histories, and practices from flows of capital, information, and value.

Rather than interpret remains as a sign of national pathology, this book thus asks how, why, by whom, and in what ways the past becomes pathologized as a problem in the first place, and how this self-reflexive perception of a challenging past can be the source of present-day cultural productivity. I show how the worry of not dealing with the past properly would provide new opportunities in both public and everyday life for Hungarians to narrate not only the recent experience of state socialism but also the bright hopes, persistent anxieties, and increasingly sharp critiques that emerged from ongoing encounters and negotiations with global modernity.

Although my scope is limited to the Hungarian context, my analysis of socialism's remains is ultimately a study of modern historical subjectivity and the overlapping, incommensurable, and conflicting narrative horizons that compose it. Symbolizing that which was excluded in the formation of Hungary as a new postsocialist subject, remains became sites to articulate new positionalities vis-à-vis both an unwelcome past and a long-anticipated present whose fantasies of democratic transparency and consumer plenitude would soon be disenchanted. The challenge of remains would provide a crucial way for Hungarians to voice growing concerns about the place of the nation in the new global order—as well as the fear that Hungary itself might be left aside and discarded as a mere remain of globalizing neoliberalism.

The Structure of This Book

During my fieldwork in the 1990s and 2000s, there was hardly a sphere of political or public culture that was not saturated with attempts to discredit or enshrine almost every important historical figure from Hungary's turbulent twentieth century. Their stories were often embedded in broader national narratives of mourning, martyrdom, victimhood, and defeat: during the twentieth century, Hungary lost two world wars, was invaded by two major foreign powers (Nazi Germany and the Soviet Union), and lost two-thirds of its territory in the 1920 Trianon peace treaty imposed after its defeat in World War I. As István Rév observes, Hungary's narrative of national selfhood has thus been one of "battles lost, and consequently a continuous history of executions, exiles, and political suicides. The normal public rituals of Hungarian history are, accordingly, not victory parades but funerals and reburials" (Rév 2005, 41–42). Moreover, these political upheavals also brought about profound social and economic transformations. Hungary went from being a multinational empire dominated by Hungarian elites to an almost monoethnic state with significant parts of the ethnic Hungarian community becoming minorities in neighboring countries. The country also underwent two significant economic reorganizations: the communist nationalization of the economy and collectivization of agriculture in the 1950s and 1960s, and then the shift of that wealth back into a new set of private hands in the 1990s.

Although I cannot do full justice to chronicling the events that define the history of modern Hungary, a brief chronological summary is necessary to ground the discussion in the chapters that follow. At the beginning of the twentieth century, Hungary was a European middle power that ruled with Austria over a vast multinational empire that stretched over much of today's Central and Eastern Europe. The Austro-Hungarian Monarchy collapsed in the final days of World War I, and Hungary became a democratic republic in 1918; a Bolshevik Soviet republic for several months in 1919; and then a constitutional monarchy led by Regent Miklós Horthy, a former naval admiral, who would remain in power until after the Nazi occupation in the final days of World War II. Horthy's interwar government was politically conservative, and its policies were driven and justified by the demand for a return to pre-Trianon borders. This goal of territorial revisionism would lead Hungary to ally itself with Nazi Germany during World War II (although Horthy's government would later unsuccessfully try to reach out to Allied powers late in the war). In 1944–1945, Hungary was occupied first by Nazi Germany and then by Soviet troops. The country emerged defeated in 1945 with its capital city severely damaged, its territory returned to its post-Trianon borders, and with casualties of nearly 900,000, including almost 500,000 of Hungary's Jewish citizens killed in the Holocaust.

After the war, Hungary became a democratic republic, but Hungarian communists, with support from the Soviets, worked to undermine their political competitors and the integrity of the election process. By 1948 the communists managed to gain almost total control, and in 1949 they practically eliminated opposition parties and passed a new constitution modeled after that of the Soviet Union. Over the next four decades of communist rule, both the nature of political authority and its means of legitimation would undergo several transformations. The harsh measures favored by Mátyás Rákosi, in power from 1948 to 1953, fell out of favor after Stalin's death, and he was replaced by the more reform-minded Imre Nagy before then retaking power in 1955.[18] The post-Stalinist thaw paved the way for Hungary's brief popular uprising against both the returning Rákosi regime and Soviet rule in 1956, but this revolution was brutally suppressed by Soviet troops.

Over the next three decades, János Kádár would lead Hungary, and the first years of his rule were ones of violent retaliation for the 1956 revolution. Beginning in the 1960s, however, Kádár's regime gradually liberalized and attempted to reconcile with Hungary's citizens by offering them a higher living standard (increasingly subsidized by foreign loans) that would eventually make Hungary the "happiest barracks in the Soviet bloc." The regime's economic foundations were ultimately untenable, however, and after Kádár's forced retirement in 1988, the reformers who replaced him acceded to pressure from the democratic opposition and began negotiations for multiparty elections that were held in 1990. These elections pushed the communists out of power, and Soviet troops left the country by June 1991.

This book begins in these early years of postsocialist transformation, as Hungarians sought to make remake themselves as new national subjects amid the remains of multiple discredited pasts and failed historical trajectories. Chapter 1, "Banishing Remains: The Statue Park Museum," explores how politicians, activists, and public officials initially conceptualized the problem of socialist remains in terms of physical remainders: monuments, statues, street names, and other objects and architecture now perceived to be emblematic of the former regime. These competing groups battled to "spring clean" such remains of the communist past in order to restore Hungary to the "authentic" course of national history and to present themselves as harbingers of the nation's triumphant future. The chapter focuses on the debates that resulted in the removal of Budapest's socialist-era statues to a Statue Park Museum on the outskirts of the city. Supporters justified the creation of the park as a democratic solution to the outrage that communist monuments inspired. Yet the removal of these statues was not a response to a crisis of defacements and public dissatisfaction, but an attempt to cover up the fact that little such crisis existed. Instead, many people viewed the statues with fondness, amusement, or indifference. The creation of the Statue Park Museum thus ironically helped to produce the very problem it claimed to solve, by renarrating comfortable landmarks of urban life into newly disruptive remains.

Meanwhile, as new political parties and activist groups sought to put the remains of an unwanted past to rest, they simultaneously revived the remains of previous eras in order to lay claim to these histories' renewed moral legitimacy. They recuperated statues and monuments, heroes and symbols, and historical narratives and vocabularies that state socialist authorities had officially rejected as fascist or reactionary, and they disinterred and reburied long-disparaged historical figures in order to consolidate their place within the new historical landscape of Hungary. Chapter 2, "The Hole in the Flag," examines two significant attempts to replace the remains of communist history with new democratic content during the first decade of postsocialism: first, the political battles to claim the revolutionary inheritance of Hungary's failed rebellion against Soviet rule in 1956, and second, the commemorative activities of the center-right Fidesz coalition in power between 1998 and 2002 (epitomized in the 2000 celebrations of the millennium of Hungary's statehood and Christianization). In different ways, each of these efforts strove to transform a national community united by pessimism and perceptions of victimhood into a victorious, forward-looking citizenry. But, like the Statue Park Museum, these attempts to create new historical foundations for postsocialist Hungary would also struggle with the recent memory of Kádárism.

By the late 1990s, attempts to master the recent past would take a surprising turn. Chapter 3, "Nostalgia and the Remains of Everyday Life," argues that the various attempts to distance the past described in the previous two chapters became the condition for its return in the form of nostalgia for socialist mass and popular culture. It thus shifts the discussion of remains of socialism from anachronistic monuments and devalued historical narratives to the detritus of an everyday life now on the brink of vanishing: from candy bars and soda pop to the songs of the Young Pioneers. Despite appearances, this nostalgia did not represent a wistful desire to return to the previous era, nor simply the gleeful impulse to laugh at state socialist kitsch found years earlier. Rather, these consumers used nostalgia for the detritus of an everyday life now on the brink of vanishing to both distance the past and give it new value. By detaching fond communal memories of these objects from the political system that produced them, nostalgia recuperated socialist remains as a novel form of national inheritance. This ironic invocation of the international discourse of cultural heritage to legitimate the trash of the previous era enabled Hungarians to redefine themselves as both savvy capitalist consumers and cultured democratic citizens: equal—if not indeed superior—to their Western counterparts.

By the second decade of postsocialism, widespread disenchantment with the experience of "transition" would replace such claims to victory with new laments of victimization that revived the buried past in the hopes of breaking with it anew. The final three chapters of this book examine this transformation in how remains were conceptualized in party politics, cultural debates, and everyday discourses of complaint. As both explanation and evidence of the failure of transition's promised transformations, the persistence of remains would enable various political and social groups to give voice not only to their past victimization by state socialism, but also to their contemporary frustrations with capitalist transformation, new forms of social inequality and stratification, and the pressures of membership in the European Union, which Hungary joined in 2004.

Chapter 4, "Recovering National Victimhood at the House of Terror," explores how the center-right Fidesz-led coalition government revived remains as a looming threat in Hungary's postsocialist culture and politics at the time of the 2002 elections. Key to this shift in the politics of memory was Fidesz's creation of a controversial museum to commemorate Hungary's victims of fascism and communism: the House of Terror, located on one of Budapest's most elegant boulevards. If the Statue Park Museum, opened nearly a decade earlier, was created to lay the socialist past to rest by mastering its visible remains, the purpose of the House of Terror was to revive the remains of socialism as a hidden danger that threatened Hungary once more. And although the Statue Park Museum's democratic preservation of socialism's monuments ultimately attracted few visitors, the House of Terror's rhetoric of victimization would make it enduringly popular with a public that increasingly blamed the persistence of socialist remains for the failure to enter transition's promised future.

Chapter 5, "Secrets, Inheritance, and a Generation's Remains," demonstrates how this rhetoric of communist terror and the danger of its return would soon extend past party politics to encompass intimate friendships and family relationships. The problem of the communist regime's informers—and their moral responsibility to both the past and the present-day—increasingly inspired public debate in the second decade of postsocialism. One crucial way these conflicts took shape was through the charged idiom of family and generational conflict, whether that entailed betrayal by cultural elders (as in the case of the celebrated filmmaker István Szabó) or actual parent (explored in the work of novelist Péter Esterházy). By phrasing the call to accountability as a matter of generational inheritance, Hungary's cultural "children" reconceptualized the problem of socialism's remains as not only the challenge of banishing the past, but the fear of reproducing it in the future.

As the twentieth anniversary of 1989 approached, new political and economic crises appeared to threaten the success of Hungary's postsocialist transformations. In 2006, on the fiftieth anniversary of the 1956 revolution, right-wing demonstrators protested the socialist-led government, which had admitted to lying to win the election. Two years later in 2008, the global financial crisis hit Hungary with disproportionate force, leading to the first-ever International Monetary Fund bailout of an EU country. Chapter 6, "A Past Returned, A Future Deferred," examines how the experience of these crises fueled renewed complaints that remains of socialism prevented Hungarians from attaining a "normal" life of political civility and economic prosperity. As Hungary approached the twentieth anniversary of 1989, the memory of the transition now only inspired the lament that "communism never ended."

The conclusion discusses the transformations in Hungary's politics of memory since the 2010 return to power of Fidesz, which has now become a right-wing populist party. Fidesz hailed its electoral victory as enabling Hungary to finally achieve transition and leave the socialist past behind. Yet its critics argue that beneath the government's anticommunist rhetoric lie authoritarian policies that have turned back the clock on many of Hungary's postsocialist democratic transformations. This chapter examines Fidesz's recent attempts to redefine Hungary's political and memorial landscape and discusses the opposition to these efforts. Ironically, both Fidesz and its opponents have revived the threat of socialist remains to warn of present and impending danger: whether in the form of an EU bureaucracy that Fidesz compares to the Soviets or in the ways that those who oppose Fidesz's policies liken contemporary social and political conditions to life under late state socialism. These strategies suggest that remains of socialism—as sites to enact mastery of the past and to imagine desired and dreaded futures—will endure in years to come.

Background and Methods

This book draws on fieldwork and archival research conducted in Budapest and a village in northeastern Hungary over the past twenty years.[19] Its origins, however, lie in my first trip to Hungary in 1993 as an English teacher in a small village located a ninety-minute train ride from Budapest. Like many young people who came of age with the fall of the Berlin Wall, I was eager to travel to the former Soviet bloc and dismantle the Cold War fears and fantasies that had structured my childhood. During my time in the village, as I taught classes of children and adults the rudiments of English vocabulary and grammar, I lacked both the linguistic and cultural knowledge to fully make sense of the ways the transformations of postsocialism were influencing the material and imaginative worlds of the people I met and lived with. My diary and letters from that time instead present a catalog of post–Cold War clichés that sought out the most visible signs of change, contradiction, and difference compared to what I considered to be North American norms. I noted that many villagers had satellite dishes, yet the entire village had only one telephone, and I marveled at the heterogeneity of the built environment even in the center of Budapest, where signs warned of crumbling building facades next door to glossy new business centers. I also recorded, without entirely understanding, how the economic challenges of postsocialism were dislocating its subjects, whether the Russian-language instructors at the school where I taught who were frantically trying to learn English in order to transfer their teaching skills to a more marketable language, or my own host family's sudden purchase of a variety store on the outskirts of the village during my weeks living in their home, through which they hoped to supplement their professional salaries.

Most of all, I was struck by the way my status as a mixed-race visitor, from a country (the United States) commonly considered to lack culture or history, inspired many of the people I met to want to educate me about the defining events of Hungary's past: from the elderly couple in the village who invited me into their home to present with great ceremony a framed map of the territory of Greater Hungary, to the acquaintances who dismissed my questions about Holocaust memorials with the argument that Hungarians had suffered longer and worse under communism, to the filmmakers I interviewed a few years later who emphasized the Hungarian origins of some of old Hollywood's most famous directors. Others, of course, rejected these claims or minimized their significance, but I soon realized that even the fact of passionate disagreement embedded them in the same interpretative community, anxiously concerned with the task of remembering or forgetting *properly*. These self-reflexive discourses signaled concerns not only about what constitutes authentic national history but also about the status of the nation engaged in such historical introspection.

When I first began research for this book, I was eager to put these experiences into a broader context, using this question of memory as a lens through which to understand how the political transformations had demanded equally far-reaching changes to the ways Hungarians lived and narrated their lives. Specifically, I was concerned with the materiality of memory, such as new museums, memorials, and the topic that would become the first chapter of this book: Budapest's Statue Park Museum of communist-era statues. During my initial field research, however, I soon discovered that for the most part such official sites of memory had become well-established and were no longer active topics in public discourse. This would soon change with the opening of the House of Terror in 2002 and the shifting political circumstances that would give the "problem" of official representations of the recent past renewed urgency in Hungary's second decade of postsocialism. Nonetheless, this initial challenge forced me to reconsider the very assumptions that structured my project. Why, at that moment, did such official relics of the socialist past no longer interest the people I worked with—at least, not framed in the way I first presented it?

Initially, I continued to pursue my original research strategy on state attempts to materialize new historical narratives and visions of collective memory in Hungary's cultural landscape: traveling to sites and events, collecting archival materials, and gathering life histories oriented around questions of personal and historical remembrance. In so doing, however, I soon realized that the apparent absence or "failure" of certain forms of memory—and the commentary such absences inspired—were themselves topics of analysis. Moreover, my desire to locate the cultural process of working through the past in the most obvious and literal remains of socialism was excluding other more ambivalent and dynamic ways through which memory and knowledge of the socialist era were taking shape.

My focus thus shifted from what was enshrined as cultural heritage to include those physical and symbolic remainders that were being excluded as trivial, valueless, and/or culturally "inauthentic." Attentive not only to what was (and was not) being said but also to when and in what contexts, I decided to track the production of remains of socialism across a number of registers: from monumentalized histories to ephemeral media events, and from official narratives of historical martyrdom to the circulation of jokes, rumors, gossip, and complaints. I also expanded my scope to trace the trajectory of postsocialist memorial practices over a time span of more than two decades. My focus on the longitudinal aspects of cultural memory helped me to trace the various ways specific remains shifted in and out of cultural focus, as well as how these remains responded to the provocations of other conflicting and overlapping commemorative practices: whether competing claims to victimization or attempts to demonize other memories (such as socialist nostalgia) as pathological.

As a result, my research strategy expanded to examine a more contested and heterogeneous set of cultural objects and discursive sites. I also spoke with a more varied range of interpretative communities (from representatives of political parties and activist groups to filmmakers and other artists, and from museum curators and visitors to marketers and consumers of "socialist nostalgia"). I conducted semistructured interviews that included life histories as well as interviews on more specific topics that ranged from retro pop music fandoms to the cultural heritage policies of various government regimes. My interview subjects included members of Budapest's cultural and political elites—including well-known intellectuals, artists, film studio heads, and government officials—but I focused my efforts on selecting individuals from both Budapest and the village who would provide a sample that was as representative as possible of age, occupation, and political affiliation within Hungary's highly polarized political spectrum (from far-right supporters to members of the Hungarian Workers' Party).[20] I interviewed some people only once; I met with others repeatedly over the span of many years.

In addition, I conducted research at the Budapest General Assembly and local district archives to collect minutes of parliamentary debates concerning the fate of Budapest's statues, and I collected media reports at the Open Society Archives and the library at Hungary's Parliament in order to chronicle the battles to determine the contours of national memory during the years preceding and directly following the political transformation. I also performed site and event analysis at locations that included the Statue Park Museum, yearly film festivals, the Magyar Millennium celebrations, all-night nostalgia parties, and musical performances.

Perhaps most importantly I participated in the textures and routines of Budapest's everyday life—from meeting friends and attending lectures, festivals, and performances to shopping for groceries, attending exercise classes, and standing in line at the post office to pay my bills—in order to immerse myself in the social life of the city and the circulation of urban knowledge and gossip. I also balanced my involvement in the life of Hungary's capital with regular visits to the villages where I had taught English before beginning my fieldwork. Visiting village friends and my former host families periodically not only gave me the opportunity to participate in the family life of my former hosts and to attend village events, but also provided a sense of community and continuity sometimes lacking in the more socially fragmented environment of Budapest.

Finally, my sources included contemporary books, newspapers and magazines, film, television, advertisements, museum exhibitions, and internet discussions and websites. I drew on these materials as both primary sources and cultural artifacts through which to analyze the emergence of Hungary's democratic postsocialist public culture. In particular, I was interested in media events and scandals as "revelatory incidents" (Fernandez 1986, xi) that illuminated—however temporarily—ongoing spheres of public debate. Their very newsworthiness and atypicality provided the means to better understand the cultural norms these stories violated (or epitomized), and they also provided another idiom through which my interlocutors offered cultural commentary and reflected on their own experiences.

The first chapter begins with one such "problematic semiotic object" (Dominguez 1989, 43): Budapest's Statue Park Museum of communist-era monuments, opened during the tumultuous yet optimistic early years of postsocialism. The outcome of heated debates among politicians, art historians, and city authorities, the creation of the park in 1993 transformed everyday landmarks into threatening remains, and thus helped to make "transition" a visible fact on the landscape of the city. And like the opening of the pizzeria Marxim, this performance of mastery over an unwanted past would provide a spectacle that appealed not only to residents of Budapest but also to a Western media eager to confirm their own post–Cold War fantasies about the triumph of democracy and market capitalism.

BANISHING REMAINS

The Statue Park Museum

"What has value when it falls?" asked the newspaper *Magyar Hírlap* in early 1990. "The symbols of a former regime." What had been painful for the East, it reported, now meant business for the West: huge red stars were selling for 4,000 deutschmarks and small Lenin statues for 80–120 (*Magyar Hírlap* 1990, 3).

Written just weeks before Hungary's first democratic elections in more than four decades swept the communists from power, this article joined an abundance of both local and international media coverage that eagerly cataloged how Hungarians were already engaged in the process of "spring cleaning" the physical traces of communism from both public and everyday life.[1] The red star was removed from the Parliament building two months before the elections, and for local governments across the country, the process of renaming hundreds of streets and squares (usually to their precommunist names) was well under way. Busts of Lenin, military medals and uniforms, and other once-ubiquitous artifacts of communist rule also began to swiftly disappear from homes, schools, offices, and factories.[2]

Embedded in these stories of the ignoble fates of state socialist-era relics were hopes about the nature of the political transformation and the future yet to come. The appeal of such anecdotes to both international observers and newly democratic postsocialist citizens is that they not only decisively announced a break with the recent past but also confidently prophesied a future free of its influence. The speed and ease with which Hungarians and their former Soviet bloc neighbors removed the detritus of the past regime's ideology seemed to guarantee that other, more intractable legacies might be as rapidly overcome. And the marketability of these objects seemed to be the harbinger of a future in which all could be redeemed within a capitalist economy, however politically worthless.

Across the former Soviet bloc, no image better encapsulated this desire for a quickly mastered past than that of a fallen monument. Whether in news articles, artworks, or scholarly books, photographs of toppled statues and headless Lenins helped to prop up a narrative of the political transformation as popular revolt, in which assaults against the visual symbols of Soviet rule represented the rebirth of national sovereignty.³ These spectacles of national agency had particular reso-nance in Hungary, where one of the key moments of its failed 1956 revolution against the Soviets was the destruction of a statue of Stalin in one of Budapest's main squares. Protestors sawed the statue from its boots, dragged it through the city streets, and eventually hacked it into souvenirs.⁴

I highlight the fantasies of historical mastery invested in monuments and other physical remainders in order to denaturalize the commonsense assumption that after 1989, these objects simply represented a problem to be solved—whether through revolutionary destruction, ironic commodification, or simply their sale as scrap metal. Instead, our investigation of socialism's remains begins by asking the ways such seemingly self-evident relics of Soviet rule emerged as a "problem" in the first place. This chapter examines how politicians, art historians, and city authorities struggled to determine the fate of Budapest's communist statues, mon-uments, and memorial plaques. These debates reveal the cultural, political, and imaginative labor necessary to transform everyday landmarks into intrusive re-mains of an unwanted past.

Monumental Time and Everyday Life under State Socialism

Traditionally, monuments "face two ways in time": they cast the past in metal or stone so that its memory will endure for posterity (Anderson 1990, 174). Each statue, memorial, or commemorative plaque thus represents a bid for eternity, by projecting a future that is the fulfillment of the past's aspirations. This ability to signify both the nation's historical depth and future permanence makes the monument a powerful tool for political legitimation. It is also what makes revo-lutionary iconoclasm so compelling to witness: destroying the monument as a physical object also represents the violent rejection of the future that the monu-ment prophesied.

Yet by signifying the inevitability of both the past and future, monuments render the present static and unchangeable. As a result, monuments tend to go strangely unnoticed in everyday life. In the famous words of the Austrian novelist

Robert Musil, "There is nothing in this world as invisible as a monument": its stillness and durability seem to "repel attention" (1995, 61).[5] Instead, the monument's memorial value usually inspires attention only as a marker in cyclical time: a site to commemorate holidays within the official calendar.

In capitalist democracies, the temporal completion of the monument is at odds with the cycles of novelty and obsolescence that drive the ways different commercial and political claims compete for public attention. But for authoritarian regimes, monuments are a key element of what Alexei Yurchak terms the regime's "hegemony of representation," in which signs and symbols do not represent their literal meaning. Instead, their very ubiquity signifies the immutability of the system itself (1997, 165–166). In daily life under state socialism, most people may have been unaware of or indifferent to the specific ideological content of each monument that they passed on the street, whether a statue of a liberating soldier, a memorial plaque to a street partisan, or a stone relief commemorating heroes of the workers' movement. But although these monuments may have failed as commemorations of particular individuals or events, their very invisibility and taken-for-grantedness represented the success of the regime's claim to permanence.

To protect this bid to eternity, monuments were not allowed to accrete the effects of time. Instead, rumor had it that if statues needed repairs, communist authorities would whisk them out under cover of night and replace them with replicas. One perhaps apocryphal example is Budapest's first statue of Lenin, donated by the City Council of Moscow and erected outside Hungary's center of heavy industry, the famous Csepel Iron and Metal Works, in preparation for a 1958 visit from Nikita Khrushchev. Because of the poor quality of the statue's construction, the metal soon began to corrode, and in 1970 it was reportedly secretly removed and recast. No newspapers covered the event: a silence that both preserved the prestige of the statue's Soviet donors and denied the monument's own vulnerability to the depredations of chronological, historical time.[6]

Over the decades of communist rule, the static, eternal temporality of the monument and its role in reinforcing the immutability of everyday life would come to replace other, potentially more revolutionary temporal orientations. Communist ideology was determinedly oriented toward the future, breaking with national tradition to hurry history to its inevitable fulfillment. Even when it celebrated figures and events in the national canon so as to give historical justification to communist rule, what these new histories ultimately demonstrated was the regime's mastery of the past itself and the ability to mold it to its will. And if the past was the servant of the politics of the present, the present was to be sacrificed to a constant will to progress—what Michael Buroway and János Lukács call the myth of the "radiant future" (1992, 145), at once imminent and yet always out of reach.

The routinized rhythms of everyday life thus initially posed a challenge for communist ideology. In the early years of state socialism, Soviet authorities sought to revolutionize the quotidian with interventions such as the communal apartment, which declared war on bourgeois notions of privacy and domesticity (Boym 1994, 124–125). Following the years of retaliation after the 1956 revolution, the Kádár regime changed course to pursue a policy that sought to provide in advance some of the rewards that communism had long been promising. It offered an unspoken compromise: in exchange for abstaining from political participation, Hungarians could enjoy a raised standard of living, increased autonomy at work, the opportunity to earn extra income in the private sector ("second economy"), and relative freedom from harassment in private life.

Although more peaceful than previous decades, this everyday life during the Kádár era was characterized by a sense of inertia, insignificance, and eventlessness—a feeling of being on the sidelines of international trends and outside the global course of history. By the 1980s, many Hungarians would describe the temporality of late socialism in terms similar to that used to describe monuments themselves: defined by utter stasis and the perception that nothing would ever change. Indeed, one of late socialism's most popular and critically acclaimed films was titled *Time Stands Still* (*Megáll az idő*; Péter Gothár, 1982). The film takes place during the early years of normalization after the 1956 revolution, but its title—borrowed from a love song of that era—was applicable to late socialism as well: expressing the frustrated longing for rebellion and escape that the film's teenaged protagonists experienced. Even communism's promise of a beautiful future fell silent, to be replaced by the everyday concerns of "existing socialism." In the words of the historians András Gerő and Iván Pető, "Time seemed to have stopped: socialism was being built, but the construction process appeared to be uncompletable, never ending" (1997, 7).

Meanwhile, public statues, rituals, and political symbols continued to buttress the faltering regime's ideological self-justification until almost the last days of its rule. Occasionally, these statues offered an opportunity for political critique; for example, a piece of bread spread with lard (*zsíros kenyér*) was anonymously placed in the outstretched hand of the Csepel Lenin statue to protest the rising prices of everyday goods in 1980 (Prohászka 1994, 168). In most cases, however, the intended meanings of the monuments went relatively unnoticed. Instead, they endured as indexes of the unchanging nature of everyday life itself, taking on prosaic and often ironic meanings in the urban environment they helped to organize.

For example, István Kiss's monument to Hungary's short-lived 1919 Soviet Republic reproduces the imagery of a famous propaganda poster from that era: a sailor caught mid-stride, waving a red flag and calling "To arms! To arms!" Rendered in bronze, the charging figure was placed near Budapest's City Park on the site of a former church, standing next to one of Budapest's several statues of Lenin. Rather than inspire awe or even indifference, however, the enormity of the statue made its dynamic pose look comical, and it became the target of urban humor that compared the sailor to a cloakroom attendant, rushing after a customer to give him his coat (Réthly 2010, 47).

The End of Revolution

> Then suddenly it was over. Mostly it rotted away on its own, plus there was Gorbachev, after all. We began to live in a different world—in a matter of minutes, what had presented itself as a continuous, timeless present suddenly became a finished past. "The era died like an enormous, huge carcass," and amidst the old scenery, the same human material began to do something radically new.
>
> —Tibor Keresztury, "We Are Those People"

Hungary enjoyed a steadily growing national income and level of consumption throughout the 1970s. By the mid-1980s, problems with foreign trade debt necessitated Western loans and austerity policies that threatened the regime's post-1956 promise of an ever-increasing standard of living. Gorbachev's perestroika thus found a welcome reception by reform-minded communists who hoped that increasing pluralism within the one-party system would help to reestablish their legitimacy on political rather than economic grounds. In 1988, these reform communists forced the retirement of General Secretary János Kádár, who had led Hungary for the past thirty years. Over the following months, they pursued a policy of increasing openness and political restructuring that ultimately permitted other political parties to form. In March 1989, the democratic opposition groups and parties established an Opposition Round Table, which was to spend the next year in negotiations with the communist government to determine the nature of Hungary's new parliamentary democracy. Eight months later, Hungary was declared a democratic republic; free elections followed in March and April of the next year.

The end of socialism in Hungary thus did not represent revolution, but rather—as István Rév argues—the apparent end of the age of revolutions.

> In Hungary there was no revolution in 1989, not even a velvet one, as in Prague. There were no strikes, no large-scale demonstrations, no signs of massive popular unrest. Hungarians skeptically watched the not-so-dramatic suicide of the system. The dictatorship of the proletariat, in its own version of history, had started with the seizure of power. Perhaps this was why, in 1989, nobody wanted to begin again with "all power to the Soviets," or something similar. (Rév 2005, 30)

No shots were fired and few monuments were vandalized as the regime dismantled itself in negotiation with its democratic opposition. Instead, after forty years, Hungary's era of state socialism simply appeared to "melt like butter in the late summer sunshine" of 1989 (Rév 2005, 30).

In life history interviews I conducted in the late 1990s and early 2000s, many people remembered the end of communist rule as seeming to have happened of its own momentum. Although some had participated in protests or had been active in opposition movements in the final years of state socialism, many others remembered feeling that the political changes were disconnected from the pressing concerns of their own lives: whether holding down several jobs to support their families, or studying in what Laura, now a lawyer, remembered as the "closed and carefree" world of university in a small city far from Budapest. There was also now little agreement on what might even be considered the defining political events of that era. The years leading up to the system change had been marked by peaceful attempts to reclaim national history, such as the demonstrations to commemorate the anniversary of the Hungarian Revolution of 1848 on March 15 and the state reburial of Imre Nagy (former prime minister and a martyr of the 1956 revolution) attended by hundreds of thousands in Budapest on June 16. Yet nearly an entire year separated these actions from the democratic elections that finally removed the reform communists from office. As Laura added, "We knew something important was going on," but in retrospect, she like many others seemed to feel that she had "missed" the event, that she had not been present to it. "By the time people began to realize it," argue Gerő and Pető, the political era "was already over" (1997, 12).

In everyday life, any sense of having "missed" the political demise of the system would quickly be replaced by the euphoria of new possibility and the urgent need to adapt to the new economic and social pressures of postsocialism. That is, the static, monumentalized temporality of late socialism transformed into the exhilarating and disconcerting forward motion of chronological time. A former journalist, Anikó Farkas, recalled that the early 1990s felt as if the entire country was suddenly energized by the drive and momentum of youth. "All that describes the essence of being in your twenties was vibrating in the air: everything is possible, everything stands open, there is strength, energy, mood, belief, and talent for everything—and the bad experiences that might turn us back from taking serious steps forward had not yet happened" (2009, 30).

But for Hungary's emerging political parties and actors, the challenge was to imbue a sense of eventfulness and popular sovereignty to what had been a negotiated and bureaucratic transformation. Statues and monuments would play a crucial role in these politicians' attempts to reenact the originary break from the socialist era—and thus to portray themselves as the rightful inheritors of the public's political will. Two problems would confront these efforts. First was the task of enacting historical rupture. What made the political change of power such a radical divergence from the upheavals of Hungary's recent history was its peaceful and democratic character. To return to the established political symbolism of violent uprisings would undermine Hungary's crucial break from precedent. Instead, the task was to find new, "civilized" solutions to the problem of communist monuments to prove that the nation had not only abandoned its past but also had already succeeded in entering a peaceful and prosperous future determined by shared Western values of democratic consensus and historical preservation.

The second problem involved what Mikhail Yampolsky has termed "temporalization": the abrupt descent into historical time of what had previously existed as an "islet of eternity" (1995, 97). Monuments that outlast the regime that erected them usually meet one of two fates: they crumble into ruins or they are destroyed by revolutionary iconoclasm. Ruins make visible the triumph of nature's corrosion over human aspiration (Simmel 1959, 259); their deterioration robs the monument of its specificity and instead represents only the inevitability of decay. The history of revolutionary defacement and demolition, on the other hand, is one of popular sovereignty against suddenly visible emblems of a hated regime: whether the destruction of a monument to King Louis XV during the French Revolution, the decapitation of a statue of Tsar Alexander III by Russian revolutionaries in 1917, or Hungary's own demolition of a Stalin statue during the 1956 revolution.

Yet while images of toppled monuments and decapitated statues may have dominated both local and Western media representations of the demise of communism across the former Soviet bloc, Hungary entered a new era with most of its monuments unscathed by the forces of revolutionary transformation. Indeed, it was the communist city authorities themselves who removed the main Lenin statue from Budapest in spring 1989, ostensibly for maintenance (Prohászka 1994, 174). As a result, local city governments and Hungary's new political parties were not merely faced with the question of what to "do" with the problem of communist monuments, but to what extent they even represented a problem to be solved in the eyes of Hungary's newly democratic public. Neither ruins nor defaced idols, the "temporalization" of Hungary's monuments into anachronistic remains was not an inevitable consequence of political transformation. Instead, like all remains, they would only become visible as the contingent outcome of cultural and political battles to transform relatively unnoticed landmarks of everyday life into visible relics of history.

Architects of Democracy

Sixty-five political parties registered for Hungary's 1990 democratic elections; twelve were admitted to participate; and six eventually won parliamentary representation. Of the six parties in Parliament, half were inherited from the recent twentieth-century past: two were right-wing parties that had been active before the communists took power (the Christian Democratic People's Party [Kereszténydemokrata Néppárt, KDNP] and the Independent Smallholders' Party [Független Kisgazdapárt, FKGP]), whereas the other (the Hungarian Socialist Party [Magyar Szocialista Párt, MSZP]) was one of the two successor parties to the communist party. The other three parties represented a variegated spectrum of ideologies, historical politics, and visions of Hungary's future. The Alliance of Free Democrats (Szabad Demokraták Szövetsége, SZDSZ) was composed of left-liberal, Western-oriented members of the former opposition, and the Alliance of Young Democrats (Fiatal Demokraták Szövetsége, Fidesz) was a liberal alternative youth party that would later turn to the center-right after the 1994 elections. Finally, the Hungarian Democratic Forum (Magyar Demokrata Fórum, MDF) was a center-right conservative "national-Christian" (*nemzeti-keresztény*) party whose policies were often perceived as attempts to revive the values and historical rhetoric of Hungary's interwar period.

The MDF ultimately won Hungary's first postsocialist democratic elections, and it formed a conservative government in coalition with the FKGP and KDNP. It promised "peaceful power" (*nyugodt erő*) rather than the anticommunist radicalism of the SZDSZ (the largest opposition party at the time) or Fidesz. Nonetheless, for both the new government and its citizens much depended on making tangible the demise of a political system that seemed simply to have crumbled from within. The question of how to undertake the work of "national spring cleaning" trumpeted by the MDF's campaign poster would thus occupy politicians, city authorities, and art professionals alike in the early years of postsocialism.

Although this task of cleansing Hungary's public spaces of socialist remains would prove to be primarily a bureaucratic process, it is important to note that a small number of politicians and protestors did attempt to revive Hungary's previous history of revolutionary iconoclasm. In the summer of 1989, members of the Hungarian October Party (Magyar Október Párt), a small radical social organization led by 1956 participants, called on the Budapest city council to change the name of a street that honored Ferenc Münnich, a communist politician who played an important role in crushing the 1956 revolution. In a series of demonstrations, these activists painted over and removed street signs containing his name, and—in a tribute to the destruction of the Stalin statue in 1956—ultimately sawed off a statue of Münnich at his boots.[7] Representatives from SZDSZ, Fidesz, and the conservative FKGP also participated in a joint action to move the Csepel Lenin from its pedestal to the factory museum in March 1990 (Népszava 1990).

Such acts of revolutionary iconoclasm may have revived the memory of similar protests in 1956, but they did not face the same danger of retribution. And far from being spontaneous actions performed in the heat of revolutionary fervor, these isolated incidents were often orchestrated media events. As the art historian László Mravik pointed out, it was no coincidence that television cameras were present at many of these "spontaneous" demonstrations (1990, 10). Such defacements thus represented not only retaliation against symbols of the former regime but also attempts to garner public attention and symbolic capital at a time when competing political actors were striving for public visibility. As we shall see in more detail in the next chapter, the memory of 1956, whose maintenance had once been a form of resistance to the socialist regime, now functioned as a stake in a contemporary struggle for political power and moral legitimacy.

Although actions such as the October Party's political demonstrations hoped to turn the system change into a revolution that would purge the remnants of communism (or at least, give the appearance of promising to do so), such initiatives failed to capture broad public enthusiasm. 1989 was no 1956, and, in an attempt to maintain the peaceful nature of the transition (*békés átmenet*), most politicians wanted to evoke the spirit of 1956 without actually conjuring it up as a model for action. For them, the lack of violent upheaval or widespread iconoclasm indicated what was truly "revolutionary" about the negotiated political transformation.

Art historians and other professionals, on the other hand, objected not only to the idea of defacements but also to the ongoing quiet removal of the monuments by local authorities. They argued that since memorials to Marx or Soviet liberation can be found in some Western European cities, Hungary's communist monuments should similarly be allowed to remain: whether as icons of shared Western values or as artistic and historical documents of the previous era. Historical essays appeared in a number of newspapers and journals to support this position, comparing current efforts to remove the statues to communist attempts to similarly redefine public spaces of the city by removing old monuments without public consent (Nemeskürty 1989; Sinkó 1990; Wehner 1990). The Russian artist Vitaly Komar described the long-standing tradition of Soviet iconoclasm as

> classic old Moscow technique: either worship or destroy. Bolsheviks topple czar monuments, Stalin erases old Bolsheviks, Khrushchev tears down Stalin, Brezhnev tears down Khrushchev. . . . No difference. Each time it is history, the country's true past, which is conveniently being obliterated. . . . And usually by the same people! In most cases, these

weren't passionate crowds doing tearing down—it was [the] cool hand of officials, by bureaucratic fiat. (Weschler 1993, 59)[8]

As these artists and art historians pointed out, Hungary's own twentieth-century history had already amply demonstrated that every new regime seeks to redefine the public landscape through the official destruction or removal of old monuments and the installation of new ones.[9] What would be truly new in the Hungarian context was for any removals to take place in the same peaceful and legal manner as the dismantling of the former regime, and to occur only as the result of a democratic, "European" process. "Politics should no longer decide their fate, but rather how these monuments fit into the cityscape [*városkép*]," the art historian Katalin Sinkó maintained (1990, 10). At the very least, these professionals demanded, the fate of these objects should be determined by democratic public debate, rather than by default. For example, a 1990 conference at the University of Debrecen on monuments in Hungary issued a statement emphasizing that any decisions concerning the statues should be arrived at legally and democratically, by the local government authority in cooperation with art professionals (Boros 1993, 8).

Most Hungarians, taking similar pride in the peacefulness and legality of the political transformation, were unwilling to ally themselves with the radicalism represented by the destruction of monuments—which reminded them not of 1956, but of the iconoclasm and annihilating historical politics of the communists themselves when they took power. Defining the political transformation as Hungary's entrance into democratic Europe and a return to Western "normality" after the Eastern "barbarism" of Soviet communism, they welcomed this break from the turbulence of Hungary's twentieth-century history.

Yet despite such concerns, local governments across Hungary maintained the project of "spring cleaning" remains of socialism by continuing the methodical removal of communist monuments initiated during the last months of communism. Some of these local governments carried out these changes in consultation with historians and the opinions of the community, but, for most, the logic was simpler: when the communists took power, no one asked the people if they wanted these monuments; now that the communists were gone and the people had regained their sovereignty, the monuments too must go. At issue was not only the fate of specific monuments but also the way Hungary's rapid political and economic transformation was to be understood and reenacted in the public space of the city: Should it be through democratic negotiation or an act of compensatory destruction that would give revolutionary momentum to a political process otherwise lacking in definitive public events? The very nature of the public to inhabit this space was thus also under question: Did those who sought to tear down the monuments represent valiant popular resistance or were they preemptively an antidemocratic mob?

The idea for a statue park was first raised in the summer of 1989 by the literary historian László Szörényi, in an article that appeared in the conservative journal *Hitel*. In a short piece titled "Lenin Garden," Szörényi suggested that the state gather the now-unpopular statues of Lenin in a park, which could then be used as a moneymaking tourist attraction for Budapest's World Expo (planned to be held in 1996, but canceled after the 1994 elections) (1989, 62). This suggestion was later promoted by several organizations across the political spectrum: from the Recsk Association, composed of 1956 veterans and former inmates of the Recsk labor camp (*Magyar Nemzet* 1990), to the Békéscsaba branch of Fidesz (*Népszabadság* 1990a).

City authorities soon recognized that the idea of a statue park represented an ingenious political compromise between those who wanted to demolish the monuments and those who preferred them to remain. Rather than erase the fact of the socialist era or allow the former regime's self-representations to go unchallenged, placing the monuments in a park would invest them with new symbolic content. They would function both as documents of the aesthetics, ideology, and historical politics of the previous era and as emblems of democracy and Hungarian cultural health. Creating the park would thus enable city officials to make the political transformation visible in public life, while preserving the sense of legality that distinguished this transformation from others in Hungarian history.

In June 1991 the government voted into law a resolution giving the local governing authorities the right to remove and install statues, and in December, Budapest's General Assembly met to vote on the statues one by one, according to opinions collected from local districts and the recommendations of the assembly's Cultural Committee. Invoking the discourse of European democracy and legality, officials emphasized the necessity of discovering precisely which monuments "irritated" the public, whose interests were set in opposition to the art professionals otherwise entrusted with the care of the monuments and to the vocal minority who sought to destroy them. Ultimately, the assembly decided that public opinion was best reflected through removing most of Budapest's communist monuments solely on the basis of their ideological content.[10]

Yet although the idea of a park was greatly praised abroad, it failed to appeal to everyone in Hungary. Some wanted the monuments destroyed rather than "honored" in a park, whereas others argued that such a park would function as a quarantine that represented an antidemocratic expulsion of historical heterogeneity from the public spaces of the city (*Népszabadság* 1990b). Furthermore, the reaction of the "public," whose desires had purportedly determined the fate of the monuments, was similarly lukewarm. After all, as the head of the Cultural

Committee, László Baán, acknowledged when he presented the committee's recommendations to the General Assembly, a third of the local governments had
failed to respond to queries concerning the fate of monuments in their districts.[11]
When I later interviewed András Szilágyi, the representative of the Budapest
Gallery charged with directing the monuments' removal, he maintained that the
decisions were simply based on whether there was any objection to a particular
monument—whether that objection was voiced by five people, or one thousand.[12]
Even a poll conducted in fall 1992 revealed that many city residents resented the
expenditure of public funds on such a symbolic gesture, and the majority would
have preferred nearly all the statues to remain (*Népszabadság* 1992). Nonetheless,
art professionals and city officials publicly stated their consent to the monuments'
removal and reinstallation in the park. Both the ideal of democratic consensus
and the fantasy of popular protest against the statues would persist—but as much
as rhetorical devices as reality.

Remains and the Memory of Kádárism

The decision to remove Budapest's statues to a park thus did not necessarily
represent a solution to the "problem" of defacements and public outrage at the
persistence of socialist remains in the official cityscape. Instead, this attempt to
respond to a crisis of communist monuments functioned to cover up the fact
that little such crisis existed. What was at stake in this fantasy of popular revolt
against the statues was the memory of the recent past itself. That is, the problem
of Budapest's communist monuments was not that they represented dangerous
intrusions into the public spaces of postsocialism. Rather, the risk was that the
statues were not dangerous *enough*, since by the final years of state socialism, most
of the city's inhabitants had managed to find ways to live with the regime and its
symbols. Creating the Statue Park Museum would help to disavow such knowledge, by reducing Hungary's experiences of "goulash communism" under the
leadership of János Kádár to a narrative that consisted solely of national suffering
under Soviet occupation. By transforming these statues into the remains of a history of unrelenting oppression, politicians and city authorities would be able to
avoid the more disquieting reminder that such icons of state socialist rule had
inspired indifference as well as resentment—or, in some cases, were experienced
as comfortable and familiar.

As discussed earlier, the tacit social contract of the Kádár era was based on
relinquishing political participation in order to pursue one's private life relatively undisturbed. That is, the condition of political citizenship under Kádárism
was not fanatical adherence to communist doctrine, but rather the retreat

into a depoliticized private realm and the outward appearance of conformity to the myriad public rituals, values, and activities demanded by the regime. The response of dissident intellectuals to this logic was then to target the sphere of private life and action as the most powerful site of resistance: what Czech dissident Václav Havel termed the mandate to "live within the truth" (1991, 146).

Such calls to overturn the regime's "hegemony of representation" (Yurchak 1997, 165) were morally crucial to the dissident movements. But as Yurchak argues, their logic obscured the preexisting dialectic of reproduction and indifference within which most individuals already negotiated the system of late state socialism. This strategy did not reflect simple intimidation; it also indicated a tacit acceptance of the immutability, inevitability, and ubiquity of state discourse in public life. Neither a demonstration of belief nor a rationally calculated attempt to mask dissent, the population's compliance with the signs and symbols of state socialist rule was a product of a (regime-encouraged) lack of interest and a disregard for the literal meanings of state rhetoric (Yurchak 1997, 163), which few expected even party officials to take seriously.

In this atmosphere of depoliticization and indifference, public space became a site of both political indoctrination and the production of personal meaning. Although some read the monuments as painful evidence of foreign occupation, others managed to live with the monuments as they did with the regime: a more or less peaceful coexistence that most did not experience as intolerably oppressive. This shift in the nature of the regime's legitimacy found its emblem at the site of Stalin's statue, which was never replaced after it was torn down to its boots in 1956. The empty platform remained in "Boots Square" until the end of the regime, and party leaders stood upon it for the May Day parades. (It has now been replaced by a memorial to 1956.) If the destruction of the Stalin statue epitomized the 1956 protestors' rejection of the symbols of authoritarianism, this monument to the "emptiness" that remained symbolized the unspoken contract through which citizens were able to tolerate Kádár's post-1956 soft dictatorship. As Miklós Haraszti, then a samizdat author and publisher, wrote in 1987:

> The fact that after the failure of the 1956 revolution no new statue replaced the old one shows, if you wish, that those in power had to retreat; that their victory was Pyrrhic. Their setback was thought by some to be irreversible because though they now had to stand on the platform with only the phantom weight of the boots on their necks, in fact nothing was behind them but painful emptiness.
>
> But isn't another reading of this emptiness possible? Perhaps our leaders found themselves some new form of legitimation, and their rule

became even stronger. The fathers, with the fathers of the future on their shoulders, were again ready for the annual march—this time without ideological slogans. Nor did they march, as in the past, out of fear. Neither their lives nor their freedoms are threatened if participants in today's parade don't attend. This annual pilgrimage is respectable civil investment in their careers and what society would morally object to that? (Haraszti 1987)

Thus, one reason few people attempted to destroy or deface monuments during Hungary's political transformation is that by the end of the era, communist rule in Hungary no longer derived its legitimacy from monumental claims to totality. Instead, as we have seen, the very structure of socialist temporality seemed to have taken on the qualities of a monument itself: static, unchangeable, and never-ending. As a result, people responded to communist statues not only with anger but with boredom, irony, or affection. In a series of street interviews conducted before the Statue Park Museum's construction, some respondents claimed that they had long been ignorant of or uninterested in the identity of local communist statues. While most expressed consent for the statues' removal, they viewed this task with little enthusiasm or urgency, arguing that the money for the park would be better spent on social welfare measures (*Köztársaság* 1992). "You see, I've been coming to this park for decades, and I don't even know whose statue this is," said an elderly woman, referring to a monument to the Bulgarian communist Georgy Dimitrov, one of the prominent figures of the international communist movement. "The truth is that I got used it, somehow it belongs to the area. Statue, statue, you know how it is." She then went on to remark that no one she knew was bothered by the statues, arguing that the idea of the Statue Park Museum merely reflected the agenda of "those writers or whoever who want to put everything in order—in our heads and souls, as they say. I think they're the ones who decided this. They think that they'll turn people's attention from how horribly expensive everything is" (*Köztársaság* 1992, 18).

Moreover, there were simply no more Stalins to tear down. The public space of late socialism was an increasingly heterogeneous mix of socialist-realist kitsch and artistically ambitious monuments, bland state enterprises and colorful private shops, political posters and occasional commercial advertisements. Many of the statues, monuments, and memorial plaques did not even celebrate Lenin or Russian soldiers, but reflected the shift from socialist internationalism to the commemoration of local Hungarians, both well-known and obscure.

The difficulty of the labor of transforming this diverse set of objects into mere remains of socialism is clear in the two tropes used to characterize the "problem" of communist monuments in media coverage, political debates, and everyday conversation. On the one hand, there was Lenin—not a specific monument, but the sheer quantity of Lenin busts, statues, and portraits that saturated visual space under state socialism. For most Hungarians, the ubiquity and seriality of these Lenins represented the imposition of a foreign power and the banality of socialist-realist aesthetics. The necessity of eliminating such remains—whether by destruction, mockery, or removal to a park—appeared self-evident and uncontroversial: no different from renaming "People's Republic Street" and "Liberation Square" or marketing Soviet medals to tourists.

On the other hand, there was "Osztyapenkó," a monument to the Soviet envoy Ilya Afanasyevich Ostapenko, who was killed on December 29, 1944 while delivering an ultimatum to the German forces that encircled Budapest.[13] Standing on one of Budapest's main highways at the city's border, the statue's upstretched arm and waving flag appeared to greet or bid farewell to city residents on their trips in and out of the city. Over the years, the statue became an informal emblem of Budapest, and many viewed it fondly, even domesticating its name into the Hungarianized "Osztyapenkó" rather than its official designation as "Ostapenko" or "Osztapenko." As Péter György explains:

> The Osztapenko statue meant the beginning of a *trip to the Balaton* [a popular holiday spot]: and thus for at least two generations, it meant the beginning of vacation, prosperity, the Hungarian "weekend." For the younger generation, it served as *Route 66*. This is where they hitchhiked: "Let's meet at Osztyapenkó!" . . . Captain Osztapenko meant the *genius loci*, the *phantom of freedom*, independently from who this officer of the Red Army actually was. (2000, 306)

Transforming this local landmark into a socialist remain would prove a more ambivalent task than disposing of countless Lenins. To remove Osztyapenkó would expel not only the hegemonic official culture of state socialism but also the memory of the informal ways that generations of Budapest residents had nonetheless imbued this official culture with collective significance.

Each of Hungary's new political parties and organizations had a slightly different stake in banishing such memories of the domestication of Kádárism. Some were concerned with returning to other, more distant pasts. The radical October Party and other groups of 1956 veterans attempted to revive the memory of the 1956 revolution, dismissing the intervening years of Kádárism in order to argue that 1989 represented the fulfillment of 1956's revolt against communist oppression. The ruling MDF party and its coalition partners, on the other hand, sought to draw a line of historical continuity between Hungary's conservative interwar years and the present, eliminating all four decades of state socialism as an unnatural divergence from the true course of Hungarian history.

Others were more focused on a future defined as the repudiation of what had come before. Fidesz, created as a youth party, based its claim to legitimacy on rejecting all the "sins" of the communist era, and thus prohibited those over thirty-five from joining its ranks. The SZDSZ, which had won the second highest number of votes in the election, were at that time the most Western-oriented and implacably anticommunist of the new political parties. Its members had been the most active in the opposition in the final decade of state socialism, rejecting the comforts of the Kádárist compromise in favor of "living in the truth" by fighting for human rights, freedom of expression, and democratic political participation. Some of its representatives called for the removal of statues, such as those who demanded the removal of Lenin in Csepel. Others, such as the parliamentary representative Mihály Ráday (a well-known television director and historical preservationist) lobbied for the preservation of monuments and memorial plaques by arguing they represented both urban history and the commemoration of factual historical events. Even the communist successor party MSZP disavowed direct continuity with the previous regime, by presenting its attempts to reform communism in the final years of the regime as a break with the decades of Kádár's rule.

During the meeting of Budapest's General Assembly on December 5, 1991, representatives of the MSZP, as well as some representatives of SZDSZ (Ráday) and Fidesz, supported retaining the Osztyapenkó statue and others whose cultural significance had exceeded or replaced their political content. (The Cultural Committee charged with collecting the opinions of the city districts also recommended that Osztyapenkó stay, despite the district's request that it be removed.) Conservative members of the assembly as well as other representatives of Fidesz denounced this and additional monuments as symbols of political oppression. Insisting that the General Assembly's function was to represent popular will rather than impose personal or professional viewpoints, everyone cited a different opinion of the statues to support their claims, ranging from views of colleagues to those of local districts to—in one case—the opinion of the speaker's barber.[14]

More than the statues themselves were under debate: speakers argued over the nature of the socialist past and the competing memories and experiences of that era that were currently vying for public legitimacy. Whose feelings were to be heeded: those of residents who preferred that the monuments remain or those who were "irritated" by them? Would removing the monuments erase recent history or would it simply rectify the communists' own historical distortions? As one member of the General Assembly noted, determination of the true history of the events and figures commemorated by the monuments would have to wait for historians to resolve. In the meantime, the General Assembly ultimately voted to remove almost all the communist monuments under debate—including Osztyapenkó.[15]

In thus officially effacing the difference between a Lenin and Osztyapenkó, the General Assembly's decision was probably the first to take seriously the monuments' ideological intentions since the moment of their erection. Despite the members' lively debate, the outcome of their deliberations would make no distinction between the kitsch of socialist realism and work that was significant for artistic or cultural reasons. Instead, by sentencing monuments representing different historical periods, aesthetics, and political intentions to a common fate, the removal of the statues would enact a logic of commensuration that rendered the monuments "generically representative" of the socialist era (Ivy 1995, 13). If the purpose of monuments under communism was to function invisibly as generalized signs of the eternity of the present, here the monuments would ultimately function as similarly homogenized signs of historical break.

This remonumentalization in the service of a new memorial project to disjuncture rather than continuity suggests that what was ultimately most threatening about communist monuments during the system change was not the scandalous visibility of their ideological message, but the potential *invisibility* of this content to the newly democratized city residents. After all, the very insistence that the monuments were a problem that needed to be solved was the one element common to the many different public opinions—whether voiced by city authorities, art professionals, journalists, academics, or politicians—concerning the monuments' fate. To suggest otherwise risked implying that "temporalization" had not occurred: that the socialist past was not yet over in the minds, memories, and dispositions of its former citizens, and that there was no consensus concerning the nature of the political transformation and what persisted in the postsocialist present. That is, while countless Lenins proved the infuriating fact of Soviet occupation, it was perhaps ultimately even more pressing to render judgment on Osztyapenkó, who called attention to the ways that forty years of socialism had become cozy and familiar.

The decision to remove Budapest's statues to a museum thus did not simply solve the challenge of what to do with the unwanted remainders of the recent past. By converting living presence into anachronistic remains and rewriting collective experience as distant history, it instead helped to enact the very transformation it sought to reflect. As Éva Kovács argues in her analysis of the Statue Park Museum, the park would enable forgetting as much as remembrance: "While not everyone wanted to remove the statues, there was much more desire to erase their own socialist past and their experience of socialism" (2001, 80). By reducing the statues to merely their unwanted ideological content, the removal of statues to the park would help its visitors to avoid acknowledging their ambivalent relationship to Kádárism and their own memories and attachments to its legacies. Thus, the heated debates about the monuments' future, which from one aspect appeared to be an engagement with the past, from another point of view can also be considered a "remembering in order to forget" (Esbenshade 1995). The creation of the Statue Park Museum would not necessarily solve the "problem" of communist monuments, but it provided a ritual of closure that buried goulash communism in order to ensure its demise.

A Monument to Transition

If the creation of the park functioned as a historical break from the recent past, the winning proposal for its architecture sought to celebrate the spirit of the new. The architect Ákos Eleőd designed an "anti-propaganda park" intended to subvert the totalizing mindset that erected the monuments. "I would like this park to be right in the middle: neither a park to honor Communism, nor a sarcastic park that provokes tempers, but a place where everyone can feel whatever they want," he stated to the *New York Times*. "People can feel nostalgic, or have a good laugh, or mourn a personal tragedy connected with the period" (Ingram 1993, 3). For Eleőd, the Statue Park Museum's openness to a diversity of opinions that was denied by the previous regime would embody the essence of democracy (Eleőd 1994, 24). As he told me in an interview nearly ten years after the park's opening, his intention was that the park would function as a memorial not to communism, but to the "transition" itself.[16]

To transform authoritarian icons into emblems of freedom, Eleőd designed the park to deliberately frustrate traditional expectations of the monument. Visitors to the Statue Park Museum first encounter an imposing red brick facade in the style of socialist realism, flanked by a statue of Lenin and another that commemorates Marx and Engels. No building stands behind this false front, and its gate is always locked. The poem "A Sentence About Tyranny," written in 1950 by Gyula Illyés to describe the experience of living under communist rule, is inscribed on the gate's rusting metal doors. Only a smaller side entrance permits visitors to enter the park: an architectural strategy that symbolizes the disjuncture between communism's lofty ambitions and actual practice. (It also brings to life the Hungarian concept of getting around official barriers by finding a "little side door [*kiskapu*]," whether that is through personal connections or legal loopholes.)

Once inside and past the small booth that constitutes both the ticket counter and gift shop, visitors step onto a path in the shape of three figure eights, the mathematical sign for infinity. This "infinite" path ultimately ends in a brick wall at the opposite end of the park, as another metaphor for both the aspirations and end result of communist ideology. The monuments themselves line the loops of the figure eights, organized into what the guidebook describes as "endless parades" of common themes: liberation monuments, heroes of the workers' movement, and "concepts" (memorials and events) of the workers' movement. Each loop's statues, monuments, and memorial plaques are clustered close together, deprived of the tall pedestals that usually prohibit close examination. This proximity invites visual comparison and physical engagement: a perceptual shift that undermines the original aim of each monument to overwhelm time and space, and hence to transform an event in history into the eternity of myth.

The impossibility of attaining a "monumental perspective" on the objects in the park reflects Eleőd's aim of producing an open, nonhierarchical architecture. In this logic, the transformation of the visitors' encounters with the monuments reflects the transformation of the public that purportedly demanded the statues' removal: from oppressed and atomized subjects of late socialism to active and critically engaged participants in public life. As we have seen, this desire to use the fate of Budapest's monuments to actualize the discourse of democracy is also what linked many otherwise disparate opinions concerning the fate of Budapest's statues, both in the media and in the debates that occurred at the levels of the national, city, and local government.

Yet Eleőd's attempt to celebrate popular sovereignty and democratic diversity conceals the political context of the park's creation, which reduced the history of these statues in the parks and squares of Budapest to a narrative of Soviet occupation and popular unrest. The Statue Park Museum thus became, perhaps inevitably, a site of structural tension between the story of its origins and its architectural goals. And after its opening, the park would face a new set of contradictions, torn between Eleőd's sober, demystifying ambitions and the sensationalistic demands of consumer capitalism. Rather than perform its intended pedagogical function of educating about the past and proving the success of democracy in Hungary, the Statue Park Museum would become a place to reinforce the monumental fantasies of its local and foreign visitors.

Marketing Remains

The Statue Park Museum opened in summer 1993 as part of Budapest's celebration of the second anniversary of the departure of Soviet troops from Hungary. Staged as a parody of a 1950s communist party rally, the opening received a great deal of media attention in Hungary as well as abroad. Its subsequent maintenance, in exchange for its profits, was entrusted in 1994 to a young entrepreneur, Ákos Réthly, who on the basis of the park's initial surge of visitors created a business plan that anticipated—as the Western press later reported—making a capitalist profit out of communist icons (MacLeod 1998).

Once the flurry of interest surrounding the opening died down, the park was initially unsuccessful in luring either foreign tour groups or local Hungarian visitors. And with ticket prices kept artificially low for a public accustomed to decades of state subsidies for cultural consumption, the park was dependent on state funds for the completion of its infrastructure. The park's intended political function as an end rather than a beginning, however, made it difficult to raise support for such initiatives. In fact, it was only in 2000 that the government committed to executing Eleőd's original plans for the park complex, which in addition to finishing the park's construction included the reconstruction of the Stalin statue tribune from "Boots Square" and the construction of an exhibition hall and movie theater in a building that resembles an army barracks. (This updated and renamed "Memento Park" was finally completed in 2006.)

Three years after Réthly took over management of the Statue Park Museum in 1994, I met with him on an unseasonably chilly morning in late September.[17] The park was empty when I arrived, and no visitors appeared during our long conversation sitting at a picnic table near the visitors' booth. Young, casually dressed, and energetic, Réthly appeared unruffled that, apart from an elderly woman working at the ticket counter, we were the only inhabitants of the park. "Eleőd thinks we don't have more visitors because the park is unfinished," he commented wryly. "He's wrong—there's just not that much interest!"

Réthly explained that he approached the city government about managing the park shortly after its opening. He already had plans under way to put together a "communist panopticon" tourist attraction, and he realized that the Statue Park Museum would give him a ready-made site and audience that he could—in his words—"exploit." "I don't view it as a museum or a memorial, but as an enterprise," he told me. "I thought it would be more fun than running a snack bar."

But after taking over the park, Réthly soon discovered that the Statue Park Museum's location was a deterrent to both local and foreign visitors. The park is located in a quiet suburb a twenty-minute bus ride from the center of Budapest, and thus does not fall within traditional tourist routes. Nor does it provide many amenities: before the Statue Park Museum was expanded and transformed into Memento Park in 2006, it could be easily explored in less than an hour, and there were no benches, greenery, or places to eat while visitors waited for a bus to bring them back to the city center. Travel agencies were thus uninterested in adding "Molotov cocktail parties" and "goulash communism happenings" to their itineraries without significant bribes. One agency, Réthly recalled, asked for 20,000 forints (approximately $125 in the mid-1990s): an "enormous, impossible" sum. So Réthly decided to focus his marketing on two groups: city residents who remembered the statues, and those he termed foreign "culture tourists." "Of course, there is a very small group who comes in November and sings the Internationale," he explained. "And there's another small group who raise their fists outside and spit at the statues. But most people treat it as a museum, and not a memorial."[18]

Réthly was insistent that the Statue Park Museum was a serious, "non-ideological" space—"not a joke." Nonetheless, to make a profit, he opened a gift shop at the park to sell humorous kitsch and memorabilia, including postcards, T-shirts, busts of Lenin, Red Army medals, and a tin containing "The Last Breath of Communism." This decision to frame the experience of Eleőd's demythologizing antipropaganda park with the consumption of communist-themed kitsch has undoubtedly made the Statue Park Museum more marketable for the Western European "culture tourists" that the park targets. Over the years that I have been coming to the park, their comments to me and as recorded in the guestbook have tended to interpret the park as proof of both the oppressed socialist past that feared and hated these statues and the democratic present that is free to laugh at them. U.S. media reports of the park's opening similarly played into these fantasies of monumental oppression and current ignominy: describing the park's architecture as a humorous "theme park" (Kaufman 1993, 2); "Leninland" (Beck 1992, 53), or "Commie World" (USA Today 1993, 8), and romantically locating the park on a "bleak hilltop" (Boland 1993, 8). Some journalists even compared the Statue Park Museum to a popular film released at about the same time the park opened: Steven Spielberg's Jurassic Park (1993), which portrays a theme park of living dinosaurs, genetically revitalized from their fossilized traces (Boland 1993, 8; Waugh 1993, 21).

But although the narrative pleasures of Spielberg's film stem from its park's inability to contain the menace unleashed by the reanimation of deadly dinosaurs, most of the Statue Park Museum's forty-one monuments, memorial plaques, and statues are neither scary nor silly. This absence of drama is perhaps one reason the Statue Park Museum initially struggled to attract visitors. The park's opening ceremony, with young women in red neckerchiefs and overalls singing workers' movement songs, may have humorously evoked the kitschy atmosphere of a 1950s party rally, but most of the monuments date from the latter decades of state socialism and, as György Szücs points out, few partake of the excesses of socialist realism (1994, 106). Many monuments simply commemorate local Hungarians: Stalin is nowhere to be found, nor is János Kádár, who discouraged personality cults.

While Western media representations of the park were factually inaccurate, such comparisons to Disneyland and Jurassic Park nonetheless provide a window into understanding what made the marketing of communist kitsch so compelling for international tourists and visitors. Just as the city authorities' desire to deal with monuments in a "civilized" manner revealed their fantasies about entering a more peaceful, prosperous, and European future, many visitors now

brought to the park their own mass-mediated memories and Cold War precon-
ceptions concerning the triumph of Western capitalism over the aesthetic and political barbarism of the communist past. In other words, what may have driven
the fascinated gaze of the West was the possibility of seeing its own burnished
reflection in the remains of a toppled regime.

This imaginative investment was made comically clear to me during a visit in
2002, when I discovered that the Statue Park Museum had been temporarily taken
over by an English-speaking film crew and several carloads of blonde Hungarian
models dressed in 1980s-style jogging shorts and sweatbands. In response to my
questions, the crew told me that they were shooting a music video for a band from
the United States, and they showed me how they had set up the stage in the center
of the park, with the statues that commemorated Ostapenko and his fellow Soviet envoy, Miklós Steinmetz, looming in the background. Unaware of (and clearly
uninterested in) the statues' layered history, the young video director explained
their appeal as "Cool—he's got his arm up waving, like he's saying, 'Hey!'" In this
encounter, the statue's symbolic journey—from the Soviet memorial dedicated
to Ostapenko, to the local emblem of weekend travel and adventure known as

FIGURE 1.1   Memento Park (formerly the Statue Park Museum). From left to
right, statues and monuments to the Buda Volunteers Regiment Memorial, Ilya
Afanasyevich Ostapenko, and Captain Miklós Steinmetz. Personal photograph,
2018.

"Osztyapenkó," to a mere remain of communist ideology—appeared to have reached its final destination. In an ironic inversion of monumental invisibility, the statue was reduced to pure form, untroubled by any content except its ability to provoke the visitor's curious gaze. As an empty figure, beckoning his viewers by waving a flag, Osztyapenkó thus served to prop up a visual story told by, for, and about consumers in the West.

Remembering to Forget

Réthly's kitschy marketing of the Statue Park Museum offered a different appeal to its local visitors. As we have seen, consuming the past in humorous quotation marks became a fashionable cultural practice in Hungary long before the park opened: the communist-themed pizzeria Marxim opened in 1991, and on November 7, 1990, the city of Szeged held a socialist realist ball (Gy. Szücs 1994, 102). The magazine *Magyar Narancs* also hosted a "memory-canteen" public action, where Budapest locals could again taste the kinds of food once served in socialist factory canteens (György 2000, 304). The very speed with which these remains of socialism became trendy demonstrates that their popularity had little to do with a nostalgic desire for restoration or return. Rather, they helped to produce the difference between the communist past and Western present by rewriting the socialist era solely in terms of Soviet occupation. Making the soft dictatorship of yesterday equivalent to that of the repressive Stalinist 1950s—a period that for decades had already been experienced as past—helped to distance an everyday suddenly consigned to the dustbin of history.

Many of the Hungarian visitors I spoke with or observed thus treated the park's statues with the same distanced and ironic enjoyment they displayed in consuming other relics of communist kitsch. Over more than twenty years of making periodic visits to the park, I have seen visitors climbing on the statues, holding mock socialist rallies, and taking photographs as they gleefully repeat the exaggerated poses and gestures of the statues. One group of friends in the late 1990s, for example, drew my interest because they were dressed much more formally than other tourists—the men in suits and ties and the women in dresses and high heels. With cameras in hand, they marched from monument to monument shouting communist slogans and pretending to declaim speeches to an invisible crowd. "It's his birthday," one of the men explained, pointing to his friend who made a fierce face as he struck a heroic pose next to one of the workers' movement monuments. "He's a very right-wing sort of person [*jobboldali valaki*], so we thought it would be funny to take him to the most left-wing place there is." Such mocking and mimetic gestures both summoned the past and pushed it away, reviving memories of the statues' political function while draining them of the potential to inspire any response but laughter. If the creation of the park had enabled politicians and local governments to distance the ambivalent experience of Kádárism by transforming everyday landmarks into anachronistic remains of Soviet rule, then here the pleasures of mocking communist kitsch covered up such official forgetting through the appearance of remembrance.

But the Statue Park Museum is more than a place for the good-humored ridicule of the relics of Soviet rule. Some visitors leave flowers at the base of the statues, whether out of loyalty to the past regime or to honor the sacrifices of the Soviet soldiers who died liberating Hungary at the end of World War II. One friend, who had not grown up in Budapest and was unfamiliar with most of the statues in the park, was shocked to discover that it contained memorial plaques to fallen Soviet soldiers, as many of these plaques were originally erected at the site where these soldiers' bodily remains had been interred. Although she was unsympathetic to those with positive memories of communist rule, she argued with tears in her eyes that these plaques functioned as tombstones and that their removal thus represented a desecration of the graves they once marked.

Other visitors treated the park as a museum of the communist era, with a more unified, pedagogical, and distant relationship to the past than the democratic diversity that Eleőd envisioned. Some parents brought their children, explaining to me that the purpose of the museum is to educate the next generation. (One young woman who lived in the neighborhood nearby told me in 2002 that she took her newborn infant for strolls along the borders of the park—not out of any interest in the statues themselves, but because she considered it to be a "cultured place.") A common complaint in the guestbook during the first years after the park's opening was that the park does not contain every one of the socialist statues of Budapest. And where are the former street signs? The red star from Parliament? Rather than accept the park's mandate to present a representative collection of communist statues, these comments suggest disappointment in the park's failure to provide a comprehensive archive of communist material culture implicit in its rhetoric of democratic preservation. This sense that "something" is missing challenged the park's logic of forgetting through memory, which denies the recognition of loss itself.

Overall, however, relatively few Budapest residents I have spoken with have evinced interest in visiting the Statue Park Museum in the decades since it opened. When I interviewed Réthly in 1997, he claimed that at least half of the park's visitors are Hungarian, and in an interview in 2011, one of his employees repeated this estimate. My own impression, based on both periodic visits to the park since 1995 and discussions on this topic with locals, is that this figure is much lower. Although most people I spoke with accepted the park as a unique and "civilized" solution to the problem of communist monuments, over the years they have repeatedly told me that it is too far away from the city center to be worth a trip, and anyway, they already know what the statues look like—or are not curious to learn.

"I don't feel any need to go there," Eszter explained to me a few years after the park opened. Then in her late twenties, she worked part-time as a secretary in a branch of a multinational firm while she earned her college degree. She remembered some neighborhood complaints when a monument to Béla Kun (founder of the Hungarian Communist Party and leader of the short-lived 1919 Hungarian Soviet Republic) was installed in 1986 in Vérmező park near her family's home in Buda. The last—and perhaps most artistically ambitious—communist monument to be erected in Budapest, the modernist metal sculpture was created by the renowned artist Imre Varga, and presents Kun standing on a platform, urging to action a mixed crowd of working-class demonstrators, Hungarian Red Army soldiers, and urban bourgeoisie. "Some people hated it, but I was proud to have work by such a famous sculptor nearby," Eszter recalled. "It's a shame that they took it down because it's artistically very significant, and after all, Kun and communism are a part of our history, too." But when I asked her if she would go to the Statue Park Museum to see the monument again, she just looked at me incredulously. "No. I don't need to see it again. But I did take some [foreign] colleagues there, because they were curious."

As disparate as the different reactions to the Statue Park Museum may seem, what they have in common is that each enacts a relationship to the past that does not draw on the personal or cultural memory of the statues in socialist-era Budapest, but instead assumes the irrelevance of such prior knowledge. Each constitutes a distancing gesture—whether triumphant mockery, respect for the unknown dead, the curiosity of a museum visitor, or simple indifference—that replaces acknowledgment of the everyday lives of these statues with a focus on their historical context and ideological function. That is, although the architecture of the park is democratically open to a variety of responses to its statues, its actual uses tend to reflect the park's performative function as an end rather than a beginning: the transformation of elements of a living urban landscape into remains of a finished past.

This logic is thus distinct from the reburials of various historical figures found across the former Soviet bloc in the early years of postsocialism. In the case of these reinternments, the point was to finally do it right: to consolidate and rectify remembrance. Here, the point was to forget, and to forget doubly: to expel both the monuments' ideological content *and* the memory of the myriad strategies with which individuals and communities had carved out personal significance from the hegemonic official culture of state socialism. And in thus performing a ritual of mastery over socialism's remains, the Statue Park Museum offered its visitors the possibility of overlooking—however temporarily—all that might still persist from state socialism in institutions, behaviors, and structures of feeling, as well as in the landscape and material culture.

For a time, these lived memories of communist landmarks were nonetheless more difficult to banish than their physical presence: in my early visits to Hungary in the mid-1990s, for example, some people I spoke with still referred to central streets and squares by their old names, whether "Felszab" (short for Felszabadulás [Liberation]) Square instead of Franciscan Square, or "Maja" (short for Majakovszkij [Mayakovsky]) instead of Király Street. But over the years, these names passed out of general circulation without comment, as new (or revived) political and social geographies overwrote the socialist-era names and significance of these sites. The rare exceptions became newsworthy, such as when an internet blog reported in 2011 that McDonald's was keeping alive the memory of Osztyapenkó, since a restaurant located near the former site of his statue used his name to denote its location on printed receipts. "In a former socialist country, one of the best known American symbols and a dead hero of the Soviet Union together transcend the grievances of the Cold War," the blog post declared, "Gorgeous" (Gorbacsov 2011).

But although the example of the Osztyapenkó McDonald's represents the fantasy of overcoming the oppositions between communist East and capitalist West, past and present, memorialization and commercialization, the Statue Park Museum struggled to reconcile such tensions. In particular, the contradictory architectural and marketing strategies of the park reveal the frictions between the two competing visions of the Hungarian public emerging in the early years of postsocialism: citizens versus consumers (Harper 1999). In emphasizing capitalism over democracy—the "individual satisfaction of commodifiable desires" rather than participation in "political decision making processes" (Harper 1999, 109)—the park's marketing lost the possibility of debate or the desire to build consensus. Those who found the park's playful marketing strategies painful or offensive to their own memories of socialism could simply choose not to visit or buy its products. Thus, while the park was built to collect competing memories, this logic of individual consumption evaded the possibility of dialogue or confrontation.

Monumental Fantasies

Over the years of visiting the Statue Park Museum (and its current incarnation as Memento Park), I have taken numerous photographs of its monuments, as well as observed the ways its visitors encounter the space and use snapshots to represent that encounter to others. In accordance with Eleőd's desire to produce a democratic architecture, it is striking how difficult it is to produce images that achieve the stately and totalizing effects of the monumental. Many shots include houses, power lines, or a nearby water tower in the background, or weeds growing in the gravel that lines the paths. Close-ups that isolate a monument from its neighbors risk fragmenting or distorting the image, and thus breaching the perceptual distance that monuments traditionally demand. The prospects are no less discouraging if a wide shot is attempted, perhaps standing on the highway that borders one side of the park. This reveals many of the monuments as improbably and poignantly small, no longer supported by the enormous bases on which they once stood.

Over the years that the park has been open, however, its promotional images have told a different story. Whether official posters, postcards, guidebooks, or photographs on the park's website and informational CD, these images often advertise the park with dynamic montages that present the statues photographed from dramatic angles, excised from their physical setting against a backdrop of communist red. In these images, the monuments appear menacing, oppressive,

FIGURE 1.2 Memento Park (formerly the Statue Park Museum). Lenin statue that once stood at the entrance of the Csepel Iron and Metal Works. The sign in the background advertises a gardening store. Personal photograph, 2018.

FIGURE 1.3 Memento Park (formerly the Statue Park Museum). From left to right, three monuments from the park's "Endless Parade of Liberation Monuments": a liberation monument by István Kiss, the Hungarian-Soviet Friendship Memorial, and a statue of a liberating Soviet soldier that was once part of the liberation monument on Gellért Hill. Personal photograph, 2018.

and forbidden: a visual strategy that seemingly counters Eleőd's explicit aim to deconstruct the effect of the monumental and present the monuments neutrally, as documents of the aesthetic politics of the previous regime and evidence of democratic tolerance.

As in the international reports of the park's opening, these images fail to document the physical reality of the park. In doing so, however, they illuminate one of the imaginative investments in remains of socialism. This is the temporality of the *ghost*: a trope apparent in some of the international media coverage of the park, which viewed it as a "gulag" or "graveyard" of dead statues, only to reanimate these figures as "poor giants," "forlorn," and "adrift in a suburban wasteland" (Plachy 1993, 48–49). If the Statue Park Museum was created as a memorial to the transition, then it too became susceptible to monumental invisibility; ghosts, on the other hand, intrude on and demand attention, warning of improper burial and unfinished business. As paradigmatic instances of the uncanny, ghosts thus do not reflect confusion between fantasy and reality, but rather the "excessive and terrible certainty" occasioned when that which has been expelled and forgotten reappears (Ivy 1995, 85; Dolar 1991).

The power of this trope of ghostly danger and unwanted return is that it conceals the relative lack of eventfulness in the political transformation that brought the park into being. Instead, it writes the statues back into the triumphant monumental history that the park's architecture sought to deconstruct. Projecting both a past that never happened and a future that was never realized, these promotional images function as photographs without a referent. In so doing, the images patch over an even more disquieting awareness: what was so dangerous about the statues in the early years of postsocialism was that few found them threatening at all. That is, these images of the Statue Park Museum are able to play humorously with the threat of haunting precisely because at the time of the park's creation, there was little fear that the monuments or the ideology they were perceived to embody would return.

Supplemented by images that reveal the lack of ghostly danger in the original, the statues and monuments of the Statue Park Museum may thus disappoint many of its visitors precisely in their failure to evoke the uncanny. But the park's inability to attract many local visitors does not mean that Hungarians soon lost their interest in fantasies of a triumphant future forged from the remains of an unwanted past. Rather, the park—as both a physical and discursive space— appears inadequate to the task. Over the years, the park's architecture of democracy would swiftly fall out of date, as its potential visitors became increasingly disenchanted with both the economic and political aspirations visible in the park's design—the hope that embracing democratic principles and values would translate into a prosperous future unencumbered by past legacies. As we will see in the later chapters of this book, the postsocialist future the park so confidently prophesied would ultimately seem as irrelevant and anachronistic as the statues themselves. First, however, we will continue to examine the first decade of postsocialism, as political parties, historians, and activists battled to replace socialist remains with a new historical canon.

THE HOLE IN THE FLAG

"Hungary has survived everything," Béla told me in an interview I conducted during the first months of my fieldwork. "Hungarians know how to get by [*Életképes ez a nép*]." We sat in a lushly appointed small conference room in the home office of his daughter, who had just finished renovating her apartment to include space for her burgeoning legal practice. Recently retired, Béla was visibly proud of his daughter's professional and financial achievements, and he compared her promising legal career to the difficult choices he had faced as a young graduate in 1960. Unable to find a position as a lawyer, he had reluctantly become a public prosecutor and eventually rose to the position of attorney general in his county before retiring earlier that year.

> There's a joke that the Russians asked the Turks after 1956 how they had been able to remain here for 150 years without the Hungarians attempting to overthrow them. The Turks responded that the secret was not to make Hungarians celebrate their own occupation. "You always make them celebrate on April 4 that they've been liberated [from Nazi Germany]." This is just a joke, but there's a lot of truth in it. The Russians did politics very badly.

> *So did these holidays bother you?*

> No. They were nice holidays. There were programs, and not just on April 4, but on May 1 [International Workers' Day] too. On November 7 [the anniversary of the October Revolution of 1917], there weren't as

many because that was still a Russian holiday. There were wieners, beer, nobody thought about the holiday, but rather how much fun they had. Nobody bothered themselves about what kind of holiday it was.

I was initially surprised by the disconnect between Béla's critique of Soviet holidays and his remembered enjoyment of the events—as well as the fact that he did not perceive this as a contradiction. Béla's career as a public prosecutor meant that he had worked in one of the most entrusted—and thus loyalty-dependent— positions that one could hold after the 1956 revolution.[1] Yet he nonetheless offered a politically critical remark that addressed the ideological foundations of the regime he had served, before then resolving this tension by insisting that his personal experience of these celebrations was free of such considerations.

At first, I assumed that Béla's ambivalence simply reflected his experience of the previous system, in which accommodating himself to the limited prospects available to him had ultimately brought him professional prestige and satisfaction. (It also perhaps evidenced his desire to now portray himself as untouched by a discredited political ideology.) But I soon discovered that many other people of different ages, class positions, and political affiliations often offered similarly benign remembrances of communist holidays like May 1, regardless of their criticism of the regime more generally. As we saw in chapter 1, one answer to this apparent paradox lay in the ways many of my interviewees now remembered the political subjectivity of late socialism. The unspoken social contract under Kádárism that dichotomized the relationship between ideology and the everyday now enabled many people to claim that they had navigated even the most prominent symbols of an unwanted regime—whether holidays or monuments—with relative indifference.

As with Budapest's communist statues, the past regime's holiday calendar and its depoliticization in everyday life would thus present a challenge for Hungary's emerging political parties eager to demonstrate their break from the past in the early years of postsocialism. And just as the Statue Park Museum attempted to replace the communist monumental landscape with a democratic memorial to transition, many of the most important events of the system change would strive to replace the remains of communist history with new national narratives that would transform Kádár's resigned subjects into a newly democratic citizenry. After the elections in 1990, the first sessions of Hungary's new Parliament were devoted to determining the new national holidays and coat of arms. And as Budapest authorities changed street names and removed communist statues, they also reworked the Hungarian historical and monumental landscape into an ideological patchwork of new monuments to heroes of the distant past alongside those reinstalled after spending the socialist era in warehouses (Gy. Szücs 1994, 101). Even literal as well as metaphorical bodies were on the move. In the final years of state socialism, state authorities held a ceremonious reburial of the renowned composer Béla Bartók, and in 1993, the heads of Hungary's first postsocialist democratic government attended the reinternment of the controversial interwar leader Miklós Horthy.[2]

But nothing was more crucial to the historical politics of the system change than the recovery of the memory of Hungary's 1956 revolution: a two-week countrywide uprising that briefly raised the hope of national independence before it was brutally suppressed by the Soviet Union. In the 1980s, attempts to honor the revolution in public memory helped to organize opposition to the regime. This pressure on state authorities ultimately led to perhaps the most important symbolic event of the change of system: the official rehabilitation and reburial of the revolution's martyred prime minister, Imre Nagy, and his associates on June 16, 1989. By the mid-1990s, however, political battles would instead make the memory of 1956 a symbol of the fragmentation and polarization of the former opposition, as well as the source of increasing skepticism and disengagement in the general public.

This chapter examines the task of creating new histories—and the new national citizens produced by those histories—in the first decade after the end of socialism. It looks at how competing parties, politicians, and activists struggled to eliminate the experience of state socialism from both official history and public remembrance, by replacing socialist remains with national content summoned from the more distant recent past. First, I analyze contested attempts to repair the recent past by recovering the memory of 1956 as the symbolic foundation for a new democratic Hungary. Second, I explore the historical politics of the center-right Fidesz-led coalition government in power between 1998 and 2002 and the commemorative events it sponsored, such as the celebrations of the "Magyar Millennium" in 2000–2001. These commemorations sought to remake both history and the nation itself: transforming what Fidesz considered to be defeated and depoliticized Kádárist subjects into confident, optimistic citizens ready to enter the postsocialist future. Yet such attempts to create new histories would encounter the same challenges that the efforts to eliminate old ones did—the ambivalence with which most Hungarians now regarded their memories of the recent past, a time of both political oppression and a degree of material and existential security that was now quickly vanishing.

My goal is not to adjudicate among various claims to historical truth and national authenticity: a battle that those on the right tended to frame as the forces of historical justice against communist amnesia, and that those on the left portrayed as reactionary nationalism. Indeed, one of the most pervasive complaints I encountered during my fieldwork was the perception of the overpoliticization of everyday life in general, in which the polarization of left and right, and the historical ideologies these positions represented, had filtered down into even prosaic interactions with friends, partners, and families. Many people complained to me that it was impossible to talk about anything important because each side demonized the other and there was so little common ground on which to debate these issues fruitfully.

Such complaints only helped to reinforce the perception that Hungary had a pathological relationship to its recent past, which then prompted further attempts to master socialism's remains. The title of this chapter—"The Hole in the Flag"—thus refers literally to the flags waved during the 1956 revolution by protestors who excised the communist coat-of-arms from the traditional Hungarian tricolor. But it also describes more broadly how attempts to eliminate remains of socialism from Hungary's history would leave holes in the symbolic fabric of national identification—and how the heated battles to determine how to patch it up would ultimately reinforce the perception of lack.

The 1956 Revolution

To explain the importance of the memory of 1956 during the end of communism in Hungary—as well as the surprising decline of its relevance in the first decade of postsocialism—historical background on the revolution and its memory under communism is necessary.[3] In the wake of Stalin's death in 1953, the Soviets replaced Hungary's hard-liner prime minister Mátyás Rákosi with Imre Nagy, who began undertaking economic reforms and releasing political prisoners. Rákosi, who had remained the head of the Party, returned to power in 1955, before then being replaced by one of his close associates, Ernő Gerő, in 1956. In this atmosphere of uncertainty, when it seemed that the previous tentative liberalization would be reversed, there was an increasing demand—first among young communist intellectuals,[4] later among students in general—for a return to the reform-minded policies represented by Nagy and, ultimately, for a more fundamental democratization.

On October 22, 1956, students of the Technical University of Budapest issued a set of demands ("Sixteen Points," modeled on the "Twelve Points" issued during the 1848 Revolution) that called for, among other things, the immediate withdrawal of Soviet troops, the reinstatement of Nagy as prime minister, and the reorganization of Hungarian economic life (Békés, Byrne, and Rainer 2002, 188–190). On October 23, students and members of the Writers' Union participated in a demonstration to show solidarity with Poland, where the reform attempts of the new party leadership resulted in a standoff with Moscow. This grew into a massive march through the streets of Budapest, during which protestors cut out the Stalinist state emblem from the Hungarian flag and toppled the Stalin statue at one of the city's main squares, before proceeding to the Hungarian Radio building to broadcast their demands. Violence broke out when members of the secret police (ÁVH) fired on the crowd, and the demonstrators began to fight back.

Over the next four days, protestors organized into armed militias and fought Soviet troops in both Budapest and the countryside. Nagy was appointed prime minister on October 24, and on October 28, he formed a new cabinet, thus signaling that he endorsed the main demands of the uprising. Nagy declared a ceasefire, and in the coming days, he withdrew Hungary from the Warsaw Pact, demanded the withdrawal of Soviet troops, released political prisoners, and called for a nonaligned multiparty social democracy.

Although the Soviets were initially willing to negotiate with Nagy, they soon switched course, and on November 4, Soviet troops invaded Hungary. Fighting lasted until November 9 when the rebellion was entirely crushed. János Kádár, who had been first secretary of the Communist Party under Nagy and seemed to be his ally, made a turnabout and accepted the role given to him in Moscow to form a new government and consolidate power. Nagy was imprisoned (and later executed), and thousands of Hungarians fled the country, with most ultimately settling in Western Europe and the United States. Several years of harsh repression and retribution followed.

Once the immediate threat of rebellion was quelled, however, Kádár changed tactics to pursue a strategy of "consolidation." In the early 1960s he began releasing political prisoners and attempted to reconcile citizens to communist rule by shifting state investment from heavy industry to consumer goods in order to support a rising living standard. Hungary's exhausted and traumatized populace acquiesced to this policy of material stability and the depoliticization of everyday life, which would continue for more than three decades until the final years of the regime.

Throughout this time, government authorities rigorously controlled both public remembrance and the production of historical knowledge about the events of 1956. Officially, they termed it a "counterrevolution" that linked the uprising to the "reactionary" adherents of the conservative government in power during the interwar period. Enforcing this interpretation was crucial to maintaining the regime's legitimacy, insofar as the suppression of the rebellion was the condition of Kádár's own ascent to power. In practice, however, the authorities avoided mentioning 1956 as much as possible, in order to circumvent the resistant personal and collective memories that public discussion might inspire. The silence around "56" would come to represent a structuring emptiness in public discourse: its absence signified the regime's fear of a rebellious populace as well as its citizens' own desire to avoid painful reminders of the executions, imprisonments, and persecution suffered by thousands after the revolution's suppression.

From Public Secret to Public Memory, 1956–1989

We have seen that under late socialism, economic stagnation and the conviction of a better life elsewhere produced the common perception that time had stopped. Not only time, but history itself stood still under Kádárism. Yet despite the "enforced historical amnesia" (Gyáni 2006, 1199) that prevailed in public discourse under socialism, 1956 did not entirely disappear from collective discussion, popular culture, or historical research.[5] Resistant interpretations or memories of 1956 could not be spoken publicly, but they did not go forgotten—whether represented elliptically in film and literature or in the private recollection of participants and their families. Moreover, the very necessity of avoiding 1956 in public speech paradoxically functioned to reinforce its memory, by preserving the knowledge that something was being evaded.

This tension between official amnesia and private recollection reflected the dichotomous political subjectivity that the Kádár regime encouraged in its subjects more generally. For example, as Júlia Szalai and László Gábor describe from their study of how adolescents in 1992 understood 1956, teachers under socialism were trained to discourage public discussion of 1956 with their students. Instead, they emphasized that individuals were entitled to their own personal opinions, provided that such beliefs remained "private" and did not enter the public political realm (1997, 30–31). There were thus no points of connection between the sparse official narratives offered at school and the vivid "history lessons" that some students might receive at home, where parents provided both factual information and the social knowledge that made life under the Kádár regime intelligible As Szalai and Gábor observe, "Nothing else was needed but to explain over dinner who the present boss had been 'in those days,' why X was promoted or decorated while Y would have truly deserved it instead, why G and Z do not talk to each other even today, why half of the family lived in the West, why they fled and from what" (1997, 39). Thus, 1956 functioned as "a symbol of the absurd duality of life," in which private and public knowledge were sharply divided (31).

But the shared experience of official amnesia did not necessarily mean that everyone was eager to preserve the memory of 1956 or that they experienced state socialist life as one of "absurd duality." Some former participants kept 1956 alive in personal and family recollection, but others sought to forget what they perceived as a painful trauma that destroyed, uprooted, or separated families and stigmatized those who remained. Moreover, some of those not personally touched by 1956 were simply content to accept the official party line that it was a reactionary counterrevolution. One friend, who came of age at the time of the system change, remembered that his older colleagues at the library where he was then employed were upset at the sudden revaluation of the history of 1956 in the late 1980s, and that they complained about the "big-mouthed opposition" (*nagyszájú ellenzék*) that had succeeded in pressuring the government to rebury Nagy. Change, my friend recalled, appeared to be moving almost too quickly: the dizzying tempo of political transformation was overtaking the stately pace of scholarship, reviving painful memories that were best left to history.

But although the *interpretation* of 1956 might divide Hungarians across generational, political, and even familial lines, the remembered *experience* of 1956 (and the subsequent years of reprisals) shared a sense of national and personal trauma: what the historian János Rainer M. describes as "a tangled, feverish, confused and opaque situation, when life was jerked out of its normal rut for a while" (2002, 220). As a result, Rainer observes, what patched over these diverging interpretations during the socialist era was a shared understanding that the revolutionary events represented "troubled times" that no one wanted to repeat (220). In the 1970s, the regime similarly attempted to shift its political interpretation of 1956 into an emotional register, by calling it simply a "national tragedy" (211).

By the mid-1980s, 1956 nonetheless began to reenter public discourse as the symbol of national resistance to communist rule as well as the injustice and illegitimacy of the current regime. This was primarily due to the efforts of two overlapping groups: (1) 56-ers and relatives of those who died during the revolution or the retribution that followed, and (2) Hungary's intellectual opposition more generally. These groups were numerically small and divided by ideological concerns, but they were united in their demand that the regime reexamine 1956 and recognize the claims of its victims and veterans.[6] Their call to rehabilitate national history thus became the lens through which they envisioned both the end of communism and their hopes for the future that would follow. For example, one key way these groups sought to restore the revolution to public memory was by attempting to rewrite the state holiday calendar, replacing communist holidays with ones that celebrated Hungary's national sovereignty.[7]

Because Kádár had been implicated in the execution of Nagy, prime minister during the revolution, no change in the regime's policy toward 1956 was possible before Kádár's forced retirement in 1988. In 1989, however, the reform communists who replaced Kádár began to accede to public pressure to reevaluate 1956. In January, the leading party functionary Imre Pozsgay made the unexpected public statement on a popular weekly radio program that Hungary's

1956 "counterrevolution" was in fact a popular uprising.[8] This interpretation, which threatened the legitimacy of communist rule, sparked two weeks of heated public debate and party infighting before a compromise was found between party leaders and the more radical faction of reform communists Pozsgay represented. By engaging in such public debate and acceding however half-heartedly to Pozsgay's views, though, the regime also capitulated to the demand to bring 1956 back into public discussion (Dienstag 1996).

This reevaluation of the 1956 revolution was followed by the state reburial of Nagy in June 1989, on the anniversary of his 1958 execution. Nagy and his associates had been sentenced to death at a non-public trial, buried in secret, and placed face down in unmarked graves. In the weeks preceding the Pozsgay affair, the government gave permission to the relatives of Nagy and the other victims to hold a private funeral. But under increasing pressure from the opposition parties, the regime now restaged the reburial as a state event that attracted a crowd of 200,000 mourners and was broadcast on state television. Attended by the prime minister and the speaker of the national assembly, and opened with speeches by 56ers (such as Imre Mécs, a founding member of SZDSZ [the Alliance of Free Democrats]), as well as the young leader of Fidesz, Viktor Orbán, who spoke on behalf of Hungary's youth, the reburial of Nagy allowed its diverse attendees and participants to attempt to align themselves with the revolution's legacy. The opposition considered the revolutionary acts of 1956 to be inspiration for similarly far-reaching political changes in 1989, whereas the reformers presented themselves as the true heirs of Nagy, who had sought to maintain socialism while correcting both its past excesses and the plans for its future direction (Rév 2005, 37).[9] The participants thus each sought not only to forge a new interpretation of national history but also to write themselves into that history as its proper inheritors. Moreover, the liminal character of the commemoration enabled speakers, politicians, and everyday attendees alike the opportunity to collapse the decades between then and now (Rév 2005, 42), and thus to symbolically erase the memory of Kádárism from public remembrance.[10]

But despite the reform communists' attempts to use Nagy's reburial to assert their own political legitimacy, their rehabilitation of the memory of 1956 would accelerate the regime's demise, playing a key role in what many Hungarians otherwise perceived as a fairly remote process of dismantling state socialism. In the months that followed, the party negotiated with the opposition the creation of the multiparty electoral system that would ultimately remove it from power. In keeping with Hungary's much-heralded return to historical truth and national authenticity, the new republic was announced on the thirty-third anniversary of the uprising, October 23, 1989, and the first act of the freely elected Parliament in 1990 was to establish the new canonical definition of 1956 as a "revolution and

war of independence" like that of 1848. Former political prisoners and participants created new political parties and groups (such as the October Party and the
Recsk League), and scholars who included both former participants and a younger
generation of historians founded a new research institute devoted exclusively
to studying the revolution (the Institute for the History of the 1956 Hungarian
Revolution [Az 1956-os Magyar Forradalom Történetének Dokumentációs és
Kutatóintézete]).

The events of 1989 appeared to signal new life for the memory of 1956, by
reinserting it back into public discourse and establishing it as Hungary's new
historical canon through which national identification could be forged. Yet although
1956 had served as the knot to tie together many otherwise disparate personal and
political agendas at the moment of communism's demise, once this unspoken
memory—or public secret (that is, what is widely known but cannot be stated
publicly [Taussig 1999])—was revealed, it lost much of its power (Rév 2005, 39;
Gyáni 2006, 1201). By the mid-1990s, it had already become a truism in academic
and public discourse that the 1956 revolution had failed to become the foundational myth of a newly democratic Hungary.[11] Rather than representing a new
beginning, Nagy's reburial appeared to mark the end of 1956 as a possibility for
unifying the national community.

Contested Legacies, 1956 after 1990

A number of factors explain why the memory of 1956 retreated so quickly from
its central role in the symbolic politics of the system change. One concerns the
changing role of the memory of 1956 after the fall of communism. Under late socialism, to invoke 1956 was to invoke the regime's war against historical truth
itself: the very name of the events (that is, "revolution" rather than "counterrevolution") could not be uttered in public speech. To call the revolution a popular
uprising thus functioned as a tool of political criticism, symbolizing both national
resistance to Soviet rule and the injustice and illegitimacy of the current regime.

Nagy's reburial represented the first moment when the ideological schisms
within the opposition became publicly visible, as new political parties and groups
fiercely battled to claim the revolution's legacy in order to assert their own political legitimacy. From that moment forward, the memory of 1956 would no longer function as a shared weapon against an unjust state, but rather as a tool of
democratic political competition. For example, even the initial act of the first
democratically elected Parliament after the 1990 elections, which put into law the
official definition of the 1956 revolution, omitted the name of Nagy. (His desire
to reform rather than abandon communism delegitimized him in the eyes of the

right-wing politicians who pressured for this change.)[12] And by the time of my fieldwork in the late 1990s, yearly commemorations on October 23 had become explicitly fragmented and politicized, as each party held separate events to legitimize its own programs and policies.

At stake was not only who could claim the legacy of the revolution, but what the revolution even consisted of. Due to the limits that had been placed on historical study of 1956 under state socialism, much scholarly work still needed to be done in the early 1990s in order to understand the revolution.[13] Under socialism, the fight against a common enemy had concealed competing understandings of what the suppressed "true" memory of 1956 actually entailed—a reform communist movement, a workers' uprising, a national revolt, or an agent for more radical change.[14] Now, given the lack of a preestablished canon, the flexible interpretation of the revolution meant that it not only could be cited to support competing political platforms, but that its main actors, events, and aims could be selectively chosen to buttress specific claims. Árpád Göncz, a 56er who later became the president of Hungary from 1990 to 2000, may have famously declared that there were as many memories of 1956 as Hungarians (*ahány ember, annyi 56*), but this diversity was not hailed as part of Hungary's collective heritage. Rather, it represented competing and mutually exclusive claims to historical and present-day victimhood, heroism, and legitimacy.

This challenge of determining the meaning of 1956 was only compounded by a more general interpretative problem: the lack of public consensus as to what Hungary's new postsocialist national identity, as reflected in and founded by 1956, should comprise. As Szalai and Gábor point out, little connection could be drawn between the political motivations and social values of the revolution and the present day (1997, 47). For example, according to the main dissident narrative, the future that the 1956 revolutionaries had been battling to attain was that of democratic socialism. But because the reform communists had tried to portray themselves as the heirs of this legacy in the final year of the regime, this vision became irrelevant even before the demise of state socialism in favor of capitalist democracy. Moreover, as discussed in chapter 1, most Hungarians were proud that the end of the regime was accomplished not through revolutionary turmoil, but through peaceful negotiation.

For this reason, although Hungary's new political parties appealed to the memory of 1956 for moral and political legitimacy, they did not draw on its legacy in formulating their own programs. The desire for a peaceful political transformation was one factor in the 1990 electoral victory of the conservative MDF (Hungarian Democratic Forum), whose coalition government with the KDNP (Christian Democrats) and the FKGP (Independent Smallholders' Party) offered an alternative between the communist successor parties and the perceived radicalism of SZDSZ. Staffed by a number of professional historians,[15] the MDF-led coalition government was ultimately less concerned with maintaining the memory of the 1956 revolution than with obliterating the socialist past entirely by reviving the conservative "national-Christian" heritage of interwar Hungary. In doing so, it thus sought to portray all four decades of communist rule as a foreign imposition by the Soviets, and hence a divergence from the authentic course of Hungarian history (Rév 2005, 44).

The MDF coalition's attempt to restore national continuity by rehabilitating the interwar period, expressed through what many perceived as nationalist and populist rhetoric, would reach its symbolic apex in the reburial of Admiral Miklós Horthy in the summer of 1993. (This funeral was not an official state event, but it was nonetheless broadcast on state television and attended by many members of the government.) Horthy governed Hungary from the interwar years through the final years of World War II. His reburial thus served as a symbolic challenge to the reburial of Nagy four years earlier: an implicit effort to reenact the political transition by making postsocialist Hungary the direct heir of Horthy's conservative historical tradition rather than the contested legacy of 1956. Yet although Horthy was undoubtedly a more complex historical figure than the fascist he was portrayed as during the years of communist rule, he had nonetheless governed Hungary during its alliance with Nazi Germany, and he was in office during the Nazi deportation of Hungary's rural Jewish population. The MDF coalition's attempt to rehabilitate him as a Hungarian patriot thus met with controversy both locally and abroad.[16]

Such anachronistic historical politics contributed to a backlash in the 1994 general elections. With the initial optimism of political transformation quickly tempered by the economic stresses and uncertainties of Hungary's entrance into a market economy, voters elected to power the main successor to the communist party, the MSZP (Hungarian Socialist Party), in coalition with their former opposition, the SZDSZ.[17] The MSZP's victory was commonly considered to represent not the triumph of a competing ideology, but rather the endorsement of a practical-minded, technocratic former elite who had reinvented themselves as a modern European social democratic party while boasting of their previous "expertise" in governing. Thus, although the MDF was elected in 1990 under a slogan that pledged the swift removal of Hungary's socialist remains—"National spring cleaning! [Országos tavaszi nagytakarítást]"—the MSZP won precisely by claiming continuity with the recent past: "Trust it to the experts! [Bizza szakemberre!]." (Meanwhile, although the left-liberal SZDSZ offered an alternative national history of revolutionary political opposition—encompassing 1848, 1956, and the dissident movements of late socialism—the party overall was more concerned with entering the future than engaging with the past, and thus emphasized narratives of progress and modernization over the restoration of national authenticity.)

Yet the MSZP soon demonstrated itself to be socialist in provenance only. Instead of reinstalling some of the social safety nets of the previous regime (one of the few spheres of governance in which state socialism had earned legitimacy), its leadership sought to establish themselves as neoliberal European moderniz-ers, undertaking austerity measures (the "Bokros package") tougher than those proposed by any other party. The MSZP also discarded its rhetoric of economic pragmatism over historical politics when it marked the fortieth anniversary of the 1956 revolution in 1996 by pushing through a bill declaring Nagy to be a Martyr of the Nation. (This bill was planned to coincide with the erection of a monu-ment in Nagy's honor at Martyrs' Square [Vértanúk tere] near Parliament.) The MSZP's highly contested attempt to portray itself as the heir to Nagy had a his-torical basis, insofar as it could argue that Nagy's endorsement of democracy and independence from Soviet rule, while still believing in a socialist system, made Nagy a precursor to the reform communists who would constitute the MSZP after 1990.[18] Nonetheless, many Hungarians perceived the MSZP's efforts to lay

FIGURE 2.1 Statue of Imre Nagy erected in 1996 at Martyrs' Square (*Vértanúk tere*) near Parliament. The monument was removed from this square in 2019 and relocated several blocks away. Personal photograph, 2018.

claim to Nagy's historical legacy as highly cynical and transparent. Some viewed the appropriation of Nagy's memory by the successors to the very regime that had executed him to be the epitome of the way 1956 had been exploited by present-day political ends. For others, Nagy's status as a communist meant that he did not merit such commemoration in the first place. (The other parties in Parliament, including the MSZP's coalition partner SZDSZ, thus refused to support this measure.)

As a result of this controversy, in the years that followed, the MSZP would increasingly avoid historical politics. And the left-liberal SZDSZ, whose leadership contained several prominent 56ers, would increasingly find its claims to anticommunism delegitimized due to its coalition with its former enemy, the MSZP. Indeed, the SZDSZ's decision to align itself with the MSZP reflected a broader transformation in the postsocialist political landscape, in which the initial divide between the new democratic parties and the successors to the old regime was replaced by an ideological split between left and right. This shift also impacted the political orientation of 56er organizations such as the Committee for Historical Justice (Történelmi Igazságtétel Bizottság, TIB), which had previously been successful in fighting for Nagy's reburial and for adequate government compensation for the revolution's veterans. In 1992, however, the committee became split over issues that included the punishment of communist crimes, the role that TIB should play in contemporary politics, and who had the right to speak in the revolution's name. Those who preached moderation ultimately left the TIB, and other activist organizations would similarly become radicalized (Nyyssönen 1999, 229–233).

Thus 1956 would increasingly become the province of the right wing, which rejected the "universalist, rights-based" anticommunism of the SZDSZ and instead conceptualized anticommunism along conservative and nationalist lines (Fowler 2006, 103). Now 1956 represented a nationalist revolution against Russian occupation; its failure was just one of a litany of Hungarian tragedies, like the Treaty of Trianon. And, as Rainer notes, those who did not share this political affiliation were branded as communists, even if they themselves had fought in 1956 or had been active in the dissident movement under late socialism (2002, 220).

Family Memory and Troubled Times

At the time of my initial fieldwork in the late 1990s and early 2000s, my interviewees and interlocutors all agreed that 1956 was a significant event in Hungary's recent history, but there was increasingly little interest in its possible relevance for present-day Hungary. This sense of disengagement may have reflected the success of the memory work at the time of the political transition, which revived and corrected the memory of 1956 in order to rebury it in its proper place in history. But it also indicated my interviewees' discomfort with the current political battles to claim the revolution's legacy, as well as the lack of consensus concerning how to interpret it.[19]

For some, conversations about 1956 became conversations about the politics of even mentioning it. Csaba, a professional who identified as politically conservative, told me that his parents were children in 1956 and thus too young to understand the gravity of the events. Instead, they remembered viewing the revolution as an opportunity to miss school and—in the case of one parent—to camp out with neighbors after the family apartment was damaged during the Soviet invasion. "They don't make a big deal out of it now and they don't complain," he said, professing himself to be somewhat mystified by their matter-of-factness. "It's just something that happened—they don't over-dramatize it." One of his colleagues jumped in with a comment about how rare she perceived such understatement to be, in light of how eagerly people claimed veteran status in order to demand authority to determine the legacy of the revolution. "It's interesting that how the years go by, there are more and more 'freedom-fighters,'" she remarked wryly, noting that members of this generation were already entering their sixties and seventies. "You would think it would be the other way around!"[20]

Csaba and his colleague considered his parents' reticence to be unusual compared to the instrumentalization of 1956 in public and political life. But in interviews and everyday conversation, many of the memories shared with me similarly emphasized the primacy of personal experience and tended to avoid addressing the revolution's broader political context (whether vis-à-vis its original goals or its potential fulfillment in 1989).[21] Although I was not able to interview anyone who identified as a participant in the revolution, many of those I spoke with considered themselves to have been affected by the revolution in some way: from those like Béla who had attended demonstrations in 1956 to members of younger generations who mentioned relatives who had been imprisoned, who had emigrated abroad, or whose everyday lives had otherwise been shaped by the rebellion and its brutal suppression. My conversations with people across the political spectrum on other contested historical topics that were still alive in public and family memory (such as Trianon, the Holocaust, or World War II) were often richly imbued with historical affect and a sense of irresolution, whether that took the form of enduring grief, defiant pride, anger at abiding injustice, or the trauma of loss and political persecution. In contrast, even those who had lost family members to emigration or possessed their own childhood or teenaged recollections of the events in 1956 described them as personally painful and significant but with little direct relevance to Hungary's challenges in the present: 1956 represented important but finished history.

For example, Ágnes, who worked as a schoolteacher and private tutor, told me that one of her uncles became a dissident in 1956 "but by accident." He participated in a demonstration at the university in Sopron in western Hungary, and when the Soviets invaded, he joined many of his classmates and professors in fleeing across the border to Austria. "And that was enough," she said, explaining that he never returned. "He was just eighteen years old." As a child in the 1970s, Ágnes remembers that her grandparents suffered because of her uncle's absence: "My grandmother cried for years, and from then on, my grandfather's life was very difficult, professionally." But the sense of finality and irreversibility of this loss was such that (unlike many other 1956 émigrés), her uncle had chosen never to return to Hungary, even after the end of state socialism. "He has his own life in Canada now." For Ágnes, 1956 thus represented a family tragedy in the past, but it was one that—unlike many other tragedies in Hungary's recent history—no longer appeared to have significant connections to the concerns of the present. Similarly, Szonja, another interviewee, also had an uncle who emigrated to Canada after 1956, and she told me in a life history interview that he did return for visits beginning in the late 1970s. But what made her memories of her uncle personally meaningful now did not concern his involvement in the revolution and subsequent escape, but rather the glamour he would later represent as a relative visiting from the prosperous West. "He brought me jeans and made me the best-dressed kid at school," she recalled with a smile. Such memories of high-status consumption and access to the perceived better standard of living in the West spoke poignantly to Szonja's current economic struggles as a single mother of two in a way that the seemingly distant family history of political revolt did not.

Other interviewees were reluctant to associate personal experiences of fear and suffering in 1956 with the current battles to claim its heroic legacy. That is, state socialism may have ended, but the perception that memories and opinions of the events were best left to the private family realm appeared to remain. Mária, then in her late fifties, had worked as an office administrator for decades, but after her firm closed in the early 1990s, she was unable to find a similar position and now worked part-time as a housecleaner. Like Csaba's parents, the childhood memories of the revolutionary events that she chose to share with me were characterized by naiveté and incomprehension ("When the Russian tanks came, we children were excited, but our parents were terrified"), and as an adult, she told me, she did not feel comfortable discussing 1956 because she did not think she knew enough concerning how to speak about it. "First they said it was a counterrevolution, and now it's not." The mother of a friend simply chose to summarize her youthful memories of the revolution and its aftermath as a "gray time, when even children did not have enough to eat," before concluding, "I don't like to talk about it."[22]

As a consequence of these various strategies that avoided, depoliticized, or minimized the contemporary relevance of 1956, a new generation was growing up whose lack of knowledge about the revolution may have been more extensive than those who grew up under communism. Under late socialism, although some Hungarians accepted the official narrative that 1956 represented a "counterrevolution," many other families considered knowing how to navigate the fraught memory of 1956 to be crucial in deciphering political and public culture. Now, however, tutoring the younger generation in such interpretive labor was no longer an urgent necessity. For example, on the morning of October 23, 2000, Zsófi—one of my former English students, then in her early twenties—phoned me from her village, using the national holiday as an opportunity to catch up and chat. When I asked her if she had planned anything for the holiday, she demurred, saying that it did not mean anything to her, "but maybe to others." There were no local commemorations in her village, and as a result, her only connection to the events was through the state broadcast of the commemorations in Budapest. Yet, although Zsófi had happily spent another national holiday—the previous August 20—watching televised fireworks and celebrations as a way "to feel everything as one . . . to experience everything as part of the nation," the more somber occasion of October 23 did not arouse similar feelings of patriotism and belonging.[23] The celebration of August 20 has gone through several shifts of interpretation under different political regimes, but its content was less meaningful for Zsófi than the continuous way the holiday was commemorated: with fireworks, festivals, and a shared sense of ritual celebration with an experiential and historical depth that the new and politically contested legacy of October 23 lacked. "We've always celebrated August 20," she explained. Now, instead of watching television, she told me, her family was hard at work preparing for November 1 (All Saints' Day), by making wreaths and cooking.

Zsófi later explained that her extended family and other members of the older generation did not discuss the revolution with her. Nor was such knowledge necessarily available from other sources. Although 1956 is taught in public schools, over the course of a student's education, only a few lessons in eighth and twelfth grade are devoted to discussing the revolution, and the extent to which teachers actually cover this material varies. (The events of the socialist era come at the end of the school year, when twelfth-grade students are busy preparing for their graduation (*érettségi*) examinations.) And in the first decade after the end of socialism, when Zsófi was in high school, many teachers may also have felt hesitant about how to approach the topic of the revolution, given that their own education under the communist system did not equip them with either the factual knowledge or conceptual tools to teach to teach post–World War II history with nuance (Pető 2002, 119).[24] As a result, at the time of my conversation with Zsófi, some students hardly encountered 1956 in the classroom at all, and those who did tended to emerge with a highly simplified understanding of events that appeared remote and unrelated to their own present-day concerns. In 2001, for example, a poll revealed that 33 percent of those between the ages of eighteen and thirty-four "didn't know" who among the main protagonists played the most positive role in the 1956 revolution—a proportion significantly higher than in older generations (Csepeli and Medgyesi 2001).[25]

But another key reason for the quickly waning relevance of and interest in 1956 in the first decade of postsocialism may not have concerned the revolution itself. Rather, at stake was what the suppression of the revolution made possible: the relatively peaceful years of Kádárism, which represented the longest period of stability and material well-being that many had experienced. During my interviews in the late 1990s and early 2000s, people often contrasted the chaos of 1956— both the events themselves and their postsocialist politicization—with the relative calm and prosperity of the Kádár era. Even Zsófi, who had only childhood memories of the final years of state socialism, spoke positively of the era's material security and entitlements—a narrative, unlike that of 1956, she had inherited from the steady comments and complaints of her parents and grandparents. In most cases, these recollections did not represent a simple endorsement of the past regime or the desire to return, but they made visible widespread ambivalence about the condemnation of Kádárism in political and public culture. And although they all agreed about the importance of returning 1956 to its "proper" (helyes) place in history (whatever that might be), few of them expressed interest in the details, which they perceived as irrelevant to their daily concerns and to their own memories of life under Kádárism.

For this reason, as Rainer argues, the "troubled times" concept continued to structure private discussion and recollection of 1956 after the end of state socialism. During the socialist era, this euphemism had provided a way to reconcile disparate memories of 1956 and the way they conflicted with the official government narrative of 1956 as counterrevolution. Now, using "troubled times" to avoid participating in debates about 1956 also enabled people to refuse to pass judgment on the memory of Kádárism (2002, 220–221). In other words, during the first decade of postsocialism, the challenge of the memory of 1956 perhaps ultimately resided in the challenge of the period that followed. As Mária remarked to me in 2001, "1956? I don't know. It would have been nice, but Hungary was abandoned [by the Western powers many Hungarians had assumed would aid them] and left to fight the Soviet Union by itself. There really wasn't an opportunity for any change. But still, something began [valami megindult], because afterwards the system really wasn't as strict."[26] That is, although most people agreed on the importance of 1956, they were also able to value what its very failure had made possible. Attempts to sweep away the remains of communist history by replacing them with the memory of 1956 to organize national identity would fail not only because of 1956's conflicting uses by party politics, but also because of the ambivalent relationship between the memory of the revolution and the experience of the system that followed it.

"Let There Be a Hungarian Dream Again!"

As we saw with the seeming contradiction in Béla's quote that began this chapter— the political joke about holidays versus the emphatically depoliticized memories of how he had experienced them—the post-1956 compromise offered by the regime did not necessarily force people to "celebrate their own occupation." Rather, the regime's emphasis on material security and a peaceful, "normal" life sought to convince its subjects to overlook the ideological foundations of the regime as being irrelevant to their personal concerns. This tension between memories of revolution and reconciliation characterized the challenge of remains in the early years of postsocialism. Many politicians and government officials attempted to resolve this tension by simply excising the memory of Kádárism from historical chronology: whether the creators of the Statue Park Museum who reduced the meaning of Budapest's monuments to relics of communist oppression, or the participants at Nagy's reburial, who rhetorically collapsed the time between 1956 and 1989. But, as we have seen in both cases, although this strategy was effective in announcing a decisive end to state socialism, its rejection of the ambiguities of lived experience of that era would make it less useful as the basis for a new way forward. The resultant perception of the "failure" of such memory work would only reinforce anxieties concerning Hungary's relationship to its recent past— and thus inspire renewed attempts to identify and eliminate remains of socialism.

I now turn to the way Fidesz, which led the government coalition in power between 1998 and 2002, responded to this challenge by attempting not only to replace a pathologized past, but also to transform the national subjects produced by the past. Fidesz entered the political scene in 1988 as a youth movement that offered a liberal alternative to the communist youth organization. It initially limited its membership to those under thirty-five, who would presumably be less tainted by the communist regime. After the 1994 victory of the MSZP-SZDSZ coalition and the resultant fragmentation and decline of the right wing, Fidesz shifted its ideology toward the center-right, redefining its mission in terms of *polgári* (bourgeois citizen, in the sense of the German *Bürger*) values and changing its name to the Fidesz—Hungarian Civic Party (Fidesz—Magyar Polgári Párt).[27] In contrast to the MSZP's painful austerity policies, Fidesz offered a populist, family-oriented program aimed at strengthening Hungary's emerging middle class, and it vowed to defend Hungary's national interests in the ongoing preparations for accession to the European Union in 2004.

Headed by the charismatic Viktor Orbán, Fidesz won the 1998 elections in coalition with the MDF and FKGP based on its ability to unify a highly variegated right wing with the promise of a Tony Blair–style revolution in Hungarian politics. Its slick campaign, which plastered close-ups of young, good-looking candidates across the signposts and billboards of Budapest, seemed to usher in a new kind of Western politics, concerned not only with policy but also with a public relations strategy that would present a new image of Hungary at home and abroad.

Despite its future-oriented, youthful appeal, however, Fidesz put history at the center of its political communication during its time in power between 1998 and 2002. Its strategy rejected the historical politics practiced by the previous two governments. As we have seen, both the MDF-led right-wing coalition (1990–1994) and the MSZP-SZDSZ left-wing coalition (1994–1998) made competing attempts to restore national history to authenticity. The MDF attempted to discard four decades of "Soviet occupation" by reviving the history and values of Hungary's interwar period. The MSZP, in turn, tried to redeem its participation in the previous regime by celebrating Nagy as a fellow reform communist. Fidesz responded to both these efforts with an avowedly anachronistic historical politics that superficially represented a return to the MDF's attempt at national renewal by distancing the socialist era and reestablishing links with a more remote past. Yet what distinguished Fidesz's attempts to free Hungary of socialist remains is the way it formulated the object of its intervention.

For Fidesz, the problem of postsocialist national identity was not merely the result of corrupted or contested histories. It also reflected the lack of an appropriate historical consciousness in the Hungarian public, whose national spirit had been dulled by the comfort and pragmatism of the Kádár era. To remedy this, Fidesz sought to eradicate the remains of socialism not only from Hungary's public spaces, official histories, and holiday calendar but also from Hungary's postsocialist citizens and all they had inherited from the experience of Kádárism. That is, if the MDF's historians had sought to educate the Hungarian public by lecturing them with revisionist historical narratives, Fidesz sought to use such narratives as the basis for vision and action. More than just a tool for political legitimation, history would thus provide Fidesz the opportunity to reform national subjectivity itself.

One crucial element of this strategy was the commemoration of the Magyar Millennium, celebrated from January 1, 2000, to August 20, 2001, as the thousandth anniversary of Hungary's conversion to Christianity by its king Saint Stephen and the founding of the Hungarian state. Its activities, headed and organized by a Millennium Commission run by the well-known popular historian István Nemeskürty, included the erection of hundreds of monuments across Hungary, the construction of a long-planned (and much-contested) National Theater, and the funding of several historical pageant films chronicling episodes from Hungary's history and the lives of great men. In addition, the government organized the controversial transfer of Saint Stephen's crown from the National Museum to Parliament and attempted to institute a law that many interpreted as making the crown, and not Hungary's citizens, the source of postsocialist constitutional legitimacy. The millennial year ended with the traditional fireworks display on August 20, 2001, celebrating both Saint Stephen's Day and the founding of the Hungarian state, under the slogan "Let there be a Hungarian dream again" (*Legyen újra magyar álom*), which played on the similarity of *álom* (dream) and *állam* (state).[28]

What was this new Hungarian dream, and what distinguished such celebrations from Fidesz's predecessors? Miklós, an early member of Fidesz who worked for the party during its first term in Parliament between 1990 and 1994, explained that the difference was the result of a "professionalism" that distinguished Western-style politicians from the academic historians who had staffed many key positions under the Antall government:

> Fidesz takes a far more pragmatic approach to history. They are guys who respect, but learned to *use* history. The MDF government could only respect history. The Prime Minister of the MDF government, [József] Antall, would go to Washington DC and give a historical lecture in the Rose Garden of the White House, talking twice as long as the president of the US did. The prime minister of the Fidesz government would never do that. Because they're better professionals, they respect but they use history, so they wouldn't deliver a historical lecture.
>
> I used to receive guests, international visitors in my office, between '90 and '94, and it was quite often that, that you know, a guy would come to me right after he went to the prime minister, to Antall, and many of them, they were coming in late, furiously, telling me that the reason why I'm late for this appointment is because your prime minister or your foreign minister gave me a history lesson instead of talking about what I was interested in talking about. So it is a key difference. So it's far more pragmatic and far more professional in what these guys do.

For the Fidesz representatives and supporters I interviewed during Fidesz's 1998–2002 term in office, being "professional" (*profi*) was a crucial way they articulated the party's claim to political legitimacy. At times, it seemed as if they placed their emphasis more on surface execution—doing things the "right" way, following Western models—than on what such policies actually constituted. My conversations with more traditional political conservatives during that period often consisted of history lessons that recounted nationalist narratives of Hungary's political victimization, outstanding cultural achievements, and embattled national pride. In contrast, I was often bemused by the extent to which many Fidesz supporters and staff made clear their lack of interest in the historical narratives and ideologies that their party sought so strongly to inculcate. For this reason, many of the party's critics dismissed their historical politics as mere political opportunism. By embracing the historical concerns and political rhetoric of Hungary's traditional conservative constituencies (whether the interwar nostalgia and conservativism of the Christian middle class or the heritage of populist [*népi*] nationalism), Fidesz was able to unify a fragmented right wing against the MSZP-SZDSZ coalition.

But the promiscuity of Fidesz's historical references, which were in some cases gathered through telephone polls,[29] demonstrated that Fidesz was less indebted to the specific ideologies embedded in particular historical narratives and symbols than to the values of national belonging and historical continuity itself. That is, what Fidesz took seriously was not history itself, but its role in encouraging Hungarians to view themselves and their place in the world differently. Communism, Miklós argued, had made it a crime to be nationalist—to be "proud of being Hungarian." "The key message," he went on to explain, "is that now we should learn and realize that it's good to be a Hungarian. This is what it is. So there is no specific kind of national identity, what they're trying to teach people, or talk about. . . . It's not a specific national identity—it's just . . . *national identity*."

Although all particular nationalisms are also abstract nationalisms (Anderson 1998), what was thus crucial about this "national dream" in the Hungarian context was the very fact of daring to have one. For this reason, central to the Magyar Millennium was a notion of cultural heritage as a practice as well as an object, which demanded enactment as well as monumentalization. Many of the activities of the Magyar Millennium were thus temporary and local in nature, designed to encourage the local performance of national narratives through a number of countrywide initiatives, such as the ceremonial handover of commemorative millennium flags (*zászlóátadás*) from government representatives to individual cities and villages. (These ceremonies were also less expensive to undertake than the extensive new monumental architecture that had characterized the 1896 millennial celebration of Hungary's conquest of the Carpathian Basin, particularly since these events were often planned to coincide with preexisting celebrations, such as state holidays, religious commemorations, or local events such as harvest festivals.)

Such efforts to remake Hungary's national subjectivity perhaps reached their apex in the creation of a Country Image Center (Országimázs Központ). Although the center was established to publicize Hungary abroad, its focus soon turned to marketing a new vision of Hungary to Hungarians instead.[30] In keeping with Fidesz's focus on a Western-style professionalization of government communication, many of these tasks were subcontracted to private marketing companies and public relations firms, particularly the aptly named Happy End, Ltd. Each holiday thus became the target of a national advertising campaign, complete with posters and slogans. These highly polished campaigns reflected the way the democratization of memory had become commodification, in which Fidesz's brand of national heritage sought to push rival visions out of the national marketplace of memory. The Country Image Center now commemorated 1956, for example, as a civic bourgeois revolution (*polgári forradalom*) fought by the "Pest lads" (*Pesti srácok*) who had participated in the city's street battles.[31] Those who fought in the revolution were primarily members of the working class rather than the emerging middle class that Fidesz targeted in its rhetoric, but this emphasis enabled Fidesz to avoid the problematic historical legacy of Nagy and thus eliminate the left-wing aspect of the 1956 revolution. Instead, this narrative of civic/bourgeois rebellion portrayed the events of the past as merely the anticipation of Fidesz's plans for the future.

Regardless of the specific historical narrative being invoked, the primary mission of these efforts was to promote national self-esteem, by transforming the famously pessimistic Hungarian national character into a happy, forward-thinking citizen who would serve as an advertisement for Hungary in the West—and an endorsement for Fidesz at home. In 2001 Edit Kiss, one of the staff members at the Country Image Center, met me at the food court of the recently opened West End City Center Mall (then the largest and most central of Budapest's shopping malls), to explain the center's activities and share promotional materials.[32] Like many of her colleagues, Kiss had worked in market research and public relations before joining the Country Image Center. Then in her mid-twenties, she seemed to embody the new national citizen that the Country Image Center sought to produce: ambitious, energetic, fashionably dressed, and fluent in multiple languages (English, Italian, and French, as well as her native Hungarian). As Kiss sipped cappuccino and fielded text messages during our conversation, she dismissed the criticism from Fidesz's left-wing opposition that the Country Image Center was engaged in political propaganda. Instead, she compared its activities to those of Hungary's tourist board, foreign ministry, and other institutions concerned with Hungary's reputation abroad.

The task of the Country Image Center, Kiss told me, was to counter international assumptions that Hungary was either mired in a gray and decrepit socialist past or it represented a rural country characterized by "horses and goulash." Instead, she and her colleagues planned national and international campaigns that sought to portray Hungary as dynamic, youthful, and cutting-edge: the home of thirteen Nobel Prize winners and the site of scientific and technological innovation that had produced the discovery of "Vitamin C, the personal computer, matches, diesel engines, and so much more!" Such campaigns sought to place Hungary within a new symbolic geography where it no longer stood at the margins of Western modernity but represented the heart of Europe, "where all the roads meet," as Kiss explained. (The national pavilion at the 2000 World Expo in Hanover, Germany, thus promoted Hungary with the slogan of "Meeting Point" [*Treffpunkt Ungarn*].)

But to accomplish these goals, the center also needed to change attitudes within Hungary. "Hungarian people see themselves as pessimistic and negative: the victim of Europe, and we always fought for the freedom of Europe, and it's just never going to be better," Kiss told me. "We like to complain, and it's just so bad for us. . . . But if we want tourists to come to Hungary and then come back again, they don't want to see negative faces. They want to see smiling faces and happy faces. And if you want the image of successful Hungary to be transmitted abroad, then we have to show that within the country, too." Kiss thus explained the Country Image Center's holiday poster campaigns and other such engagements with historical politics as serving a reparative function. First, these initiatives fueled the process of replacing old communist holidays with new ones by imbuing the experience of celebrating national holidays with positive affect. "For forty years, people were told how to behave: you had to go to May 1 celebrations with your flag and it was compulsory. And now you can do it for fun and have a good time." Second, by emphasizing moments of optimism and political agency in Hungary's embattled national history, these campaigns would help to restore Hungarian national consciousness and pride, thus enabling Hungary to boost its image abroad and enable its citizens to succeed at home. "Because if I say that I'm not going to make it, I'm not going to make it," she explained. "If you don't believe in yourself, you're not going to do it. You have to believe that you're happy—and then you're going to be happy!"

Such appeals to national optimism—perhaps best encapsulated in the Magyar Millennium's exhortation to "Let there be a Hungarian dream again!"—were a key aspect of Fidesz's political messaging more generally. Sándor Holbok, then the chief of staff for the Fidesz faction leader, József Szájer, similarly told me in an English-language interview,

> We are ideologically opposing a very important Marxist thesis, which is that, in Hungarian at least, a *lét határozza meg a tudatot*. This is a very

important Marxist definition, which says that *lét*, the being, *meghatároz*, defines, *a tudatot*, the way you are thinking. And it's not true. We think that the *tudat* sometimes *meghatározza a létet* [The way of thinking sometimes defines the state of being]. Not always, but sometimes.[33]

This performative logic, which sought to make optimism the condition for and not the effect of national prosperity, would also later be visible in one of the posters for the Fidesz coalition's 2002 reelection campaign. It featured the photograph of a joyful, laughing child with a slogan that announced that the remains of the past had decisively been put to rest: "The future has begun!" (*A jövő elkezdődött!*)

Performing the Nation

In 2000, the village where I had taught English scheduled its millennium flag ceremony to coincide with its yearly festival (*búcsú*) scheduled on the Feast of Assumption. This semireligious festival annually attracts locals and visitors to enjoy folk dance and classical music performances, market stalls selling local pottery, woodwork, and leather goods, and exhibits celebrating the village's agricultural products. My friend Vera, a librarian then in early forties, was charged with creating an exhibition about the village's history for the village library. She later reported that the various events were well-attended, and the flag ceremony itself attracted a crowd of at least two hundred spectators.

Although local newspapers and village residents praised the festival as successful, it was unclear what role the millennium flag ceremony specifically played in the high turnout. Across Hungary, such annual village festivals traditionally represent one of the most important events in the local calender, and they were even celebrated under state socialism, albeit primarily in secular terms. For Fidesz and its coalition partners, the flag handover ceremony represented an opportunity to display their ideological commitment to the Hungarian countryside versus the metropolis (a long-standing divide in Hungarian politics). By sending members of the government to attend each ceremony and entrust the flag to a local representative, the Fidesz coalition sought to demonstrate that its high-ranking politicians were deeply concerned with even the smallest villages, which rarely were the target of such direct attention. In so doing, the Fidesz coalition could thus present itself as the very means through which the connection between local experience and Hungary's thousand-year national history was reiterated and reforged.[34]

But the aspects of the ceremony that were specific to these political goals were the ones that seemed to provoke dissatisfaction among those I spoke with. The organizers felt disrespected by the visiting government official (a representative of one of the coalition parties), who refused to follow their plans to meet him at the entrance of the village and escort him on foot to the site of the ceremony. In addition, Vera later told me, the visiting politician did not even read the speech he prepared and submitted beforehand, but instead made up something new on the spot. "He didn't treat it as an honor," Vera later recalled, "but just something to do before he got back in his car and went to the next village." She thus challenged the notion that the village should be grateful for the mere fact of the government's attention—"as if all we do is agriculture and we live one hundred years in the past!" Indeed, although Vera and my other friends in the village agreed with the importance of celebrating the millennium and seemed to appreciate the opportunity to receive the flag, several of them also questioned its usefulness (and even asked me, in my status as visiting anthropologist, to explain the flag's symbolic significance). "What does the government want us to do with the flag?" Vera asked rhetorically, before concluding, "The money would be better spent on a nursery."

Needless to say, Vera's ambivalence was not representative of everyone who attended or participated in planning the millennium events in the village (and nor, we can assume, did every visiting politician disappoint his or her hosts). But Vera's frustration at the condescension of urban politicians, as well as her pragmatic dismissal of symbolic politics in favor of material concerns, is nonetheless reminiscent of the skeptical reactions that also greeted the construction of the Statue Park Museum and the contestation of 1956 in public memory. Kiss may have contrasted the pleasures of postsocialist holidays with the semi-compulsory participation in May 1 events under communism. But both bore the imprint of the Kádárist compromise in which, as we have seen, the regime encouraged Hungary's citizens to keep their distance from political concerns: whether by permitting semireligious village traditions or providing the weiners and beer that made the experience of waving banners and marching in parades more palatable. Fidesz's historical politics sought to use these holidays as the opportunity for national pedagogy that would eliminate remains of socialism from the historical consciousness of the participants, and in so doing, recruit potential voters. As Vera's comments make clear, however, such attempts to transform local traditions that had long been experienced as outside the sphere of state politics into vehicles for political aggrandizement risked alienating village constituencies—particularly when, in her eyes, these politicians appeared to be offering little in return.

"The Past Has Begun!"

The Fidesz coalition's 2002 reelection campaign sought to celebrate the achievements of the present as the fulfillment of the dreams of the past: whether that was a millennium of Hungarian statehood or international recognition as the "meeting point" of Europe. But this glorious future, Fidesz warned, was threatened by remains of the communist past in the form of its political enemies: the MSZP-SZDSZ coalition. As a counterpoint to its project of restoring national optimism, Fidesz's rhetoric thus also emphasized Hungary's recent experiences of historical victimization, drawing direct links between the injustices of the communist era and Fidesz's contemporary left-wing opponents. (These efforts included funding the creation of a museum dedicated to the victims of fascism and communism, the House of Terror [*Terror Háza*], which I discuss in chapter 4.)

Such warnings of the danger of communist return would become particularly emphatic after Fidesz's surprising loss during the first round of parliamentary elections, due to factors that ranged from government corruption scandals (including accusations of financial mismanagement at the Country Image Center) to a general desire for change that had similarly removed the incumbent in each previous postsocialist election from office. In a speech at a rally next to Parliament that drew an estimated 500,000 supporters, Orbán harshly criticized the MSZP-SZDSZ's previous government in 1994–1998, and portrayed his opponents as relics of the communist past (Gavra 2002). A former English student of mine, Vera's son Ádám, now attended university in Budapest and told me that he found Fidesz's rhetoric of embattled national pride under threat strongly compelling. As he told me during this lead-up to the final election, "If Fidesz doesn't win, it will be like 1989 never happened!" And the day after the Fidesz coalition lost, I opened my email to discover a message from Ádám that interpreted the failure of Fidesz's promised future as the return of socialism's remains. Instead of the future, the email lamented, "the past has begun [*a múlt elkezdődött*]."

As a result of this narrow defeat, Fidesz would abandon both its narrative of civic/bourgeois (*polgári*) Hungary and the transformative rhetoric of national optimism that celebrated both the distant past and the bright imminent future. Instead, the party reinvented itself as a countrywide civic movement united in its perception of historical victimization by past and present communists. Fidesz thus replaced the fantasy of overcoming remains of socialism with the warning that transition had failed to fully break from communist rule. And this logic, which blamed Hungary's inability to enter the future on the irresolution of its dangerous past, would ultimately extend to the memory of the 1956 revolution, whose politicization and ambivalent relationship to Kádárism had challenged its ability to replace the remains of communist history with a new founding mythology. As we shall see in chapter 6, during the 2006 protests against the MSZP government, Fidesz supporters and other right-wing demonstrators drew on the memory of 1956 in their demands to depose the "communists" from power. Their (sometimes absurd, sometimes violent) reenactment of iconic incidents from the 1956 revolution attempted to rectify both the problem of 1956 after 1989 and the problem of transition itself, by claiming that their actions would finally accomplish the change of regime promised a decade and a half earlier.

Thus far, we have examined the problem of socialist remains by looking at attempts to banish and replace memories of the socialist past in political life, public culture, and—in the case of the Fidesz coalition's 1998–2002 historical politics—the hearts and minds of Hungarian citizens themselves. Chapter 3 analyzes a set of memory practices that represents a different response to the challenge of an ambivalent recent past that characterizes all attempts to master socialism's remains, torn between memories of both painful oppression and cozy domesticity. The phenomenon of nostalgia for popular and material culture of the socialist era would celebrate rather than condemn such remains of socialism, by renarrating them not as relics of oppression but as domestic objects free of political content. By overturning the logic of the memory practices we have analyzed thus far, nostalgia enabled its consumers to envision a future in which relinquishing the past was not the condition for attaining the future. Instead, the nostalgic consumption of these remains of socialism could become the very proof of having entered it.

NOSTALGIA AND THE REMAINS OF EVERYDAY LIFE

In the early summer of 2002, I met a group of friends at West Balkán, a newly popular open-air bar. Tucked into a wooded area of Buda, West Balkán was so far off the beaten path that its owners hired bicycle rickshaws to ferry passengers from the street to the bar's location. As we sat chatting in the early evening, my friend Róbert suddenly stood up and walked over to a nearby table where two teenaged girls were loudly complaining as they struggled to open bottles of Bambi soda. A citrus-flavored soda produced in the 1960s as a Hungarian socialist alternative to banned Western brands such as Pepsi and Coca-Cola, Bambi had been recently rereleased by the mineral water bottler Pannon-Aqua '95 Rt and was briefly available in the soda's original distinctive swing-top bottle (*csatos üveg*). Its return was part of a growing nostalgia industry in Hungary that sought to capitalize on fond memories of the material and popular culture of the socialist past. As I watched, the teenagers laughed as Róbert quickly showed them how to flip up the wire cage that surrounded the bottle cap. Róbert, then in his early fifties, returned to our table with a shrug. "Well, why would they know how to open it?" he commented as he returned to his own beer. "They didn't grow up with it."

From previous discussions, I knew that Róbert had suffered personal and professional hardships under the communist regime. Yet, as we settled back into our conversation, he merely shrugged at the sudden experience of expertise based on his own childhood as a socialist consumer. "I never thought there would be anything useful about what I learned under communism," he joked.

Bambi was not the only remain of socialism to make a comeback more than a decade after the end of the regime. Beginning in the late 1990s, nostalgia for socialist mass culture became a popular marketing trend not only in Hungary but across the former Soviet bloc.[1] In Budapest, entrepreneurs furnished new coffeehouses and restaurants with carefully salvaged furniture and objects from the former era. Hungarian manufacturers reintroduced Bambi and other snacks and beverages from the 1960s and 1970s, while advertisers revived old socialist-era television spots or created new ones that attempted to target similar memories. A number of films, invariably narrated from the limited perspective of a child or teenager, managed to win local audiences back to Hungarian cinema with their sympathetic narration of the conflicts and everyday pleasures of life under late socialism. And, just as several popular books and museum exhibitions cataloged the material culture of the recent past, collections of official socialist-era songs also topped the charts.

Even the word "nosztalgia" itself became fashionable, giving its name to parties, raves, bars, and even new business ventures without explicit reference to what, if anything, was intended to be the target of this emotion. As Róbert's experience at West Balkán suggests, the success of marketing socialist nostalgia may have derived precisely from the ambiguity of nostalgia's references and ideological content—and thus its ability to mobilize different consumers with very different relationships to the socialist past. For the teenagers who could not open the bottles of Bambi they had ordered, the appeal of such nostalgic marketing lay in its exoticism: objects that represented a temporal remoteness as glamorous as the spatial inaccessibility of the trendy West Balkán and the geographical region its name invoked.[2] For members of the older generation, particularly those dispossessed by the social and economic uncertainties of postsocialism, nostalgia offered an idiom through which to voice longing for the safer and more secure material circumstances of late state socialism. And for others like Róbert, who explicitly denied any desire to return to the injustice and oppression of the past (and who perhaps, as Róbert insisted, never enjoyed the taste of Bambi anyway),[3] nostalgic marketing prompted the bemused recognition of a set of skills and experiences, however unwillingly acquired, that was suddenly acquiring ironic new value from the capitalist recuperation of socialist-era mass culture.

The previous two chapters examined official efforts to master remains of socialism by banishing relics of communist ideology. Beginning in the mid-1990s, however, consumers in Hungary turned to what remained in everyday material culture: not to eliminate it, but to redeem it. Their nostalgic enjoyment might seem to have little in common with the emphatic disavowal that characterized earlier efforts to transform the everyday into history. But the practices of nostalgia and debates about its politics would reveal a discomfort with the ambiguities of the Kádár era similar to that visible in the battles to determine the fate of communist statues and national holidays. The difference here was that nostalgia simply inverted the previous logic through which many sought to reconcile competing memories of material security and political oppression. Rather than repudiate remains of the past era as overdetermined by their ideological purpose, nostalgic consumers would insist that the objects of their enjoyment possessed little political content at all.

Moreover, what all these practices shared was the fantasy of an easily distanced past and the optimistic future that soon awaited. If the Statue Park Museum preserved the physical memory of communism in order to materialize democracy, nostalgia similarly celebrated the consumer culture of the socialist past in order to assert the victory of capitalism. Nostalgic marketing gave new capitalist value to remnants of the past era recently discarded as the trivial, worthless, and inauthentic leftovers of Soviet occupation, and thus now irrelevant to Hungary's democratic present. And as Róbert's sudden experience of "expertise" demonstrates, nostalgia would also revalue everyday skills, habits, and memories of the past era that were themselves on the brink of vanishing—and thus enable its consumers to resist being themselves devalued as mere communist leftovers as Hungary entered the global market economy.

Nostalgia and the Fantasy of the West

Nostalgia's etymological meaning is "homesickness": from Greek *nostos* and *algia*, a longing for home. Despite its seemingly antique origins, the word is a recent invention, introduced in the seventeenth century to describe the physical illness experienced by sailors, soldiers, and other military sent far from home (Boym 2001, 3). The meaning of the term soon shifted, however, from the individual pain of spatial displacement to the more pervasive sense of loss and alienation produced by the transformations of modernity, "with its alienation, its much lamented loss of tradition and community" (Hutcheon 2000, 205).

This transformation from an individual medical condition into a cultural response also entailed a transformation in the object of nostalgia's longings. Once cured by a trip home, nostalgia now mourns the impossibility of returning to the past. It is thus, as Svetlana Boym reminds us, a "historical emotion" (2001, 10): the product of a particularly modern temporality that views individuals and societies as caught up in a destructive and irreversible flow of time. Nostalgia responds to the subject's perception of exile from the present by imagining the past as the site of a lost and utopic "immediacy, presence, and authenticity" (Hutcheon 2000, 107 discussing S. Stewart 1993, 23).

Such longing can take the form of a recuperative, virulent nationalism: what Boym calls "restorative nostalgia," which insists on the unattainable project of resurrecting past presence. But, as she argues, nostalgia can also be "reflective," focused on the breach between then and now, rather than a desired return (2001, 49–50). For while nostalgia is often interpreted as the insistence that the past be made present again, it is in fact the impossibility of returning to the past that makes such longing possible. Nostalgia, in other words, is defined by "its inability to approach its subject" (Fritzsche 2004, 65)—by the irreversibility of time and the irretrievability of its object.

Communist ideology was emphatically antinostalgic, locating its utopic yearnings in the future rather than in a largely discredited national past.[4] Yet Soviet citizens were not immune from a nostalgic longing that fantasized overcoming spatial instead of temporal distance: the imagined dream of the West and the mobility and abundance it represented. For the ordinary citizen, such aspirations were as unattainable as the space travel produced by communism's imperialist ambitions. As Boym argues, remembering her childhood in 1960s St. Petersburg, "it seemed that we would travel to the moon much sooner than we would go abroad" (2001, 60). Possibilities of emigration or exile were thus so circumscribed that they retained the sense of irreversibility and finality that characterizes temporal nostalgia (Nadkarni and Shevchenko 2004, 492).

Such fantasies of mobility were modulated in the Hungarian context by Hungary's exceptional status as "the happiest barracks in the Soviet bloc," with greater access to Western goods, media, and travel than many of its socialist neighbors. Hungarians thus articulated their dreams of escape in terms of material consumption and a Western standard of living broadly perceived as superior to what socialism offered. One study from the mid-1970s, for example, quotes a factory worker who defined his fantasized life in the West not in terms of democracy and freedom of expression, but as "living with two cars of my own" (Halmos 1978, 131–132, cited in Pittaway 2006). And even in the early years after the end of socialism, people I met were eager for me to evaluate their possessions and furnishings in comparison to a Western standard that they considered Hungary still struggling to achieve. The middle-class family who hosted me during my first visit in Hungary in 1993 (a schoolteacher, engineer, and their two young children) lived in a split-level two-story house that they had constructed in their village during the last years of socialism. Walking me through the sunlit and spacious rooms—which included separate bedrooms for the children, a formal parlor, and a TV room where I slept and prepared my lessons—the schoolteacher Orsolya compared it negatively to homes in the United States, asking me, "This is where a factory worker would live, isn't it?"

Ironically, it was the socialist regime's own policies that encouraged the emerging consumer consciousness that made such comparisons possible (Fehérváry 2002, 2013; Pittaway 2006; Valuch 2000). As we have seen, one way for the regime to distance itself from the hated Stalinism of the 1950s was to emphasize consumption and an ever-increasing standard of living as the basis for its political legitimacy. As Krisztina Fehérváry argues, the regime reconceptualized its project of modernizing Hungary as a specifically material one, in which the production of a utopian society necessitated transforming both the lived environment and the material expectations of Hungary's citizens (2013, 4–5). This policy would help to produce modern consumer subjectivity in Hungary's socialist citizens, even as the state system lacked the products to fully satisfy this demand. By the time Hungary opened its border to Austria in the last days of communist rule (to enable East Germans to escape through Hungary to the West), many Hungarians had already been taking advantage of lax regulations to make shopping daytrips to Vienna for years. On the anniversary of the Russian Revolution in 1989 (November 7), for example, 10 percent of the country's population was estimated to be in Vienna doing their Christmas shopping (Böröcz 1992, 207).

The Western standard of living became the benchmark of the "normal" (normális) through which Hungarians developed consumer consciousness (Fehérváry 2002, 2013). As a result, many Hungarians articulated their critique of the regime precisely through the idiom intended to stave off their dissatisfaction: that is, consumerism. The lower quality of Hungary's mass-produced goods, perceived as cheap imitations of Western ones (such as Trapper, socialist Hungary's brand of designer jeans) became emblematic of the lower quality of life within the Soviet bloc more generally. Many people thus recalled the innocence with which they had endowed Western products with a magical and transformative capacity based on their perceived higher quality, unavailability, and the prestige in their consumption. My friend Levente, whom we met in the introduction, remembered fantasizing about Tic Tacs and Mars bars because they were advertised on Austrian television and only available in foreign currency shops. Gazing at them in the window of the one foreign currency shop in the town where he grew up in Western Hungary, he would long for "just one dollar!" with which he could go in and purchase these forbidden treasures. Utopia thus appeared to be located just outside Hungary's borders, in a Western European and North American consumer culture characterized by unlimited Coca-Cola, bananas, and consumer choice.[5]

With the demise of socialism in 1990 and the entrance into democracy and the free market economy, many Hungarians initially hoped that they would quickly gain not only the political freedoms but also the consumption patterns and living standards of the West. Enthusiasm for all that was Western and new thus characterized the advertising and consumption during the first years of postsocialism, as Hungarians sought to counter the image of being backward, dowdy socialist neighbors and to repudiate a perceived past identity as consumers of both socialist ideology and inferior material culture. To return to the example of "national spring cleaning," many people greeted the disappearance of socialist products in favor of new Western goods and advertising with far more enthusiasm than the removal of statues and communist monuments from public spaces.

But the economic challenges of postsocialism soon disenchanted this dream of consumer plentitude—as well as the romantic vision of the West that had undergirded the fantasy. After the initial euphoria of entering the world of Western consumerism, Hungarians quickly discovered that access to such products was still limited by financial constraints, if not political ones. Moreover, after decades of knowing how to read between the lines of official state discourse, many people told me that they found themselves suddenly ill-equipped to decipher the claims of Western advertising with the same skepticism. Mária, whom we met in chapter 2, was a former office administrator who lost her job in the early 1990s and now worked as a housecleaner. Many of our conversations concerned the hardships she and her husband, both in their late fifties, faced due to rising prices, the end of many state subsidies, and their loss of economic security and social status at a time when Hungarian society was becoming increasingly stratified. "We were all so innocent then," she recalled to me in an interview in 2001, as we discussed her naiveté in the early years after transition. "For years [under socialism], we had seen all those advertisements on Austrian TV, and we thought they were true." Although Western brands still remained popular, people like Mária now insisted that the quality of these products was not necessarily superior to local ones. She was thus able to justify buying cheaper Hungarian products not only in terms of her need to economize but as evidence of her growing capitalist consumer sophistication.

One of the first commercial successes of Hungary's postsocialist film industry was a nostalgic revival of outdated fantasies of Western consumerism: the low-budget musical *Dolly Birds* (*Csinibaba*, 1997). Set in the early 1960s to evoke both the privation and optimism of the first years of normalization, the film's loose narrative chronicles the activities of the members of a socialist housing block under the bumbling supervision of the block warden Uncle Simon. Inspired by the chance to win a trip to Helsinki in a talent contest, a group of teenagers forms a rock band, dreaming of an escape to a West imagined as a fantastic surplus of commodities: Coca-Cola, Chesterfield cigarettes, and the spectacular figure of Anita Ekberg (whose projected image sparks a riot in a theater showing *La Dolce*

FIGURE 3.1 Film still from *Dolly Birds* (*Csinibaba*, directed by Péter Timár, 1996).

Vita). These fantasies of escape—epitomized in various characters' performances of old pop hits from that era—are crushed when the group learns the talent contest has been rigged, and the state has chosen a "traditional" women's choir to represent Hungary abroad. The film nonetheless ends on a cheerful note: the teenagers shrug off the contest, a new couple falls in love, and, after much nagging, the block warden Uncle Simon finally agrees to play a children's game with an older neighbor in the park—a salient metaphor for the limited pleasures available under state paternalism.

Dolly Birds is a film about the losses and fantasies experienced under state socialism—dreams of a Western "normality" impossible to achieve—but its enthusiastic reception reflected distinctly postsocialist realities.[6] The film mourns a specific configuration of the "West" as an object of longing around which socialist-era subjectivities were constituted. By mythologizing the now-lost pleasures of everyday life in early 1960s Hungary—outdated fashions, teased hair, Bambi soda, and the popular hits of the day—it revives the dreams of that era: a time when both the socialist utopia predicted by communist ideology and the fantasy of self-fulfillment promised by Western consumerism had not yet failed to materialize. Its local success (unusual in the context of the 1990s film industry that specialized in art films for international festivals) paved the way for a plethora of nostalgic phenomena that began to emerge in the late 1990s. This included not only a number of films that similarly conjured up the fantasies and imaginative constructs of the past era,[7] but the recuperation of the remains of state socialist everyday life that Hungarians had previously rejected as inauthentic.

Remains of the Everyday

The marketing of such nostalgia was indeed particularly suited to Hungary's entrance into the temporality of the market economy, with its accelerated obsolescence and the commodification of age value (Jameson 1991). Capitalism makes a fetish of authenticity: the auratic perception of an object's singularity, which, as Walter Benjamin (1968) reminds us, only arises at the time of its reproduction. As we have seen, the production of socialist remains by commodifying relics of official state culture began even before Hungary's first democratic elections took place. The very speed with which such communist kitsch became fashionable demonstrated that it had little to do with a desire for restoration or return. Rather, it helped to produce the difference between the communist past and the "Western" present by rewriting the socialist era solely in terms of Soviet occupation.

The wave of nostalgia that appeared in the late 1990s differed from this earlier phenomenon, which used ironic humor to invoke the past in order to break with it. Instead, nostalgic consumers sought to commemorate a way of life they now viewed as irretrievable, through gentle, more affectionate attempts to recapture the fantasies, knowledges, and practices embedded in objects of socialist everyday life. What drove this nostalgia was not the desire to re-create or recover the socialist past. Rather, this nostalgia reflected the fundamental logic of nostalgia as the "desire to desire" itself (S. Stewart 1993, 23). That is, these consumers paradoxically attempted to recapture the structure of fantasy under the previous regime by projecting it onto a new target: socialist-era consumer and material culture now assigned the same emotional value once invested in foreign goods. Once reviled as cheap imitations of the West, these remains of socialism now appeared auratic and desirable compared to now-familiar Western brands and products.

In some popular cafés, Coca-Cola stood alongside not only Bambi but the local grape soda Traubi (which became the object of litigation by two competing firms who both claimed to own the rights to this socialist-era product). The formerly despised Trapper jeans reappeared, and Tisza sneakers (Hungary's 1980s answer to Adidas) became trendy again thanks to viral marketing among club DJs too young to have worn the original brand. And in an underground passage across from the Kálvin square metro entrance, the popular Cha-Cha-Cha Eszpresszó tempted nostalgic consumers with a stylishly retro interior and murals based on black-and-white photographs. Its use of Westernized spellings made visible the recursive nature of socialist nostalgia, in which conjuring up the

FIGURE 3.2 Interior of (now closed) Cha-cha-cha Eszpresszó in 2002. The neon sign borrowed from the Italian spelling of "espresso," and the name of the café itself was a Westernized "Cha-cha-cha" rather than the Hungarian "csac-sacsa." Personal photograph, 2002.

atmosphere of 1960s Hungary also necessitated evoking fantasies of that era: the longing to appear glamorously Western to both locals and tourists, as well as the desire to participate in Western levels of consumption.

Meanwhile, a number of popular books and museum exhibitions presented collections of socialist-era mass and material culture. Examples included Zoltán Poós's book *Rainbow Department Store* (*Szivárvány Áruház*, 2002), the historian András Gerő's book and exhibition series *Fingerprint of the Twentieth Century* (*A XX. század ujjlenyomata*, 2001), and the 1999 exhibition *Kitsch and Cult* (*Giccs és Kultusz*), which displayed household objects from the 1950s and 1960s. The accompanying essays functioned as inventories of the cultural emotions of a lost age, chronicling not only the cultural histories of these remains, but also the memories, fantasies, and associations these objects once inspired.

In the autumn of 2000, I attended an all-night festival dedicated to the experience of growing up as consumers of the arts and mass culture of the 1970s and 1980s: the childhood era of what I term Hungary's "transitional generation," who came of age just as the regime was ending. Held to promote the nostalgia film, *Little Journey* (*Kis Utazás*, 2000), the festival took place in the (now-closed) Almássy Square Recreation Center, which had opened as a youth and Young Pioneer recreation center in 1983 and thus evoked nostalgic remembrance of the famous concerts and other cultural events held there during the final years of state socialism. Throughout the evening and into the early morning hours, the space was densely packed with visitors: primarily those in their late twenties and thirties, but including teenagers as well. People attended roundtable discussions and walked through exhibits of socialist-era styles and material culture, while others laughed at the old television commercials and socialist public service announcements—from ads for Fabulon cosmetics and the former Etc. (Satöbbi) fashion boutique to notices regarding litter and car maintenance—that played on numerous television monitors in the dance hall.[8]

The local architecture and design magazine *Octogon* produced a publication to promote the event, featuring old advertisements and fashion spreads as well as an article that asked local celebrities and business leaders what they personally considered to be the most memorable objects from the era. Many interviewees fondly remembered the Western goods (such as Adidas and Levi's 501s) that by the 1980s had become available to those who purchased them abroad (or, in some cases, could afford them at home),[9] as well as those objects (such as the *amcsi dipó*, an "American" attaché case—sometimes called "diplomat case"—used as a school satchel) that conjured up the glamour of Western consumption. The majority of interviewees, however, emphasized the local fashions of the time, such as the *szimatszatyor*, a military surplus gas-mask bag also used as a school satchel, and the *Alföldi papucs*, a Hungarian-made closed-toe sandal (*Octogon* 2000).

Zoltán Poós, another member of the transitional generation whose collection of memories of socialist-era objects, *Rainbow Department Store* (2002), went through several editions, explained the appeal of such objects in an interview with the newspaper *Népszabadság*. His encounters with these items, which ranged from candies, drinks, and cigarettes to toys, games, and knick-knacks, lacked what he termed the "pathos" and "false elevation" found in other, more triumphalist popular memories of life under state socialism (such as Hungary's famous 1953 soccer win against England). Instead, these objects told a story of cultural invention and national idiosyncracy: "My favorites are the injection-molded plastic products made in the garages of Budaörs: the somewhat futuristic MK-27 tape recorder; the space-gun with a flint stone; the Rolli Zoli, which was a real piece of art; and the miniature car [*törpeautó*]. It was awkward, clumsy and inconsistent like the era itself in which it was made, but it still had some sort of compelling loveliness in it" (Trencsényi 2001). His affection for these remains thus included the context of their creation: what Daphne Berdahl describes as a nostalgia for an era of production itself (1999, 198–199), in contrast to Hungarians' postsocialist identities as consumers of primarily Western goods.[10]

Such nostalgia mourned a disappearing sociality as well as a lost material culture. Hungarians under state socialism were never fully cut off from Western media and mass culture, and they did their best to follow international fashions and trends. Nonetheless, the production and distribution of socialist mass culture did not function according to capitalist principles of market segmentation, product differentiation, and planned obsolescence. The experience of playing with the

FIGURE 3.3 Window display at Pont bookstore advertising the publication of *Rainbow Department Store* (*Szivárvány Áruház*, 2002). Personal photograph, 2002.

same toys, same brands, and having more or less similar access to Western goods thus enabled collective generational identities that only now became visible at the moment of their disappearance, when increasing socioeconomic stratification was resulting in very different capacities to consume both local and Western products. Remembering the consumption practices of the past era—and the now quaint envy toward those who could travel abroad, own a car, or have access to hard-currency stores—thus helped to ameliorate the new class distinctions emerging under postsocialism. In so doing, nostalgia for socialism's remains also brought glamour into the present day by reminding contemporary consumers of greater scarcity and lack of consumer choice in the previous era. Levente, who as a child in socialist Hungary had longed for "just one dollar" to take to the hard currency stores, told me that he now periodically bought himself Toblerone, although he did not otherwise enjoy eating chocolate, simply out of the nostalgic pleasure of recalling how exotic and unattainable it had once seemed. Giving shape and form to the fantasies of the past era, the appeal of such nostalgia lay in its potential to bring new value to the forgotten memories, unrealized futures, and long-dormant socialities hidden in Hungary's remains of socialism—and in so doing, enable new ways to imagine mastering the challenges of the present.

"I Only Remember the Beautiful"

Many international commentators nonetheless deplored socialist nostalgia as the uncritical attempt to resurrect past presence and imagined origins that sought to forget everything that was painful and difficult about the socialist era. Treating the status of memory in postsocialist societies as a cultural diagnostic, these critics assumed that nostalgia possessed an intrinsic political content that threatened Hungary's national well-being. As a result, each new film or fad inevitably inspired articles and reviews by Hungarian journalists who made a point of arguing that these remains of socialism had little to do with politics, and even when they did, they were not actually perceived this way at the time.

For example, Ákos Réthly, the manager of the Statue Park Museum whom we met in chapter 1, produced a collection of socialist songs called *The Best of Communism* that quickly shot to number one in Hungary for several weeks in 1997. Although the foreign media interpreted the popularity of the album in terms of political kitsch or reactionary politics (Legge and Jordan 1997; Sunley 1997), many people in their twenties and thirties explained to me that they valued these songs neither despite nor because of their political content. Their nostalgia was based on the personal and communal childhood experiences associated with these songs (such as sitting around the campfire at summer camp or stealing one's first kiss), rather than the ideology they represented. Socialist nostalgia provided an idiom through which to celebrate the experience of membership in a generation, understood not merely in the sense of life cycle or lineage, but as a specific place within—and thus relationship to—history.[11] One Dutch acquaintance was delighted to find the album to buy as a gift for his Hungarian girlfriend; he remembered that when she and her friends went out drinking, they sometimes would burst into these songs. Eszter, the student who worked part-time as a secretary, similarly told me that when she and her friends played the guitar and sang, their repertoire included both popular songs and these old songs from their days in the Young Pioneers.

Even more overtly political memories were still overlaid with the innocence of childhood. Győző, the owner of a trendy clothing shop on a fashionable street in central Pest told me that "Liberation Song" conjured up memories of being in school and celebrating the April 4 holiday (the day the Soviet army "liberated" Hungary from Nazi occupation) on one of the first warm days of spring. Local reviews of *Best of Communism* similarly emphasized personal memory over political meaning (*Magyar Narancs* 1997). An article that reviewed a dance music cover of the Soviet standard "Polyushka" (released just a couple of months before *Best of Communism*) likewise argued that the enthusiasm of the workers' movements and the free wieners and beer of the May 1 celebrations "didn't have much to do with [*nem sok köze volt*]" the injustice and repression of the past era (*Internet Kalauz* 1997, 15). From these perspectives, nostalgia was thus nothing more than the universal yearning for childhood itself as an easier, more innocent time. This position is canonized in the title of a popular ballad from the 1960s that people often invoked in this context: "I Only Remember the Beautiful" (*Csak a szépre emlékezem*). Yet explaining the appeal of such songs simply in terms of childhood memory as a transhistorical experience enabled these nostalgic consumers to misrecognize the politics of state socialism. Under socialism, the paternalist regime constructed its citizens, regardless of age, as *childlike* by encouraging them to focus on personal interests and to leave the work of politics to the communist leadership. As a result—as Fehérváry observes in her discussion of the film *Dolly Birds*—many Hungarian adults perceived the demise of state socialism as a collective coming-of-age, in which their entrance into the harsh realities of democracy and market capitalism also represented the passage from youth into the freedoms and responsibilities of adulthood (Fehérváry 2006, 55). The emergence of nostalgia under postsocialism thus reflected a broader cultural fantasy about what many Hungarians now remembered as the relative innocence and insularity of private life under socialism—and it thus stood in stark contrast to the economic uncertainties and political battles of the present day.

Although these narratives comprised a common cultural vocabulary, they spoke most directly to what I have been calling the "transitional generation": those Hungarians who came of age just as the regime was ending, and whose entrance into adulthood was simultaneously tasked with the broader national project of remaking themselves as new postsocialist subjects. As Péter Mújdricza notes, this younger generation mostly knew only from their parents the experience of policemen knocking on the door late at night, and thus "experienced the provincial forms of vulgar 'empire' culture as some magical high camp: a world of red-tie fairy tales with May-Day balloons and penny ice-cream cones—all real, and for lack of anything better, of value" (1993, 152). Tibor, a software engineer then in his early thirties, reflected:

> A few months ago on TV I saw a program with some of the so-called "smart people": you know, the founder of *Pesti Est* [a weekly entertainment guide], the president of Matávnet [an internet provider]—actually, I know some of these people. They said that this generation had the best of both worlds. Most of what they said was stupid. But not that. . . .
>
> I would have hated to have to work in college. Money from Mom was enough. I could buy beers and I could get drunk off two beers. There wasn't any thirst . . . hunger . . . to crave more. Nobody had more, everyone had Trabants. This was great for kids, not wanting more. When you're an adult, you know the Trabant sucks. But we never had to face it.
>
> Now, it's not the same, you have to pay for it. When the changes took place, we got a different chance—we didn't have to join [the] communist party, we could be creative. It's kind of magic that the system ended when my studies did.

In late socialism, films about adolescence tended to be films about political optimism and its disillusionment, as a new generation of idealistic youths confronted—and ultimately was forced to resign themselves to—the deeply tired and cynical system created by their parents and grandparents.[12] In contrast, postsocialist nostalgia films about late socialist life resembled the way Tibor recounted his memories of the era, by paralleling the youth of their protagonists to the perceived overall immaturity of Hungarian society as a whole. The young protagonists of these films invariably emphasized consumption over political participation, and they gave priority to personal rites of passage over national ones. For example, the film *Moscow Square* (*Moszkva Tér*; 2001) is a gentle comedy that follows a group of graduating male high school students in the final days of state socialism. Concerned with parties, girls, and cars (the film's slogan: *buli, csajok, verda*), these teenagers are insouciantly indifferent to the adult world of politics. For them, the fall of the regime means the chance to travel West, to purchase new exotic foreign goods, and to skip their graduation examination in contemporary history, which the recent events force the state to cancel. Even the most defining moment of this period of political turmoil fails to attract the students' attention: the 1989 televised reburial of Imre Nagy, martyr of Hungary's failed 1956 uprising, is met with apathy: "Who the fuck is Imre Nagy?"

Similarly, the *Little Journey* festival's celebration of the styles and fashions of the final decades of late socialism brushed aside the political context of such consumption as irrelevant to the commemoration of generational experience. "The festival wants to show that it's good to be young in any system, even if our history coincides with a dull and inglorious era," one journalist commented in his coverage of the event. "The essence is that 'That's when we met girls, that's when we got drunk for the first time, that's when we were young.'" In other words, he sardonically concluded, "The Kádár-era pancake was filled with crap, but on top of it, it seems, there was pudding" (Barta 2000).

Nostalgia for childhood is for a time of limited perceptions, when one is not even aware of political considerations. Yet, although the forms, practices, and structures of feeling found in Hungary's nostalgia were quintessentially postsocialist, the ideological distinctions it drew between childhood and adulthood, private life and politics, were inherited from the previous era. Nostalgic consumers may have argued that everyday life under state socialism was free from politics, but this retreat from public participation into a private realm of action was in fact the condition of political subjectivity under late socialism. Nonetheless, because those who enjoyed nostalgia considered it to be apolitical, attempts to harness nostalgic passions for political ends would fail under postsocialism.

The Politics of Nostalgia

On the eleventh anniversary of János Kádár's death on July 8, 2000, I went to Budapest's Kerepesi Cemetery to attend a memorial event in his honor, which I had seen advertised on a photocopied flyer taped to a lamppost several days earlier. As general secretary of the Hungarian Socialist Workers' Party, Kádár had led Hungary through three decades of the relative economic security known as "goulash communism." Representing the face of post-1956 normalization—epitomized in his slogan that "those who are not against us, are with us"—Kádár was known as an avuncular, plainspoken leader whose policies emphasized a steady increase in living standards, subsidized by foreign loans. Only in 1988, when political reform became inevitable in light of Gorbachev's perestroika and

Hungary's own economic crises brought on by foreign debt, did reformers in Kádár's party nudge him out of office. He died a year later.

Organized by the Workers' Party (Munkáspárt),[13] one of two successor parties to the Hungarian Socialist Workers' Party (Magyar Szocialista Munkáspárt), the anniversary event attracted perhaps a hundred mourners to the cemetery: primarily the older generations, although several of them told me that they were pleased to see a handful of children and teenagers with their grandparents in attendance as well. At the cemetery gates, members of the Workers' Youth Organization and Left-Wing Front sold red carnations, political pamphlets, and Che Guevara T-shirts, and closer to the event, the loudspeaker warned the crowd to make way for party officials to put flowers on Kádár's grave beneath banners reading "Workers' Party" and "To remember is our historical responsibility [*Emlékezni történelmi felelősségünk*]." As the crowd waited for the speeches to begin under the hot July sun, old friends and colleagues greeted each other and praised the beauty of the event or complained about a poor view, while a television reporter walked through the crowd looking for likely candidates to interview. My tape recorder and notebook also attracted attention; an elderly man beside me attempted to help me by shushing the surrounding crowd and offering to hold my backpack. I told him that I was an anthropologist from the United States and that I was interested in what people think of the communist past today. This memorial would be "instructive [*tanulságos*]" for me, the man responded, with a sweeping motion toward the rest of the crowd. "These people believed in something—something beautiful," he told me earnestly. "They received no reward, but this is common in Hungarian history. They are poor. But we will win— it's just a matter of time. It's worth it to do the right thing [*Érdémes jónak lenni*]. That's why we're born. And that's what matters at the end of your life."

The speeches that began soon afterward echoed his critique of both the quality of present-day life and the moral principles that undergirded it. "Ten years ago, we lived better than today," the head of the Workers' Party, Gyula Thürmer, declared, citing the problems of homelessness, growing poverty, declining pensions, and corruption, among many others.

> Ten years ago, we believed that all men are created equal, and what matters in this country is honest work, integrity, and humanity. Today, there is no value to honest work in Hungary . . .
>
> Ten years ago, the workers were removed from power, and in return they received so-called "rights." You have the choice to work or not to work, but only if you can find a job. If you want to go abroad, you can go, but only if you have the money. You can criticize the government and

the police won't take you away, but what you say will not get on TV. You have the right to stare at advertisements for washing powder. You have the right every four years to choose a washing powder: Fidesz washing powder, MSZP [Hungarian Socialist Party] washing powder, Smallholders [Independent Smallholders' Party] washing powder. . . .

Were we deceived? Yes! For ten years, every day, every hour. But still, I say: don't just always point at others. We too are responsible. We could not resist the temptation. We wanted a taste of capitalism. We wanted to know what private property is like, what free enterprise is like, what the European economy is like. Now we know it, we got it, and we went shopping with it, but at least now we know.

Urging his audience "not to waver" any further, Thürmer ended by invoking the legacy of Kádár to support his bid for election: not to restore the past, but to create a "modern, competitive, democratic Hungary" that would ensure the promise of a "better life" that Hungarians had once enjoyed.

Thürmer's speech did not reflect a nostalgic desire to return to the socialist era, and in an interview with me several months later, he was insistent that a return to a socialist system was neither possible nor desirable.[14] Instead, Thürmer drew on the memory of Kádár in order to launch a moral critique of the failed promises of transition and the need to envision the future in a more humane and socially just form. Yet in light of his party's lack of popularity as a contemporary democratic socialist movement, Thürmer's appeal to nostalgic memories of the previous era was clearly strategically important. It enabled him to gain support from those who did embrace the memory of Kádárism less ambivalently—such as the elderly man who stood beside me during the speeches, for whom the dream of a communist future had been only delayed, but not destroyed.

Considering the relatively small size of the crowd at the memorial and the disproportionate number of older members, as well as the marginalization of the Workers' Party in public and political debate, the stakes of such efforts to recuperate the experience of Kádárism would only become clear a year later, in the summer of 2001, when Thürmer proposed that the state permit the erection of a statue to Kádár. This suggestion to memorialize Kádár—and thus also to elevate the public profile of the Workers' Party—probably would not have registered on the public radar had it not been issued during the height of the annual political summer news drought that Hungarians call "cucumber season" (*uborkaszezon*). One of Hungary's recently established commercial television stations, TV2, picked up the story, devoting one of its most popular programs, the weekly news roundup *Diary* (*Napló*), to examining this campaign and to collecting viewer opinions via its weekly phone-in poll. To everyone's apparent surprise, 80 percent of those who phoned in agreed that Kádár deserved a statue of his own, and the question for the following week's poll ("Is it better to be young now?" [*Jobb-e most fiatalnak lenni?*]) also received an emphatic response in favor of the past.

A revised version of this catchphrase ("When was it better to be young?") later found its way back into public currency as the Workers' Party campaign slogan for the national elections in spring 2002. Yet, despite the apparent popularity of this argument in the phone poll months earlier, the party was unable to leverage the emotional capital of Kádárism into political gain. Instead, in the first round of elections, the Workers' Party once again failed to win the 5 percent necessary to gain parliamentary representation.

What accounted for the Workers' Party's inability to mobilize the emotions summoned by nostalgia for political ends? One answer concerns simple political expediency. Nostalgia in Hungary was about fantasy: both the fantasy of a more innocent past, and the past's own fantasies about what the future might bring. As a specific ideological project of restoration, however, nostalgia had little appeal in a country then already committed to joining the European Union. Politicizing the homey sentiments summoned by nostalgia would have opened the policies of the past regime to political critique, thus invalidating nostalgia's usefulness and emotional legitimacy across the political spectrum. It would subject those on the left to a condemnation of the Kádár regime's lack of democracy, and at the same time, it would also be read as a rejection of, and hence incompatible with, right-wing ideology. As we shall see in chapter 4, the Fidesz party's anti-communist rhetoric during its 2002 reelection campaign targeted such nostalgia as a particular danger. Warning that the victory of their chief rival, the MSZP (Hungarian Socialist Party), would mean the "return" of communism to Hungary, they rejected the MSZP's attempts to reinvent itself as a European social democratic party, instead portraying it as the inheritor of all the sins and corruption of the past era.

On the other hand, as long as voters could justify their fond memories solely in terms of their "stomachs"—that is, their memories of material comfort and security—the emotions summoned by nostalgia could be effective on both sides of the political divide. The MSZP, impatient to put its past behind it, could make vague reference to protecting the concerns of the "simple people" without taking responsibility for the injustices of socialism. Meanwhile, the right wing could explain nostalgic practices as merely the expression of dissatisfaction with postsocialism on the whole, rather than an endorsement of communism and hence a specific rejection of right-wing anticommunist discourse.

Public and Private Worlds

More important than the ideological incompatibility between the fantasized past and present-day ends is that those who enjoyed nostalgia viewed the domestic realm evoked by nostalgia as the absence of politics itself. As we have seen, this ideological distinction between the private domestic sphere and the public world of politics was the product of post-1956 normalization, which no longer required society to subordinate personal interests to the utopia of collectivism. The policies under Kádárism thus represented a significant shift from earlier attempts by the Soviets to revolutionize everyday life by breaking apart the bourgeois distinction between the private domestic realm and the public arena of political thought, culture, and action. As Boym describes, these efforts included interventions such as communal apartments and a revolutionary aesthetics that pathologized even rubber tree plants and kitschy bric-a-brac as emblems of the bourgeois private interior (1994, 32–38).

After 1956, the regime switched course to reinforce, rather than undermine, the public/private divide. Political compliance, rather than active participation, was the goal. One unanticipated result of the regime-encouraged enthusiasm for consumer luxuries and weekend houses (as well as the second jobs necessary to acquire them) was the production of an atomized population whose overriding concern for the pursuit of private happiness ended up being not all that different from what is found in the West (Fehérváry 2013; Lampland 1995). Yet regardless of the ideological problems this policy produced, it nonetheless served a pragmatic purpose. As Slavoj Žižek observed in an interview, by the years of late socialism, the last thing the regime wanted was for its citizens to believe in communism, because such politicization might incite them to revolt against a system that had failed its own ideals. "The paradox of the regime was that if people were to take their ideology seriously it would effectively destroy the system" (Boynton 1998, 44–45).

Instead, the insistence on a sharp division between public and private worlds enabled Hungary's citizens to maintain a sense of autonomy and moral integrity in the face of a poorly functioning and dishonest system. As Martha Lampland explains:

> All throughout the socialist period in Hungary, a stark opposition was drawn by Hungarians between the public and private domains, between what was seen as the posturing of vacuous politics and the real, substantial, truthful site of the home and hearth. . . . Everyone still engaged in public activities: wrote and fulfilled plans, built socialism in the factory, and learned lessons about party heroes in school. Once they returned

home, however, Hungarians ridiculed the plan, criticized their bosses, worked fervently in their private gardens, and forgot as much of the Communist moralizing as possible. (1995, 246)

As Lampland goes on to argue, however, this common understanding of a chasm between public obligations and the meaningful activity conducted in private only served to conceal striking continuities across both realms: whether in the ways that Hungarians thought about "human nature, personal utility, and individual interest" or the similar attitudes and practices found in the first and second economy (1995, 246, 340). At the same time, the dichotomy of public and private also effaced the significant differentiation (by class, gender, and generation, among others) to be found in different people's domestic worlds (333).

The nostalgia that appeared after the system's demise could thus claim to be free of political considerations precisely because many Hungarians experienced the material culture and everyday life of state socialism as similarly outside the sphere of politics. Yet, because this division was itself an ideological relic of the past regime, those who now defended nostalgia as politically irrelevant ironically only reproduced, rather than overturned, the political subjectivity of the previous system. And by maintaining the ideological distinction between warm memories of everyday life and the harsh context that enabled these fond recollections, nostalgia also inherited the impossibility of overcoming the tension between them.

Incommensurable Pasts

This tension was evident in the interviews conducted during *Diary*'s follow-up poll, in which the program asked Hungarian celebrities whose affiliations spanned the political spectrum about their opinions on nostalgia and whether they supported a statue to Kádár. At stake was the suitability of bringing a nostalgia based on youthful private memories of Kádár's "childlike" citizenry into the political sphere of urban monumentality.

> I had a very nice childhood. I was a Young Pioneer and I was in a pioneer camp, and it was nice. There was no ideology, but simply a very nice childhood. Okay, we didn't have beautiful shop window displays or branded items, there was only one type of things: it was a rather gray world that we lived in. But I think it was very beautiful. Then the school years came, I studied at a music gymnasium, and we played on the best instruments. The state bought me the best instruments: Steinway and Yamaha pianos. And it was the same at music academy. So I can say that I was educated on the money of the previous state. I can't say anything

bad about it. [Lajos Galambos ("Lagzi Lajcsi"), musician and host of the popular musical variety television show, *Dáridó*]

I don't like the idea that people of dubious fame get a statue, and in general, I don't really like when people are heroized, unless they were a great historical person. Kádár was a historical personality, but Hitler was too, and I'm sure there are some who would still like to raise a statue to him. . . . But I was otherwise very surprised at the results—82 percent—I didn't think that people still think of old times with such nostalgia. I see similar tendencies in East Germany. Whether it's about Erich Honecker or the era, I can't really judge, but I think that it comes from a certain level of dissatisfaction for the present and a desire for safe existence. [Gábor Bochkor, radio host]

The program interspersed these interviews with archival clips of Kádár: speeches in which he called for raising the standard of living—"not radically but consistently"—and scenes of him playing with children, with the words, "Today, there is no child whose parents have to say that my child cannot eat because 'the bread went to sleep.' If our fight did not achieve anything else but this, then it was worth it." The lack of commentary to contextualize these clips suggested that these claims were to be taken at face value—a rosy vision of socialist-era consumption that another interviewee, the right-wing rock musician Ferenc "Feró" Nagy, contested.

I don't understand—no, I do, they are nostalgic for back then, when bread was only 3,60 forints. So that was a "safe" world, but then people forget that they couldn't buy a car, couldn't buy a fridge, there was nothing really in the shops. . . .

But I understand that they cry back for the pseudo-safety. It's true, there was nothing, but you could build on that nothing, and people still live in the houses that were built on this nothing.

Any evaluation of the socialist era was thus torn between what *Diary*'s reporter summarized as "freedom" and "material security": values that the Kádár regime rendered irreconcilable. "It's interesting to see that when we asked famous people the usual reaction was anger or laughter," the program's announcer concluded. "Kádár's name still divides society."

Although the historical place of Kádár may have been divisive, it would be a mistake to merely interpret this disagreement as a split between two communities of memory: one with positive memories of the socialist past, and the other without. After all, many members of the transitional generation who enthusiastically consumed socialist nostalgia were also the same ones who, in other contexts, decried the past regime and called attention to what they perceived to be troubling social and economic continuities between the socialist past and postsocialist present. Rather, the question was one of reconciling memories constructed as free of politics with more painful (and hence explicitly politicized) experiences of oppression under the previous regime. The perceived incommensurability of these two sets of memory was what enabled most Hungarians to reject any notion of returning to the socialist era, yet still select Kádár as the most positive politician in twentieth-century Hungarian history in a 1999 public opinion poll (*Medián* 1999). It is why, as demonstrated in Feró Nagy's quote above, even those who argued against nostalgia often phrased their critiques in nostalgia's own idiom (the world of material goods), rather than explicitly political ones. A piece in the far-right weekly *Demokrata*, for example, condemned the current nostalgia trend by pointing out how the now-idealized socialist past lacked much of what today's postsocialist consumers take for granted: mobile phones, bananas and other once-exotic fruits, fresh and reliably stocked goods at the grocery store, and so on (Zs. Ungváry 2001, 41).

The film *Dolly Birds* illustrates this dilemma in its opening scene of block warden Uncle Simon broadcasting the morning lottery numbers over the local public address system. He stutters when he discovers that one of the numbers is "56" (the year of Hungary's failed uprising against the Soviets), and hastily instructs block residents to check the newspaper for the numbers instead. Within the film's narrative, of course, we are to understand that Uncle Simon refuses to say the words out of fear of political reprisals. But this scene also has a purpose outside the film's plotline. "Not saying 1956" is the film's condition for all that comes after: a portrayal of the early years of post-1956 normalization as greatly circumscribed and built on repression, but potentially joyful nonetheless.[15]

Nostalgia in the Hungarian context thus functioned as the *limit* of politics. It gave voice to broadly perceived social truths that could not be spoken in a political context because it would have subjected these claims to a critique of the past regime's antidemocratic policies. Rather than represent the desire to return to the past, the impossibility of returning to that past was what made such discourse possible: Hungarians could "afford" their nostalgic enjoyment of socialism's remains, because at that time, they saw no actual possibility of return to the Kádár era. In this way, the elegiac idiom of nostalgia impeded recognizing the ways in which the experience of political subjectivity under Kádárism continued to penetrate the present, by shaping the very possibilities of how it could be remembered.

The Workers' Party thus not only made a mistake by confusing nostalgia for socialism for an endorsement of perceived representatives of the past regime. More crucially, it failed to understand nostalgia in the Hungarian context as a specific refusal of politics—even when embodied in the figure of the country's former leader. As the *Diary* interviews made clear, support for a Kádár statue did not necessarily entail support for him as a historical actor. Rather, as many interviewees argued, the statue's supporters wanted to commemorate Kádár as a symbol of when the past itself felt safe and childlike: a time when the populace felt protected by the hand of the paternalist state, and a basic standard of living seemed assured.

Of course, many others criticized erecting a monument to Kádár, arguing that it would reverse the work of the Statue Park Museum a decade earlier by reinstating ideological content long-removed from the cityscape. But the creation of the Statue Park Museum had not simply removed communist ideology from the streets and squares of Budapest. It had been the outcome of struggles among city authorities, politicians, art professionals, and the media to transform unnoticed landmarks of everyday urban life into scandalously visible remains of Soviet occupation. This new semiotics of public space distanced the recent past by reducing the meaning and purpose of monuments to their intended political message. In turn, the proposal to erect a monument to Kádár did not simply threaten to reinsert political content into the city, as critics worried. Such criticism missed what was truly radical about the nostalgia that fueled both the Workers' Party's proposal and its enthusiastic reception. The erection of a monument to Kádár would invert the logic that created the Statue Park Museum: instead of defining the remains of the past era solely in ideological terms, it insisted that such remains were free from politics altogether.

A monument to Kádár would thus not simply be the equivalent of returning statues from the Statue Park Museum to their former locations. Rather, it would be as if Osztyapenkó, the statue discussed in chapter 1, was reerected not to commemorate Ilya Afanasyevich Ostapenko, the Soviet captain who died liberating Hungary, but to serve as a memorial to the monument's role in the everyday life of state socialism: a popular hitchhiking stop whose waving flag welcomed Budapest residents when they returned from a vacation at Lake Balaton. In this sense, a statue to Kádár would serve as a memorial to the domestication of socialism itself.

Nostalgia for the everyday life of Kádár's Hungary offered one of the few safe discourses available for talking about the past. Because it evaded being harnessed for political ends, it provided a powerful tool for collective identity that was otherwise unavailable in Hungary's polarized political and cultural climate. For some, nostalgia offered a frame to give sense and coherence to personal memories, and thus to maintain personal continuity in the face of historical disjuncture and irresolution: it enabled its subjects to integrate their memories into narrative without either endorsing or condemning an era not yet perceived to have fully resolved into history. For others, particularly the transitional generation, the emphasis was on finding a common idiom for discussing the past with others, regardless of how these memories fit into their larger family or social history during the socialist era, and independent of how positively or negatively they chose to evaluate the former system as a whole.

Indeed, the perceived incompatibility of nostalgia with such divisive political topics made the nostalgic consumption of socialist remains perhaps the *only* idiom through which to find common ground in discussions of the socialist era. Socialist nostalgia enabled Hungarians "to not talk about the past while talking about it." It permitted its consumers to retain their childhood memories while refusing to pass definitive judgment on the larger political and historical context within which these experiences took place, and thus functioned as both a counterpoint to and evasion of the highly polarized representations of the past in the public sphere. Nostalgia thus worked not merely as a discourse about the past, but as a metacommentary on what it meant to talk about the past in postsocialist Hungary. In so doing, nostalgia also offered a way to envision mastering both the troublesome socialist past and the uncertain postsocialist present: by embracing remains of socialism as both the refusal of politics and the source of uniquely Hungarian cultural value.

Remains as Cultural Heritage

One of Hungary's most popular socialist-era films, Péter Bacsó's 1969 comedy *The Witness* (*A Tanú*), tells the story of József Pelikán, a dike keeper who becomes trapped in the regime's absurd machinations in the years before 1956. Caught for illegally slaughtering a pig, Pelikán expects years of hard labor and jail time, but he is instead befriended by the mysterious party functionary Comrade Virág. Virág rewards Pelikán with a series of increasingly prestigious positions, despite the fact that Virág fails at each one. The hapless Pelikán has no understanding of the reasons for his preferential treatment—until, in the final sequences of the film, Virág orders him to provide false testimony against a friend in a show trial.

Banned for over a decade by communist authorities, *The Witness* met with an enthusiastic reception when it was finally permitted general release in the early 1980s. Its jokes and portrayal of the well-intentioned yet bumbling Pelikán (whose literal-minded attempts to fulfill the requirements of each position inevitably expose the absurdity of the system that gave him these assignments) soon gained a wide and enduring cultural currency. For example, Pelikán is put in charge of creating a haunted-house ride in an amusement park. Instructed to give the ride a socialist flavor, he produces tableaux that literalize some of Marx's most famous expressions: a clumsy mechanical ghost represents the specter of communism haunting Europe and manacled stick figures of the proletariat rattle their chains.

One of the film's most famous scenes depicts Pelikán's job of running an agricultural institute tasked with creating a "Hungarian orange." Despite the difficulty of growing such southern fruit in Hungary's continental climate (Pelikán himself says that he has not eaten one in twenty years), the institute finally succeeds in producing a solitary orange, which is then celebrated with a visit from a leading party official. Moments before the ceremony is to begin, Pelikán discovers that his son has stolen the orange and eaten it. In desperation, he turns for help to Virág, who orders him to use a lemon instead. The visiting party official tastes it and screws up his face in dismay, but—with a glance at Virág—Pelikán hurriedly explains, "It's the new Hungarian orange. It's a little bit yellow, a little bit sour. But it's ours!" With this appeal to national pride and socialist advancement, Pelikán is saved, and the official's grimace relaxes into a smile.

The ironies of the "Hungarian orange" (*magyar narancs*) caught hold of Hungary's cultural imagination in the last years of the state socialist regime. As a symbol of the irrationality of the communist system, the Hungarian orange could be interpreted a number of ways: as a demonstration of the power of the regime to determine reality; as another example of the "shared lie" of communism (summed up in the well-known joke, "you pretend to work and we pretend to pay you"); and as a critique of the unnaturalness of any attempt to plant Soviet communism in Hungary's presumably inhospitable cultural soil. In other words, the Hungarian orange became the epitome of the inauthenticity of Hungarian communism itself—so often qualified as "goulash communism," "real existing socialism," and other such terms to distinguish the lofty ideals of communism from the reality of the "new Hungary" actually produced in its name.

During the years of my fieldwork, friends and colleagues often recommended that I watch—or rewatch—*The Witness*, insisting that I could not understand the absurdity and frustration of life under communism without it. I soon began to realize, however, that pride in *The Witness* and its risible tale of the Hungarian orange reflected postsocialist realities as well. We have seen how much political and cultural labor was exerted to expel official state symbols as unwanted remains from the recent past. In contrast, the Hungarian orange became firmly established in Hungary's postsocialist cultural vocabulary. In its early years as a liberal youth party, Fidesz chose the image of an orange to represent itself as the icon of anti-communism, and a popular left-wing weekly founded in 1989 similarly used the Hungarian orange (*Magyar Narancs*) as its title. It is proof of this icon's broad appeal across political lines and the significant symbolic capital it was still perceived to mobilize that, in the late 1990s, the now center-right Fidesz launched a lawsuit that temporarily prevented the magazine *Magyar Narancs* from using its name.

But the meaning of the Hungarian orange did not remain the same. As the battle to control the symbol suggests, the primary appeal of the Hungarian orange under postsocialism no longer derived from its critique of the former regime's irrationality. Instead, the emphasis shifted to an appreciation of how the orange exemplified the resilience, imagination, and humor of Hungary's response to the imposition of communism. Most important of all was the claim to the national specificity of this response. That is, if during socialism the stress was implicitly on the humorous understatement of Pelikán's "It's a little bit yellow, a little bit sour," and on how his forced denial of reality exemplified the blindness of the regime, what resonated in the postsocialist context was the claim to national ownership and uniqueness—"But it's ours!"—that nonetheless endowed this sour lemon with value.

The saga of the Hungarian orange offers a new perspective on the challenge that socialist remains posed to the problem of mastering the previous era. Up to now, we have seen that the production of the socialist past in the form of isolated remains enabled Hungarians to distance and disavow the socialist past as merely a divergence from the authentic course of national history. In contrast, the logic of nostalgia—"But it's ours!"—made visible the cultural productivity of socialist inauthenticity, whether the Hungarian orange or the clothes and foods produced to imitate Western products. However unwanted and "unnatural" the decades of state socialist rule were for those who lived through them, the memories and meanings invested in its detritus could nonetheless inspire novel ways to envision national value, community, and identity under postsocialism.

Nostalgia for socialism's remains also provided a way to express the frustrations of Hungary's long-desired entrance into the Western regimes of cultural recognition. It did so through the language of national heritage: a global discourse of cultural value that simultaneously reinforced and challenged the ways Hungary was represented in the West—and how Hungary in turn represented itself as a new Western subject.

We have seen how the marketing of state kitsch at the time of the political transformation enabled its consumers to demonstrate their distance from a quickly receding unpalatable past. These attempts to disavow the recent era were forced to confront the Cold War nostalgia of Hungary's Western visitors, whose mass-mediated fantasies of defaced and toppled monuments had erroneously been used to characterize Hungary's bloodless and peaceful democratic political transformation. As Žižek argues, what made such imagined spectacles so compelling—and necessary—was that they reinvented democracy by reinventing the West as an object of desire: "in a likeable, idealized form, as worthy of love" (1990, 50).

> The real object of fascination for the West is thus the gaze, namely the supposedly naive gaze by means of which Eastern Europe stares back at the West, fascinated by its democracy. It is as if the Eastern gaze is still able to perceive in Western societies its *agalma*,[16] the treasure that causes democratic enthusiasm and which the West has long lost the taste of. (Žižek 1990, 50)

As the boom in scholarship and media coverage of socialist nostalgia over the past decades indicates, many Western observers have similarly interpreted the subsequent efflorescence of nostalgic practices in Hungary and elsewhere in the Soviet bloc as confirmation of the West's own fantasies about the failures and triumphs of socialism and communism. For some, the commodification of socialist-era goods has proved the victory of market capitalism. For others, socialist nostalgia offers a vision of popular resistance to capitalism that more traditional forms of political mobilization have failed to provide. Depending on the ideological stance of its observers, identical nostalgic practices can thus be interpreted as subversive or maintaining the status quo.[17]

For Hungarians, encounters with the West's own (often inaccurate) fantasies and assumptions about past and present-day Hungary have entailed a double loss of the dream of the West through which socialist-era Hungarians constructed their own identities. On the one hand, this fantasy represented the dream of utopia and a "normal life": the desire to consume Western products at Western levels and to catch up with its industrial production and consumer culture. The appeal of nostalgia thus lay in its reinvigoration of both memories of the past and a much-desired future of color, variety, and abundance: a time when, as Tibor ironically summarized in an unintentional echo of Thürmer's speech at Kádár's memorial, "your choice of washing powder could change your life."

On the other hand, what made these memories of what now seemed to be an unimaginable innocence and gullibility to the claims of Western advertising so poignant was the very optimism that had inspired them—the expectation that with the fall of communism, Hungarian citizens would soon become full members of the West in both political and economic terms. Such nostalgia symbolized the longing to be accepted and recognized as *preexisting*, rather than potential, members of the European cultural and historical community.[18] The frustrations of this were perhaps best exemplified by the Rubik's cube (*bűvös kocka*), a toy that in the early 1980s found its way into nearly every Western household just as it did in Hungary, but was rarely recognized as a specifically Hungarian invention. It thus failed to export the self-image of Hungary as a nation whose scientific skill and creativity was on par with that of more affluent countries, even as it demonstrated that its products could indeed provoke reciprocal consumer desire.

Socialist nostalgia responded to this perception of misrecognition as well as to the more general sense of disenchantment with the extravagant claims of capitalist advertising and Western consumer products and culture. Now, not only was access to products limited by price rather than politics, but also many Hungarians believed that Western firms and advertisers failed to acknowledge them as sophisticated and knowledgeable consumers. Beginning with my first trip to Hungary in 1993, my friends and interview subjects were eager to reject this perception. One spoke resentfully of a visit abroad where she was greeted as an uncultured naïf and was assumed not to know how to operate appliances such as microwaves or hair dryers.[19] Although these Hungarians may not necessarily have believed that their North American and Western European interlocutors actually looked down upon them, the risk of wholeheartedly accepting what they perceived to be "Western" values, standards, and logic was that, at best, it constructed them as inadequate imitations, and, at worst, it rendered their recent history and cultural experience pathological and inassimilable: a backward East, burdened by its discredited origins, versus the sophisticated consumers in the advanced West.

Many in the transitional generation responded to this perceived stigma by explicitly describing their shared experience and now obsolete cultural knowledge not as an unwanted legacy, but as cherished evidence of cultural intimacy and untranslatability. As one friend explained, "We know how to consume as Westerners, but we have additional knowledge that Westerners lack." A corporate executive from the United States echoed this observation when he told me with some surprise that "Hungarians want to consume like Westerners—but I don't think they want to be Western." For example, a 2001 television commercial for the popular Hungarian beer Dreher presented a dazzling selection of teenaged slang, images, and icons from the socialist 1980s with the slogan: "We speak one language" (*Egy nyelvet beszélünk*). My friend Levente, who had longed to purchase goods from hard-currency stores, praised the historical accuracy of these references, so dense in narrative, visual, and linguistic citations of the previous era that he watched, rewatched, and discussed the commercial with me for nearly half an hour in order to explain the references in this thirty-second spot.

In a rapid-fire series of clips linked by voice-over dialogue, the ad reviewed some of the defining memories of being a teenager in the last decade of socialism.

> "We did not believe when they scored the sixth against us in Mexico. Oh, how devastated we were" (*Hogy kivoltunk*).

This refers to a soccer world championship fought against the USSR; Hungary's loss was narrated as a "national disaster" that Levente jokingly compared to the Kennedy assassination in the United States. The ad then switched to scenes of Hungarian teenagers dancing in a nightclub. Levente praised both their clothing and their habit of staring at televised videos rather than each other as "very eighties," remembering also the circulation of much-copied videotapes from the West among his friends and classmates.

> "But the videodisco consoled us. We loved Zsuzsa and the "break" [break-dancing]. But Regős only loved his Walkman."

The screen then split in a nod to early music videos.

> "And you remember the first western car [verda] in the neighborhood? What was even weirder [meredek] than the color was its owner."

Levente explained that both the eighties' slang for "car" (verda) and "weird" (meredek—steep) were no longer in common use.

> "Like an actor from the horror movies we stole from your brother."

The ad showed a group of teenagers crowded around a television, screaming in gleeful fright at the events on the screen.

> "We really ate it up. [Nagyon kajáltuk]. Just like the kiwi."

Remembering the kiwi conjured up the former fascination with exotic fruits whose limited availability made them a symbol of not only economic but also cultural capital under late socialism—as illustrated in the following line, in which the advertisement cut to one man teasing another for his ignorance in not knowing how to consume the fruit properly.

> "Do you still eat the kiwi with the peel?"

The ad then ended with a shot of prosperous thirty-something yuppies sitting in a pub and laughing in reminiscence.

> Announcer: "Dreher: We speak one language."

Levente commended the ad for evoking very specific memories that only people in his generation would know, as well as for doing so through a particularly nostalgic combination of pride in present-day success and amusement at former naiveté. Levente had participated in political marches and demonstrations in the final years of state socialism; for example, he was proud that he could be seen among a sea of faces in a well-known photograph from a 1988 demonstration to show solidarity with Hungarians persecuted in Ceausescu's Romania. Nonetheless, he viewed his experience of the past regime as mostly positive, describing himself as coming from a "typical Kádárist family": "We were peasants who moved into the lower middle class. We didn't have everything, but we had enough and we had this idea that the middle-class was achievable." Each image or line of dialogue in the ad thus set off its own chain of fond personal as well as cultural memories in Levente—from watching the world championship at a high school camp (where he, as a "good leftist," chose to root for the USSR because he thought the Hungarians were playing poorly) to the videos he used to circulate with his friends to the kiwi-flavored soda that he used to love.

Similarly, Zoltán, a self-described "yuppie" in his early thirties who worked for a Western European multinational firm, praised the film *Moscow Square* not merely because it rewrote his personal biography in terms of the collective memory of his generation: as he said several times, the film "was about me—I *am* that character." The film was also "important," he argued, because it brought back to life the tiny objects and gestures that he was on the verge of forgetting. Its appeal lay in the perceived authenticity of its minuscule details that conjured up the prosaic textures of a now seemingly distant reality, such as the kind of shopping bag used by the protagonist's grandmother, or the way she, upon entering her apartment, opened a small wooden box of cigarettes and lit one with a match.

The density and the specificity of these cultural references and their meanings for the present thus stood in stark contrast to the earlier wave of communist kitsch, so easily commodified, interpreted, and consumed by foreigners and locals alike. Yet when pushed to explain the significance of such small details or to extrapolate a larger narrative of everyday life under state socialism from the memories of such scenes and objects, many people I spoke with insisted on the self-evidence of the memories themselves as a form of explanation. The mere fact of personal significance was its own justification, and attempts to analyze a larger meaning behind these memories and references would thus often lapse into what these people themselves termed banalities—reminiscent of Pelikán's defense of the Hungarian orange decades earlier. "It was stupid, but it was our life." "It had soul [*lelke volt*]." "It was ours."

On the one hand, this inability or refusal to extract broader meaning can be read as a protest against abstraction itself: against the very fantasy of pure translatability epitomized by the capitalist logic of exchange value. It thus reflected a mourning for what was now narrated as a different, more authentic relationship to the material culture of the socialist era. As Gerald Creed notes, under state socialism, commodities were not fully fetishized: the effort exerted and connections necessary to acquire them were part of their perception and meaning. Thus, even the packaging of valued or exotic goods was preserved and displayed in order to make visible "social relations and valuable connections or resources that transcended the time or period of consumption" (2002, 120).

On the other hand, the assertion of indefinable uniqueness is at the heart of that unnamable, irreducible substance that Žižek terms the "Nation-Thing" around which modern national identities are constituted (Žižek 1990, 51–53). That is, the emphasis that Hungarian consumers and audiences placed on the authenticity of the atmospheres, gestures, and memories conjured up by these objects and films—rather than their practical or narrative value—functioned to signify the uniqueness and incommunicability (which, crucially, does not prohibit the commodifiability) of the shared experience of growing up under state socialism. Many people I spoke with were thus insistent on the impossibility of foreigners understanding local nostalgic texts and references; a colleague, for example, discouraged me from watching *Dolly Birds* based on the logic that—much like the Dreher advertisement—the density of its wordplay would be too difficult for a non-Hungarian to grasp. But I soon discovered that this shared vocabulary could be impenetrable to Hungarians as well. For example, when I sought out a translator for help deciphering some unfamiliar terms in a news article that described the *Little Journey* nostalgia festival, she also did not recognize them and eventually consulted her husband, who was ten years older, to translate expressions such as *pucsít* (which he defined as to stick out one's bottom) or *tiki-taki* (a game of two balls on a string). Thus, the common insistence on the inaccessibility of nostalgia to non-Hungarians was as much ideological as factual: a way to support the fantasy of a national community that all did "speak one language" through a shared experience of history that denied both generational differences and the social stratifications under socialism and postsocialism.

As Boym observes, this logic is perhaps best epitomized by the fact that many nations insist that their word for a culturally specific kind of nostalgic longing (for example, the Czech *litost*, the Russian *toska*, the Portuguese *saudade*) is itself untranslatable: "While each term preserves the specific rhythms of the language, one is struck by the fact that all these untranslatable words are in fact synonyms; and all share . . . the longing for uniqueness" (Boym 2001, 13). From this perspective, nostalgia in Hungary was not so much a discourse *of* cultural intimacy as it was a discourse *about* cultural intimacy, which Michael Herzfeld defines as "not the public representation of domesticity . . . but the often raucous and disorderly experience of life in the concealed spaces of public culture" (2004, 320). Ironically, nostalgia offered a way for Hungarians to assert distinctiveness from the West by deploying an idiom of benign cultural heritage that was itself part of what Herzfeld calls a "globalized system of cultural value" (322).

The self-proclaimed otherness and untranslatability of socialist nostalgia thus responded to the dilemma of identity politics in globalizing capitalism: the longing to be accepted as equal partners of the West and the simultaneous desire to be seen as unique (and not a secondhand imitation).[20] The Dreher beer ad, which attempted to unify its Hungarian audience under the slogan "We speak one language" represented the fantasy of resolving this tension, by framing its scenes of the socialist 1980s through the memories of a group of successful, yuppie Hungarian thirty-somethings, enjoying their Dreher beers at a fashionable pub. It used socialist nostalgia not to mourn the past, but to suggest that its consumers could "have it all": be culturally distinctive and, at the same time, produce themselves as European by consuming and achieving at Western levels. (Not only the ad itself but the very fact of its existence suggests this, by targeting the people who had such memories as a desirable market demographic—a strategy made even more clear in its print campaign, which declared "We grew up together" alongside the slogan "We speak one language.") In so doing, this nostalgia functioned as a "narrative fetish," which Eric Santner in his work on Holocaust memory defines as a mode of representing the past that seeks to eliminate from recognition the "trauma or loss that called that narrative into being in the first place" (1992, 144). The narrative fetish offers "a strategy of undoing, in fantasy, the need for mourning by simulating a condition of intactness" (144): here, a dream of personal and cultural transformation in which everything changes, but nothing is lost.

In the early years of postsocialism, the upheavals of the market economy, loss of state subsidies, and rapid privatization forced Hungarians into a frantic struggle for social and economic positioning. Fehérváry observes that this period of ambition and anxiety was marked by a discourse of "winners" and "losers," as people fought to ensure their future stability and feared being identified as or associated with those who were downwardly mobile (2013, 188). Now, as the first decade after the change of system came to a close and people began to consolidate their social positions, nostalgia made visible two interconnected fantasies about Hungary's remains of socialism. It represented the fantasy of leaving the past completely behind and a fantasy of oneself not being left behind either—of succeeding under new economic and social demands not in spite of but *because* of one's past experience. By recovering a presumably inassimilable past as valued cultural heritage, nostalgia helped Hungarians to argue for an identity that was distinct from the Soviet past and the Western present—and, in some ways, superior to both.

This fantasy appealed most directly to those members of the transitional generation who had succeeded in joining the urban middle class. Nostalgia would enable this generation to recuperate the value of their socialist-era childhoods, while at the same time paradoxically demonstrating their mastery of the postsocialist present as savvy capitalist Western consumers. But for those who had not yet enjoyed the fruits of Hungary's political and economic transformation, nostalgia also served as a source of aspiration, and it lent legitimacy to what Boym calls more "restorative" nostalgias by an older generation dispossessed of socialist-era security and entitlements.

For the transitional generation, nostalgia celebrated the experience of bridging two incommensurable lifeworlds—and the fantasy of mastering both. The self-identified "yuppie" Zoltán thus told me he enjoyed the film *Moscow Square* not just because it commemorated his own coming-of-age at the end of socialism, but because its epilogue in modern-day Hungary accommodated his current experience of the Western European business world where he had found professional success. "It's true that by Friday I've usually had it up to my balls with globalization," he commented one evening. "But then I rest up over the weekend, and I'm ready to jump back in it again." He praised the final scene of the film, in which the now adult protagonist reports on the varied postsocialist career paths of his high school classmates and reflects on his own. The monologue ends with a reference to the opening scene of the film, when as a teenager in late socialist Hungary, the protagonist disgustedly threw away *csalamádé*—the quintessentially Eastern European pickled vegetable mix—from atop the "Western" hamburger he bought at a kiosk. "I'm fucking hungry," he now says, in the film's final, now famous lines. "I'm going to run over to McDonald's [*Meki*] and get a mad-cow burger with fries. Maybe it will eat my brain, but at least there isn't any *csalamádé* in it." Zoltán laughingly agreed with this grudging embrace of the dangers of the globalized present over the indignities of a provincialized past—but, he told me, "I still like *csalamádé* on my burgers."

The Paradoxes of Nostalgia

A number of paradoxes characterized nostalgia as Hungary's first decade of postsocialism came to a close. Nostalgia celebrated its distance from the past, even as it appeared to draw the past near. It found enchantment in remains once perceived as valueless and inauthentic, but it did so in response to the disappointments of a present that the past had once yearned for. Nostalgia's focus on the material texture and sociality of daily life enabled its consumers to interpret it as apolitical, yet this ideological distinction was inherited from the politics of the past era. And although the appeal of nostalgia lay in its ability to unify Hungarians otherwise divided by age, socioeconomic status, and political affiliation, it would find its most enthusiastic audience not among those dispossessed by postsocialism's transformations, but among those members of the transitional generation who had navigated its challenges most successfully.

But as the dream of "having it all" promised by the Dreher beer commercial suggests, the productivity of these paradoxes would be possible only as long as the present appeared to have triumphed over the past. That is, the condition for socialist nostalgia would be not only the impossibility of returning to state socialism but also the superiority of what emerged to replace it. This fantasy of a mastered past and victorious present links the different remains we have explored in chapters 1, 2, and 3. Whether remains took the form of banished monuments, outdated histories, or cherished mementos, the processes of removing, replacing, or domesticating these cultural objects enabled Hungarians to cast recent history aside and envision a triumphant and prosperous future.

As Hungary entered the second decade of postsocialism, such optimism would quickly fade. In chapters 4, 5, and 6, I explore the demise of these dreams of mastery, and their replacement by ever-increasing warnings of hidden terrors, secrets, and national crisis. Once used to demonstrate victory over the past, Hungary's remains of socialism would instead become proof that the past continued to persecute the present.

RECOVERING NATIONAL VICTIMHOOD AT THE HOUSE OF TERROR

> For decades, we have been passing by a seemingly peaceful, bourgeois apartment building, located on one of the most beautiful avenues of our capital, among palatial residences and enormous trees that never lose their cheerful character. And it never crosses our mind what this building's past might conceal. We do not even think about the fact that this house is a memento. Living pain. But there comes a day when we know. When we glance at it, when we truly see it. It stands naked in front of us, it lets us see what it has covered up, and it forces all of us to understand.

—Prime Minister Viktor Orbán's speech at the opening of the House of Terror, 2002 [*Gondola.hu* 2002]

On February 24, 2002, a new museum opened on Andrássy Street, a tree-lined boulevard that is Budapest's equivalent of Paris's Champs Elysées. Here, in a stately building much like its neighbors, the Hungarian fascist Arrow Cross Party tortured and killed Jewish and political prisoners after it seized power in a successful putsch in October 1944. Later, the communist state security police, the ÁVO (later known as the ÁVH),[1] used the same house as its headquarters and the same cells to imprison and torture political prisoners. Although the building stopped being used for these purposes after the early 1950s, according to urban legend (or, at least, the legend "revived" for the purposes of the museum), it continued to be known in the local vernacular as the House of Terror (Terror Háza). This name, in turn, was given to the museum that the Fidesz-led coalition government created within the building's walls: a historical exhibition dedicated to the victims of fascism and communism.

The House of Terror was an immediate success. The first round of the general elections was six weeks away, and the museum's opening was timed to fall on the eve of a new holiday dedicated to the victims of communism. Each morning, visitors of all ages could be seen reading conservative newspapers and discussing the upcoming election as they waited outside in line for hours beneath the museum's *pengefal* (knife wall), a stark metal scaffolding that slices the building out of its surrounding urban landscape. Andrássy Street is a protected UNESCO World Heritage Site, and its architecture and symbolism conjure up one of Hungary's

FIGURE 4.1   Line of visitors waiting to enter the House of Terror during the first weeks of its opening. Personal photograph, 2002.

historical highpoints: the frenzy of construction and monumentalization in Budapest at the end of the nineteenth century, and the economic development, political power, and national-cultural vigor that made such growth possible. In contrast, the House of Terror's knife wall casts much of the building into shadow, severing the museum from its nostalgic turn-of-the-century setting and thrusting it into the violence of twentieth-century modernity. Only cutouts in the metal allow sunlight to hit the building's facade in the shape of the word "TERROR" as well as a five-pointed star and an arrow cross. Terror thus literally haunts the building, as a once-hidden remain of socialism that the knife wall transforms into spectral possibility: a threat for the present and future.

As a memorial space that addresses Hungary's experience of state socialism, the House of Terror appears similar to the Statue Park Museum that opened nearly ten years earlier. Yet while both museums recontextualize the remains of the previous era, they do so for distinctly different ends. The purpose of the Statue Park Museum was to lay the past to rest and thus to demonstrate the triumph of democracy by containing socialism's visible remains. In contrast, the House of Terror sought to bring a hidden history of persecution out of invisibility so that Fidesz could argue that remains in the form of communist crimes and their perpetrators continued to threaten Hungary's political transformation. That is, if the Statue Park

Museum reduced the problem of the past to easily isolated physical remainders, the House of Terror would use the materiality of its location at 60 Andrássy Street as mere evidence of a more widespread contagion in political and public life. No longer were remains merely a question of the past as *past*. Rather, they took the form of a past that continued to jeopardize the present—and in so doing, called into question the very success of Hungary's political transformation.

The House of Terror would thus play an important role in the Fidesz coalition's 2002 reelection campaign discussed at the end of chapter 2. Warning of a return to communism should the MSZP (Hungarian Socialist Party) win, Fidesz presented the elections as a moral battle between those who looked ahead to the future and those who threatened to bring back the terrors of the previous era. With the Magyar Millennium, Country Image Center, and similar initiatives to reshape Hungary's national subjectivity, Fidesz attempted to replace the remains of socialist-era history with a proudly optimistic vision of national history that would serve as a model for the way forward. Alongside this tutelage in thousand-year national pride, the House of Terror functioned to remind the nation of the suffering it had recently overcome and to link the perpetrators of the past to the Fidesz coalition's left-wing political rivals in the present. The museum thus enabled Fidesz to present Hungary's accomplishments as endangered by the persistence of socialist remains that threatened to return in the form of the MSZP-SZDSZ coalition—and thus again push Hungary off the proper and authentic course of its national history.

What made this threat of communist persecution so striking is that everything the House of Terror now presented as a danger to Hungary's democratic future had already happened in past election cycles. During previous elections, the government had swung from right to left and back again—which did not necessarily reflect Hungarian voters' confidence in any particular party as much as it did the desire for change, and the public's economic dissatisfaction and political disillusionment under postsocialism more generally.[2] As we have seen, the MSZP had not only already spent a term in office between 1994 and 1998 without any threats to Hungary's democratic stability, but it had won these elections precisely by appealing to positive memories of the past regime's social welfare measures and the administrative efficiency its former bureaucrats were expected to deliver. And in 2000, two years after defeating the MSZP's bid for reelection in coalition with SZDSZ, Fidesz prime minister Victor Orbán himself declared that Hungary's transition—and thus the four decades of state socialism that preceded it—was over (Orbán 2000).

Why did the socialist past now become such a danger, and why did it seem so much nearer than a few years before? In part, the ever-increasing warnings of communist danger reflected broader ongoing shifts in the ideological landscape.

With both the MSZP and SZDSZ increasingly reluctant to engage with questions of national identity or Hungary's post-1945 history, the problem of socialism's remains could become the province of the right wing and a key element of the political rhetoric of the Fidesz coalition's election campaign. But beyond the demands of party politics, the House of Terror also sought to intervene more broadly into two circulating regimes of memory that each threatened to invalidate claims to both past and present suffering under communism. First, the museum's emphasis on the crimes of communism challenged the priority given to Holocaust memory not only by Hungary's left wing, but also by Western European memory culture, which many of my interviewees perceived as minimizing claims to equivalent victimization. Second, the House of Terror sought to tame local nostalgic desires for everyday life under state socialism, which similarly risked rendering claims to communist oppression unintelligible. Instead, by conceptualizing the problem of socialism's remains as one of continuing persecution, the museum attempted to enact an affective pedagogy that would teach its visitors to react to the material culture of the past socialist era with "terror" rather than nostalgia.

While the Fidesz coalition would narrowly lose the 2002 elections, the creation of the House of Terror would nonetheless signal a transformation in the way remains of socialism figured in public and political debate as Hungary entered the second decade of postsocialism. No longer would remains simply enable rituals of jubilant mastery of a problematic past, as we saw in the examples in chapters 1–3 of this book. Instead, the persistence of remains of socialism would become proof of Hungary's ongoing victimization, as Fidesz and other right-wing parties and political actors attempted to revive a once-buried past in order to break with it anew.

A Theater of Terror

During the first months after its opening in 2002, I made several visits to the House of Terror: on my own, as a guide for a visiting North American scholar, and with various Hungarian friends and colleagues. Each time, the wait in line to enter the museum stretched to an hour or more because the highly structured permanent exhibition required a limit on the number of visitors allowed to enter at one time. Yet the crowd, which was composed of visitors ranging from formally dressed pensioners to parents with young children to teenagers and young adults, only vocally complained once, when a group of what appeared to be visiting dignitaries was permitted immediate entrance, thus prolonging the delay even further. Otherwise, the long wait in the early spring sunshine only seemed to heighten each visit's sense of eventfulness, as did the dramatic contrast between the sunny bustle of the city outside and the shadowy, dramatically lit architecture of the museum's interior when we were finally allowed to enter. A friend who joined me on one of the visits suggested that the long wait outside was intentional: a way to augment the "political theater" of the museum. "It's like going to church," he commented quietly, as we noted the hush that had descended on the crowd when we first stepped inside.

The modernity of the House of Terror's interior renovations magnified the theatricality of this contrast. The museum's designers preserved the building's turn-of-the-century monumental exterior, but they gutted the inside of the building to transform it into a glossy contemporary exhibition space, with ominous music, video screens, and interactive elements such as a reconstructed prison cell and a 1950s voting booth. This immersive curatorial strategy, which emphasizes experience and participation over the passive reception of information, is reminiscent of other recent museums dedicated to commemorating historical trauma, such as Berlin's Jewish Museum and the United States Holocaust Memorial Museum (USHMM) in Washington, DC, with their similar mandates to appeal to the emotions and sensory capacities of their visitors (Radnóti 2003). For example, the entrance to the permanent exhibit at the House of Terror appears to take direct inspiration from the USHMM's "Tower of Faces," a three-story tower of unidentified portraits from a Jewish community massacred in 1941. The House of Terror's own imposing "Wall of Victims" presents a Soviet tank standing in a small pool of motor oil in front of a grid of nameless photographs that similarly extends two stories upward in the museum's inner courtyard.

Where the House of Terror diverges from its predecessors, however, is in the central role given to its pedagogy of affect. The museum does not encourage the representational critique found in the deconstructive architectural strategies of Berlin's Jewish Museum, which questions the very possibility of representing an event as immense and catastrophic as the Holocaust. Nor does it attempt the historical comprehensiveness and documentation of the USHMM. Instead, as the House of Terror's director, the conservative historian Mária Schmidt, explained in several interviews at the time of the museum's opening, the museum uses historical artifacts and contemporary technology to conjure up the "atmosphere" (levegő) of the past eras (Sümegi 2002) so as "to give the visitor the sensation of what terror meant" (La Bruyère 2002, quoted in Pittaway 2002).

This attempt to produce historical awareness via enactment rather than the passive reception of information is familiar from Fidesz's other interventions in memory politics at that time, such as the Magyar Millennium and the activities of the Country Image Center. In the case of the House of Terror, this appeal to affective involvement and response serves two additional functions. First, it links the reaction of the museum's Hungarian visitors to the experiences of suffering it commemorates, by inviting them to identify with a community of national victimhood. Second, by linking these experiences of suffering under two distinct regimes of terror, the museum also evokes theories of totalitarianism that similarly emphasize commonalities in the ambitions and techniques of communist and fascist rule. As both an affective stance and interpretive frame, "terror" thus unites otherwise divergent ideologies and experiences of victimization into a seamless narrative of persecution that extends into the present day.

To convey this experience of continuous terror at the hands first of the Arrow Cross and then of the communists, the museum's permanent exhibition channels its visitors through three floors and five decades of Hungarian history. Its story of "double occupation" (*kettős megszállás*) begins in the final days of World War II, after the Arrow Cross took power. A room and a hallway present information on the party and its persecution of the Jewish population. The remainder of the exhibition then details the oppression of life under communism. On two upper floors, the museum presents topics both chronological and thematic ("The Gulag," "The Fifties," "Peasants," "Justice") with interactive exhibits and reconstructions of historical interiors such as the office of the head of the secret police. This section of the exhibit concludes with a two-minute elevator ride to the cellar, during which a video screen in the elevator presents a stark interview with a former janitor who describes the process of executing prisoners.[3]

The exhibition in the cellar presents a warren of reconstructed torture cells, culminating in two rooms that explain the events of the 1956 revolution and commemorate its victims. The final room ("Farewell") celebrates the end of communism by presenting multiple video screens playing loops of television footage that include the public events that marked the end of communism in 1989 and 1990 and a speech given by Fidesz leader and then-prime minister Viktor Orbán at the House of Terror's opening in 2002. Finally, the exhibition returns to theme of the "Wall of Victims" by presenting its counterpart in the form of a "Gallery of Persecutors" (*Tettesek galériája*) besides the stairwell that leads the visitor out of the exhibition. This long narrow hallway is lined with names and photographs of functionaries from the two regimes.

During my visits to the House of Terror shortly after its opening, lengthy Hungarian and English-language handouts were available in each room to supplement the museum's history of five decades of terror by foreign powers and traitorous fellow citizens. I appeared to be the only one to consult these printed materials, but a version of these texts was later reproduced on the virtual tour offered on the museum's website (www.terrorhaza.hu). At the time of the museum's opening, it also provided free tour guides, although funding for the guides was later cut due to budget constraints imposed after the MSZP-SZDSZ coalition's victory in the subsequent election. On one early visit, for example, I watched as two miniskirted young docents earnestly provided detailed examples of everyday communist oppression ("Even one word on the phone could put you in jail!") to an elderly couple as they rested on one of the benches in the room devoted to "Communist Everyday Life."

Incompatible Histories

This argument of continuous victimization throughout Hungary's twentieth century found an eager and receptive audience among many of the House of Terror's visitors, who in my conversations with them primarily identified as supporters of one of the right-wing parties and shared the museum's critique of both the injustice of state socialism and the danger of the MSZP's possible return to power. For them, the museum was a greatly overdue opportunity to give voice to long-silenced stories of suffering. (As an elderly man insisted to me, "No one wanted to hear this before.") The museum's narrative of persecution thus encouraged visitors to identify with a community of victimhood: understood not merely as a specific experience of oppression, but as a national and political category that united its subjects across space and time (Jensen and Ronsbo 2014, 1).

Moreover, in keeping with the museum's pedagogy of affect, its exhibition strategy emphasized not only historical narration, but participation in a collective event that emphasized experience over information. Despite the lines outside the building to prevent overcrowding during the first months after the museum opened, each room of the exhibition was so packed with visitors that many of its details were initially difficult to see or decipher, particularly since the photographs and objects on display often lacked captions that would explain their significance or origin.[4] As the crowd slowly shuffled from room to room, the sounds of praise and criticism, questions and muttered historical explanations informally filled in the gaps in apprehension or highlighted perceived omissions in the exhibition itself: whether a young man who complained that the museum honored those who fought against the communists but did not mention the antifascist resistance, or an elderly couple who patiently explained to their young grandchildren that the "iron curtain" separating East and West was a metaphor, and not— as the children assumed—an actual metal curtain.

But although for some, the House of Terror provided the public legitimation of long-established family and political narratives of loss and persecution, many of those who identified as left wing refused to visit the museum at all, dismissing it as right-wing propaganda and a political tool in the upcoming elections. Such conflict was symptomatic of what Domonkos Sik calls a more general lack of "minimal consensus" (2012, 26) in Hungary about the recent past.[5] Whereas the memory of the Holocaust has been institutionalized internationally and is readily accessible through an abundance of films and literature, the experience of state socialism "does not have such rich popular cultural embeddedness" (96). The result has been little agreement in both private life and public discourse concerning the memory of the past era, particularly with regard to the experience of Kádárism (91–96).

Indeed, throughout the years of my fieldwork, many people complained to me that the polarization of both contemporary political life and memory of the past era had produced irreconcilable social rifts or fraught silences among friends, family members, and colleagues. This polarization was also the subject of much public commentary. For example, a documentary film made in the late 2000s, titled *The Fidesz Jew, the Mother with No National Feeling, and Mediation* (*A fideszes zsidó, a nemzeti érzés nélküli anya és a mediáció* [2008]) addressed this ongoing perception of a deep social divide produced by conflicting ideological positions. Contrasting the "love and hope" of 1989 with the "hate and disappointment" of 2007 (the year of its filming), the filmmakers brought in professional mediators to attempt to heal relationships divided by political affiliation. In one example, two friends who were both Jewish became estranged after one of them, a local politician, joined Fidesz. The film shows their attempt to resolve their conflict through mediation, as well as a screening of that conversation for a local Jewish community organization, where many in the audience heatedly asked the politician how he could support a party that they considered to be antisemitic. In another case, a woman became estranged from her right-wing husband and teenaged daughter after her husband had a spiritual and political "awakening" during the demonstrations in support of Fidesz during the 2002 elections. Despite the apparent good intentions of all involved, mediation did not appear to succeed in reconciling any of these strained relationships because both sides believed they had the moral high ground. In the words of a street interview the filmmakers conducted with a middle-aged man at a demonstration against the Gyurcsány MSZP government in 2006: "You can't mix spring water with shit."

Controversy

Public debates about the House of Terror were similarly torn between left-wing critics who challenged the museum's political utility and historical accuracy, and those on the right who insisted on the legitimacy of the museum's claim to continuous national trauma and the importance of this narrative to rebuilding Hungarian national identity. Because so much of the local and international press and scholarly coverage has focused on these debates in detail, I will not explore them in depth here, but will isolate some of their key points, particularly concerning the museum's funding and the historical omissions and distortions the museum was perceived to endorse.[6]

Even before the House of Terror officially opened, it provoked public and political criticism.[7] Unlike other museums in Hungary, which have to seek funding from multiple and even international sources, the House of Terror was funded entirely by the Fidesz government's Ministry of National Cultural Heritage (Nemzeti Kulturális Örökség Minisztériuma). The transformation of 60 Andrássy Street to the House of Terror—from its purchase in December 2000 by the Public Foundation for the Research of Central and East European History and Society to its opening in February 2002—thus appeared to have been accomplished with unprecedented speed. (Similar projects, such as the creation of a local Holocaust museum, had been in planning stages for much longer and yet in 2002 still remained unbuilt due to lack of funds.)[8] Moreover, the politics of these funding decisions went beyond questions of memorialization to the production of history itself. The director of the House of Terror, Mária Schmidt, was also the head of the Twentieth Century Institute, a conservative institute created by Fidesz to counter two existing historical research institutions (the 1956 Institute and the Institute of Political History) perceived to be dominated by left-wing historians. Some critics claimed that the funds for the Twentieth Century Institute came from the money cut from the other research institutes' budgets (Pittaway 2002).

Scholars and commentators critical of both the project and the Fidesz government also charged the House of Terror with misrepresenting both the history of Jewish persecution during World War II and the later experience of state socialism. In the words of István Rév, the museum deploys a "noticeably arbitrary selection and sequence (and omission) of a few disconnected brute facts" to put forward a highly partisan right-wing version of history as if it were commonly accepted and neutral (2005, 290). Specifically, the museum's emphasis on a narrative of "double occupation" by the Nazis and the Soviets effaces the key fact that until March 1944, Hungary chose to ally with Nazi Germany in the hope that it might regain the territory lost in the 1920 Treaty of Trianon. The House of Terror thus fails to address Hungarian responsibility for its history of antisemitism (which includes twentieth-century Europe's first anti-Jewish law in 1920),[9] and for the role of the Hungarian gendarmerie and other authorities in assisting the deportation of more than 400,000 members of Hungary's rural Jewish population to Auschwitz after Germany invaded Hungary in 1944. Moreover, by limiting its historical scope to the persecution inflicted by the fascist Arrow Cross after it seized power in the final months of World War II, the House of Terror's narrative entirely omits these rural deportations from its coverage—and thus excludes

Hungary's victims of Auschwitz from the victims of fascism memorialized in the museum (Apor 2014; Réti 2017; K. Ungváry 2002).

Schmidt and the museum's supporters justified this omission by arguing that the creation of a Holocaust museum was already under way, and that the story told by the House of Terror should thus begin at the point when the Arrow Cross took power in fall 1944 (Seres 2002). They defended the limited treatment of Jewish persecution vis-à-vis communist oppression as historically faithful and representationally proportionate; as Ádám, the university student, argued to me, "This is a difference of a few years [of oppression] versus decades." In turn, the museum's critics challenged this claim to historical fidelity by pointing out that the building only housed communist torture and imprisonment until the ÁVH moved away in 1956,[10] yet the museum nonetheless extends its historical scope—and its narrative of communist oppression—up to the end of the regime in 1990 (K. Ungváry 2002).

At stake in the different ways the House of Terror represents the experiences of fascism and communism was not merely a question of periodization. Rather, the museum uses the crimes of the early years of communism to characterize all four decades of communist rule—and thus to imply that communism did more harm than its predecessor (Judt 2005b, 828). To accomplish this, the museum abandons the chronological approach in its treatment of communism. Instead, most of the eighteen remaining rooms are thematically organized into what Aniko Szucs terms a "Communist theme park about everyday life in Communist Hungary in the 1950s" (2014, 235). This strategy does not make any qualitative distinction between the oppression suffered before Hungary's failed 1956 revolution against the Soviets (when 60 Andrássy Street was actively in use) and the accommodation between the regime and its citizens in the decades that followed the post-revolutionary retribution (Rényi 2003). This distinction is not only relevant to scholars, but as we have seen, it is also the main dividing line that structures the way Hungarians narrate their own experiences of the past. Instead, the museum's permanent exhibition removes the 1956 revolution from the exhibition's narrative entirely, only addressing it in two rooms toward the very end of the visitors' journey through the museum, directly before a room devoted to the system change in 1989 and 1990. By blurring the chronology of these events, the museum thus represents early socialist phenomena such as forced collectivization and religious persecution as equivalent to the relatively lenient years of late socialism—and thus morally equivalent as years of "terror."

This logic of equivalence also extends to the way the House of Terror portrays its victims and perpetrators. The two-story "Wall of Victims" at the museum's entrance does not identify the subjects of its photographs or clarify who was responsible for their victimization. Instead, this lack of specificity enables the photographs to offer a mute claim to continuous national suffering. And in a complementary logic, the museum's narrative of equivalent oppression similarly makes an equally guilty perpetrator of every individual who accommodated or collaborated with either regime in any capacity.[11] The museum argues this explicitly in the room titled "Changing Clothes": an exhibit of uniforms and old lockers that offers the (historically unsupported) assertion that those who persecuted Jewish Hungarians under the Arrow Cross later became the communist regime's most avid torturers.[12] But the contemporary political stakes of this logic are most evident in the "Gallery of Persecutors" that, along with the "Wall of Victims," brackets the visitor's experience of the museum. If the lack of identifying information on the "Wall of Victims" expands the community of Hungarian victimhood as the visitor enters the permanent exhibit, the "Gallery of Persecutors" at the end of the visitor's journey identifies the subject of each photograph to assign the blame for these atrocities to Hungary's past and present left wing. Many of the photographs represent communist functionaries, some of whom (or their children) were still active in political or cultural life at the time of the museum's opening. The House of Terror thus explicitly links the past horrors of communism to the contemporary political left to argue that the terror of the past continues to endanger the present.

The Battle for Victimhood

Many on the left who criticized the museum's historical distortions did so to dismiss the museum as a political tool of the right wing: a way to avoid discussion of Hungary's current problems and to prevent a true coming to terms with the past. One MSZP politician, László Kovács, even made the controversial suggestion that in the event of an MSZP victory, the museum should be renamed the House of Reconciliation (Megbékélés Háza) (Stefka 2002). In response, the right accused the left of refusing to take responsibility for the crimes of the previous era, arguing that the left muddied moral distinctions between right and wrong and let past injustice ebb into the grayness of recent history. Schmidt argued that the complaints about the museum's role in Fidesz's campaign were proof of the very need for a museum that would tell the truth about the past. "The unending and devious series of attacks preceding and following the opening of the House of Terror perfectly fit into the Hungarian Socialist Party's violent and aggressive campaign; they conjured up the memories of leftist power-demonstrations well known from the old party's times. To many elderly, this awoke old fears, and the old reflexes returned: 'it is still not advisable to discuss these things' and 'it's better to remain silent'" (Schmidt 2003, 197–198, translated and quoted in Szucs 2014, 241).

From this perspective, the House of Terror stood in opposition to those who sought to wipe out history and moral accountability. What made this injustice particularly acute was the emphasis that had been placed on punishing Nazi criminals and commemorating their victims. As one reader wrote to the far-right weekly *Democrat* (*Demokrata*), if the public did not forgive the Nazis after the Nuremberg trials, it should not forgive the actions of communist murderers either (Paksa 2002). The minister of justice, Ibolya Dávid, similarly complained at a conference held by the International Alliance of Those Persecuted by Communists (Kommunizmus Üldözöttei Nemzetközi Szövetség), "When it comes to the crimes of Nazism, the sentence was passed in good time, but in the case of communist crimes, only time has passed [*A nácizmus bűnei fölött időben pálcát törtek, a kommunizmus bűnei esetében még csak az idő telt el*]" (Gábor 2000).

This perception of the differential treatment of fascist and communist persecutors and victims drove much support for the House of Terror. In the eyes of many of my interlocutors, Nazi criminals had been punished and their victims commemorated both abroad and locally (whether in films and literature or memorials and official acts of remembrance). Indeed, in the first decade after the end of communism, private individuals and international institutions from Israel, Western Europe, and North America helped to fund a new Holocaust memorial beside Budapest's centrally located Dohány Street synagogue.[13] They also participated in attempts to revitalize the Jewish community in Hungary by supporting the establishment of new organizations and infrastructure, including Jewish schools, community centers, and summer camps aimed at "reviving" religious-ethnic and communal identity among a primarily urban and assimilated population who often did not know of their Jewish heritage until adolescence or adulthood (or who had learned from their parents to keep this information private) (Kovács and Forrás Biró 2011, 14).[14]

But although the memory of the Holocaust was well-established and internationally recognized, some complained, the victims of communism were in danger of being forgotten before their stories were even told. "We didn't just suffer during 1956," Miklós (the early member of Fidesz whom we met in chapter 2), pointed out, when I observed that there were a number of memorials to the victims of the 1956 revolution. "There were millions who died in the gulag." Supporters of the House of Terror thus defended its creation as a simple corrective to an imbalance of historical memory—a museum that as Hungary's only memorial to victims of communism, "should have been built 10 years ago," as Miklós insisted.

This emphasis on the importance of remembering the victims of communism in addition to the Jewish victims of the Holocaust went beyond the simple demand for commemorative parity, however. Rather, it reflected the perception that the memory of the Holocaust was threatening to *silence* the Hungarian experience of suffering under communism. This challenge of what the historian Tony Judt calls "comparative victimhood" (2005a) reflects Hungary's experience of the historical politics of state socialism. As elsewhere in the Soviet bloc, after World War II one of the original sources of legitimacy for Hungary's communists was their unimpeachable history of resistance to fascism: to be communist was to be anti-fascist. Once in power, the communist regime emphasized the crimes of fascism to reinforce the moral authority of communist rule and to make clear that only it had the power to grant Hungary, as a former Axis ally, the forgiveness of historical amnesia (Rév 1994, 4–5). This logic, which recognized victims of fascist genocide and condemned those who died fighting communism, produced two sets of victims that would thus come to constitute two mutually exclusive historical reference points: to mention one was to deny or trivialize the other.

With the end of state socialism, this competition between anticommunism and antifascism continued to mark a key ideological divide. But now, the legacy of the communist regime's polarized historical politics had the ironic effect of potentially endowing fascist and interwar-era symbols, historical figures, and narratives with new anticommunist legitimacy among Hungary's right wing. (That is, if anticommunists were once stigmatized as fascist, now fascists could be potentially redeemed as anticommunist.) For example, in 1994, under the right-wing MDF (Hungarian Democratic Forum)-led coalition government, the Constitutional Court nullified a number of provisions of the 1945 People's Tribunals Act, which had the effect of overturning the conviction of many individuals involved in the deportation and execution of Hungary's Jewish community during World War II (Braham 2014, 11, see also Rév 2005).

The majority of those who supported such acts of historical rehabilitation (which included the reburial of Miklós Horthy discussed in chapter 2) justified them as the recuperation of national values, rather than the endorsement of fascist ideology. Nonetheless, such symbolic actions—and the outrage they inspired—would function as key points of ideological reference as politicians and public figures battled to establish their positions in the emerging political landscape of postsocialism. For parties on the left (which included not merely the successors to the communist party but also the former dissidents and urban intellectuals who formed SZDSZ [Alliance of Free Democrats]), the right wing's rhetoric of national sovereignty and its perceived recuperation of the discourses of fascism and antisemitism both distorted historical fact and endangered Hungarian democracy. (As we have seen, such fears were one factor that drove the SZDSZ to become a coalition partner with its once sworn enemy, the MSZP, beginning in 1994.) For those on the right, the left wing was hopelessly tarnished by its association with communism, and its tendency to avoid national questions and emphasize the crimes before 1945 over those that occurred afterwards

(K. Ungváry 2017, 391) was evidence that it prioritized Jewish and/or international interests ahead of Hungarian ones. Moreover, the moral and political utility of the memory of fascist genocide to both the state socialist regime and the current left-wing led many on the right to view any claim to Holocaust suffering—much less a call for Hungarian accountability—as inevitably exaggerated and instrumentalized (Sik 2012, 15). Frequent warnings about antisemitism only had the effect of discrediting such concerns in the eyes of some of my interlocutors, who would argue that "no one is being sent to the camps" when I asked their opinion about what in the United States would be interpreted as antisemitic statements in right-wing political discourse. One friend observed that such sentiments might sound troubling to me, but "you [Americans] are twenty years ahead of us"—a joking denial of coevalness that he blamed not on contemporary politics but on the legacy of communism, which had "distorted everyone's thinking."[15] Others, particularly on the left, also dismissed such statements as mere political posturing: a way for those on the right to distinguish themselves from their opponents.

Indeed, regardless of political affiliation, many people across the political spectrum tended to view Hungarian Jewish claims to exceptional suffering with skepticism. For example, Mária, the former office administrator who now worked as a housecleaner, was an MSZP supporter. She emphatically told me that she had no interest in visiting the House of Terror because of its ties to Fidesz and because she would rather save her money to attend opera and classical music concerts. Nonetheless, she too expressed doubt about the extent of Jewish victimization during World War II during a conversation in which she told me how much she had enjoyed the Oscar-winning filmmaker István Szabó's English-language film, *Sunshine* (*A napfény íze*, 1999), which narrated three generations of twentieth-century Hungarian persecution of a Jewish family in Budapest. "I really liked it," Mária said. "It was interesting how it showed the history of a family, and I was especially interested in the Jewish culture—traditions, weddings, etc.—that I didn't know before. Of course, you can't really know if the war was really as awful for the Jews [as it was in the film]. But in the film, it was terrible." The film sparked similar debate in internet forums and right-wing newspapers about the historical accuracy of its claims, as well as whether its portrayal of Jewish victimization under three different political regimes in Hungary was "anti-Hungarian."[16]

Mária's uncertainty about the accuracy of representations of Jewish victimhood reflects the legacy of a communist regime that defined the victims of Nazi Germany in political rather than religious-ethnic terms. But as we have seen, it is also a symptom of the polarized historical politics between Hungary's right and left wings, which has resulted in a public culture with very little general consensus about much of the twentieth century. (This inability to find common ground in discussions of Hungary's past also helped fuel socialist nostalgia's appeal, as a way to address the experience of state socialism without being forced to engage with its political and historical context.) For some people, the unsettled nature of recent history only drove them to cling more fiercely to specific narratives of the national past, whether fueled by personal experience or political loyalty. But for many others, like Mária, such uncertainty bred an overarching distrust of historical truth claims in general: the suspicion that any attempt to invoke historical examples or precedents was biased and politically motivated.

In contrast, many of my friends and interviewees who identified as Jewish or as being of Jewish ancestry were often angered and alarmed by instances of anti-semitism, such as the publication (and popularity) of new Hungarian editions of *Mein Kampf* and *The Protocols of the Elders of Zion* at the turn of the millennium (Szőnyei 2002). Klára, for example, was a graduate student in her late twenties when I interviewed her in 1998. Like many others in the transitional generation who now identified as having Jewish parents or grandparents, she had grown up in a secularized family with parents who were members of Budapest's cultural intelligentsia. Klára told me that she was taught by her parents to view being Jewish as a "special, privileged thing" that nonetheless, like many of those in her cohort, she felt pressured to keep quiet as a child and teenager under late state socialism. (Not until the mid-1990s did she discover that some of her friends had Jewish ancestry as well.) "But I consider myself Hungarian," she told me firmly, drawing a contrast between herself and her boyfriend, who came from a rural Orthodox Jewish background and self-identified as Jewish. His parents had moved to Budapest when he was a child, and a sense of social and cultural dislocation from his schoolmates led him to become active in the revival of Jewish youth community life in Budapest in the late 1980s and early 1990s. "But when antisemitism appears," Klára added, "we both feel targeted—there is a feeling of solidarity."

Cosmopolitan Memory

The reasons for Hungarian resistance to specifically Jewish claims to victimization went beyond the polarization of national historical politics, however. They also reflect the centrality of Holocaust memory in the West, where recognition of the genocide of Europe's Jews has become the condition for European belonging as well as "the very definition and guarantee of the continent's restored humanity" (Judt 2005b, 804). Daniel Levy and Natan Sznaider have hailed the emergence of such transnational "cosmopolitan memory" (2002) as decoupling the moral imperative of remembrance from national and ethnic boundaries and thus providing, in Aleida Assmann's words, a "foundation for a global politics of human rights, based on commonly remembered barbarism" (A. Assmann 2007,

14). Yet, as Andreas Huyssen argues, this global circulation of Holocaust memory has not replaced territorialized national memory, but rather stands in tension with it (A. Assmann 2007, 14; Huyssen 2003, 148). National claims to victimization are thus forced not only to compete with the transnational memory of Jewish genocide for acknowledgment but also to navigate its established template for representing collective trauma (A. Assmann 2007, 14). As Jeffrey Olick, Vered Vinitzky-Seroussi, and Daniel Levy observe, the image of the Holocaust victim has become the measure by which other forms of victimhood are evaluated (2011, 30).

Many people I spoke with perceived this institutionalization of the Holocaust in European memory discourse as the trivialization of the suffering the country endured under communism. Right-wing scholars have similarly argued that the dominant narratives of twentieth-century history reflect only the perspective of Western leftist intellectuals, for whom the Holocaust represents a singular foundational trauma—and communism merely failed to live up to its ideals (Sik 2012, 13–14). At stake in such criticisms of Western myopia is not only the erasure of Hungary's past victimization but also the stigmatization of what many on the right consider a healthy desire to celebrate postsocialist national pride and rebirth. In the frustrated words of the representative of the Country Image Center we met in chapter 2, "Here if you're proud to be Hungarian and have national consciousness (*nemzeti öntudat*), people assume you are a fascist!"

Such complaints about Western misrecognition of Hungarian suffering go back to the post–World War I Treaty of Trianon (in which Hungary lost two-thirds of its territory), as well as Hungary's earlier loss of sovereignty under the Ottoman and Habsburg empires. But these laments have taken on new fervency in postsocialism under the pressures of cosmopolitan memory, for which claims to both political rights and moral legitimacy are often based on the recognition of victimhood (Judt 2005a). As a result, in public life and everyday conversation in the years leading up to the creation of the House of Terror, appeals to the memory of the Holocaust often inspired right-wing bids for similar national acknowledgment. For example, one of the first initiatives of Fidesz's conservative Twentieth Century Institute was to host a conference in 2001 to commemorate the publication of the Hungarian translation of *The Black Book of Communism* (originally published in 1997), a historical compendium of communism's crimes and death tolls whose chief editor (Stéphane Courtois) controversially argued against the uniqueness of Nazi genocide (2000). At the opening ceremony, the host Mária Schmidt praised the book for overturning the "double morality" that governed the way the crimes of fascism and communism were treated and argued that the establishment of gulags should be condemned just as much as Hitler's concentration camps (Regényi 2000). As the historian György Gyarmati argued at a roundtable on the book a month later, "terror" under communism was not an extremist exception, but rather a structural part of the whole system (Dombrádi 2000).

It is important to note that the attempts of these scholars and political actors to give equivalent commemorative and moral weight to the crimes of communism did not deny the Holocaust, and nor did they explicitly target Hungary's Jewish citizens as the object of contemporary national animus. Fidesz may have instituted a day of remembrance of the victims of communism, but it had also legislated a similar memorial day for the victims of the Holocaust. Later Fidesz would help to provide funding for a Holocaust museum and even attempt to collaborate with Hungary's Jewish institutions to mark the seventieth anniversary of the Holocaust in Hungary (with ultimately controversial results).[17] Such efforts enabled Fidesz to distance itself politically from the extreme right wing (which at the time of the House of Terror's opening was primarily represented by the Hungarian Justice and Life Party [Magyar Igazság és Élet Párt (MIÉP)] headed by István Csurka), while at the same time often refusing to condemn politicians or media outlets that deployed antisemitic rhetoric.[18]

Nonetheless, many on the left viewed attempts to argue that the crimes of communism were equal to—or greater than—those perpetrated by fascists to be merely covert antisemitism: a way for Fidesz to lure voters from the extreme right while still maintaining plausible deniability. The challenge for the creators of the House of Terror was thus to find a way to foreground Hungary's victimhood under communism without outright rejecting the moral primacy of the Holocaust victim in Western European memory.

A New Moral Algebra

The exhibition strategy of the House of Terror offers what was then a novel solution to this conflict. Rather than continue to oppose these two painful sets of memory of historical victimhood, it assimilates them into a continuous narrative of national persecution. By arguing that the terrors of communism emerged seamlessly out of the terrors of fascism, the museum thus provides a way for its Hungarian visitors to claim moral legitimacy within a cosmopolitan memory culture previously experienced as invalidating. Indeed, although the House of Terror borrows representational strategies from Holocaust museums in North American and Western Europe, its creators also sought to provide a narrative and architectural model of national terror at the hands of communist persecutors that would be ready for export to other European commemorative contexts.

The museum's narrative of continuous persecution no longer divided by the historical and ideological specificity of the fascist and communist regimes draws its legitimacy from the indexical authority of the site itself: the fact that 60 Andrássy Street housed both the Arrow Cross and communist police torturers. The building serves as physical evidence that, as the conservative journalist Zsolt Bayer declared at an event to commemorate the first anniversary of the museum's opening, "There was only one Hungary and one kind of suffering" (*Budapest Sun* 2003). The museum thus rejects particularistic claims to Jewish victimization by encompassing them within a broader story of Hungarian victimhood in which the persecution of Hungary's Jewish community was merely part of a larger history of terror suffered by *all* Hungarians. This strategy no longer symbolically expels Jewish Hungarians from the national community; rather, it reflects that many self-identified as Hungarian first and Jewish second.

Yet by narrating history in terms of victimhood, the museum's argument of continuous terror also enables it to conflate very different historical experiences of suffering—and different responsibilities for persecution. It draws a line of moral equivalence between the genocide of Jews during World War II and the relatively eventless experience of growing up in late socialist Hungary. By blurring together these two sets of victims (and making the historically questionable argument that the same evil band of perpetrators was responsible for persecuting both), the House of Terror externalizes the blame for Hungary's misfortunes to foreign occupiers and national traitors. Moreover, by enabling those who identify as the victims of either regime to disavow responsibility for the injustices of the past, the museum allows the victim of one historical injustice to extract moral authority from both.

The House of Terror thus rejects a "politics of regret" (Olick 2007) that would take responsibility for the segments of Hungarian society who supported Jewish oppression during World War II. And its narrative of historical victimization refuses the task of "negative remembrance" found in most European Holocaust museums, which commemorate crimes committed rather than suffered (Knigge 2002, quoted in Uhl 2009, 64).

This attempt to simultaneously minimize the memory of Jewish persecution and claim it as part of a broader experience of Hungarian suffering stands in contrast to the logic of nostalgia discussed in chapter 3. Nostalgic practices redeemed the remains of an inauthentic and disavowed past so as to assert present-day mastery—epitomized in the catchphrase, "But it's ours." The House of Terror, on the other hand, asserts ownership of a previously incompatible domain of historical memory in order to extend and support a claim to Hungary's national victimization. And by claiming a continuous history of victimhood as "ours," the museum and its supporters were also able to reject responsibility for both fascism and communism.

These two modes of formulating and dealing with the problem of socialism's remains—nostalgia and terror—were not necessarily incompatible, and they could not be easily classified along party lines. Just as some of the most enthusiastic consumers of nostalgia were otherwise highly critical of the communist regime and its legacies, some Hungarians who identified as left wing were nonetheless suspicious of claims to the exceptionalism of Holocaust memory. As much as Fidesz's election campaign may have tried to argue otherwise, the explicit politicization of history found in the House of Terror and the emphatic denial of politics found in nostalgia thus did not represent a battle between two competing communities of memory: those who condemn the past versus those who seek its return. Rather, the two forms of memory could easily coexist within the same individuals precisely thanks to their dichotomized approaches to the uneasy legacies of recent history and the incommensurability of the varied emotions evoked by the remains of state socialism. Moreover, both memory practices were in part impelled by the perception of international misrecognition, whether as naive and backward consumers or as persecutors with no legitimate claim to victimhood. "But it's ours," in both contexts, thus became a way to reassert the power of self-definition against globalized regimes of memory and cultural value.

This coexistence of cozy memories of socialist-era domestic life and highly politicized narratives of oppression thus posed a challenge for the creators of the House of Terror, whose rhetoric of victimization depended on appropriating the memory of fascist persecution and also extending such persecution through the relatively comfortable years of late socialism. To address this, the House of Terror declared war on the nostalgic recuperation of memories of the socialist era, insisting that the popularity of socialist nostalgia was evidence of an alarming continuity with—rather than triumph over—the recent past. Asserting "what is ours" would demand equal attention to rejecting what is "not ours": that is, rejecting as mere remains of socialist terror those objects, narratives, and practices already redeemed by contemporary practices of nostalgia.

Soviet Tanks and String Bags

In June 2002 I met with my friend Vera, who had come to Budapest from her village in northeastern Hungary to visit her son Ádám, then a university student of nineteen. Over the past months, Ádám, who identified as a Fidesz voter and was more politically active than his parents, had forwarded me news stories and sent email messages about the heated national elections of that spring and his participation in rallies to reelect Fidesz. Upon Fidesz's ultimate defeat at the hands of the MSZP, it was Ádám who sent me the email insisting that "the past has begun," and he now worried about both the economic and political impact of the MSZP victory.

The three of us sat at an outdoor café near the National Museum, discussing the House of Terror and furtively eating scones (*pogácsa*) that Vera had brought from home. Ádám argued for the importance of a museum that would "tell the truth about our history" by explaining the oppressive daily realities of life under state socialism. For example, he said, every Friday workers would monitor each other carefully at the canteens (*menza*), to see who declined meat and thus could be inferred to be a practicing Catholic. Among other examples of the fear and suspicion that governed the practices of everyday life, Ádám argued, were the small collapsible string bags (*hálószatyor*) that women used for shopping: they existed so that informers could see what others had purchased.

Vera burst into indignant laughter, immediately denying that either of these claims was true, at least in her experience. The three of us soon got into a discussion about where Ádám had learned such stories and why he so determinedly clung to this version of history even as Vera denied it. From earlier conversations, I knew that Vera had mostly positive memories of the Kádár era. Her family had lived within a small settlement of villages in northeast Hungary for at least five generations, and they had risen from the peasantry to the middle class under the decades of state socialism. (Her husband, father, and brother were all career military officers under the state socialist regime, and each retired after the system change.) This experience of social mobility had also nourished Vera's professional ambitions. At the time of her visit to Budapest, she was working as a librarian in her village while pursuing a master's degree in a nearby city, and she told me of her civic-minded determination to make the village library into a local hub of cultural, educational, and charitable activities. (In the following years, she was able to realize these goals by successfully obtaining funding from local, state, and ultimately European Union resources for these initiatives.)

The memories of the socialist past Vera shared with me over the years were not colored by the longing and abundance of affect that characterized the nostalgic practices described in chapter 3. (Vera was already married with two children at the time of the system change, and she thus did not belong to the transitional generation whose members viewed nostalgia through the gauzy lens of childhood memory.) Nonetheless, when I had asked Vera a year earlier what object she might choose to characterize the socialist era, she chose the neckerchief of the Young Pioneers (*úttörő nyakkendő*): not as a symbol of the past regime's political socialization of its citizens, but as an emblem of what she considered to be the past system's forward-looking optimism, work ethic, and family orientation.

In Vera's eyes, as she now explained, the ubiquity of string bags reflected the realities of shopping under state socialism, rather than state-enforced social leveling. Although life in late socialist Hungary was not characterized by the long lines and shortages experienced elsewhere, plastic bags were not common during Soviet times and the collapsibility of the string bag made it useful as a "just-in-case" bag. (A plastic bag with a Western logo, on the other hand, was an envied status symbol to be used with care for as long as possible.) Now, many people—including Vera—did their local shopping with straw baskets and paid extra for plastic bags at the supermarket, but string bags were still in common use.

On the other hand, although Friday meals at the *menza* may or may not have been subject to the community surveillance Ádám claimed, blatant displays of religious observance did carry the possibility of reprisal. For this reason, many of my friends and interviewees (including Vera and her husband) had been married in civil ceremonies and chosen to forgo an additional church wedding. A year earlier, Vera's husband, a former military officer, had shown me a photo album of his daughter's christening during the last years of state socialism, and explained that participating in such a ceremony had been a risky move for him professionally.

What is most important here is not the contested truth value of these representations, but the mythologies that developed around them. How is it that a string bag came to function for Ádám as a sign of the oppression of the socialist era? What made this everyday item into a remain of socialism unable to be redeemed by the nostalgic practices then so pervasive in Hungarian cultural life? And what about this story was so compelling that it inspired Ádám to dismiss his mother's interpretation in favor of the version that—as Ádám ultimately revealed—he had learned from a young teacher at his former gymnasium, who in turn had learned these stories from his own politically conservative parents?

The narrative of the string bag appealed to Ádám because it focused on the lack of privacy to choose and consume as emblematic of the way the regime penetrated even the most mundane aspects of everyday life. In other words, the everydayness of the string bag did not trivialize Ádám's argument—it was instead what made it so alarming. Unlike the more straightforwardly terrifying experiences of violence, persecution, and political oppression represented at the House of Terror, activities such as eating and shopping under the kinds of restrictions Ádám described were simultaneously familiar and alien: easily imaginable and yet not imaginable enough.

As we have seen, the exhibition strategy of the House of Terror was designed to appeal directly to its visitors' affective apprehension. It attempts to target the emotions and senses of its viewers—particularly the younger generations—with video installations, a soundtrack by the pop musician Ákos Kovács, and exhibits

FIGURE 4.2 "Everyday Life" room at the House of Terror. The poster advertising Bambi soda is on the upper left. Source: House of Terror Museum, Budapest, Hungary.

that emphasize experience and participation over the passive reception of information. Such techniques seek to collapse the sensory distance between then and now and to make the terror on display palpable: whether it is the sense of dread visitors feel in their stomachs as the elevator drops down into the cellar where the reconstructed prison cells are housed, or the ability to interact with the various reconstructed sets and historical tableaux that fill the exhibition spaces.

Ádám's tale of the string bag suggests that the purpose of these strategies is not just to bring the past near and thus make it comprehensible. Rather (or simultaneously), the museum seeks to pathologize the everyday life of the past system to argue that the quotidian details of socialist life were not independent of the ideology that produced them, but rather deeply implicated in the story of communist terror. For example, after an entire room devoted to propaganda posters, the museum's exhibition presents a similar room plastered with reproductions of advertisements for socialist-era products that at the time of the museum's opening had already been redeemed as nostalgia—including the recently remarketed Bambi soda discussed in chapter 3. The museum thus intervenes into the contemporary politics of socialism's remains by pathologizing these products as both relics of the past *and* objects of nostalgic consumption in the present. That is, on

FIGURE 4.3 A neon sign advertising Bambi soda inside Terv Eszpresszó. Personal photograph, 2015.

the one hand, the museum attempts to estrange memories and stories of the cozy domesticity of everyday life under late state socialism, as well as the fantasy of a private sphere free from political intervention that such domesticity represented. On the other hand, the museum also seeks to criminalize the contemporary nostalgic marketing of this era's relics as ironic kitsch or fashionable retro, particularly for young consumers who never encountered these objects in their original contexts.

It is crucial in this double logic that in neither case does the museum simply attack nostalgia directly. As we saw in the case of the Workers' Party, attempts to explicitly politicize nostalgia (whether negatively or positively) were unsuccessful because of the way most Hungarians viewed nostalgia as being free of ideological considerations. Instead, the exhibit's strategy of affective pedagogy sought to control the very desires that drive nostalgia, by imbuing its objects with painful associations that would overpower the fond pleasure they previously inspired. In other words, the task of the House of Terror is not merely to convince its visitors that both the prison cell and the concentration camp produced ideologically indistinguishable experiences of terror. Ádám's story of the string bag suggests that the targets of the museum's designated horror are also the banal details of a socialist everyday life already redeemed by nostalgia. Tanks and prison cells are thus not the only instruments of terror—so too are the Bambi soda whose poster was on prominent display and the string bag whose presumed function ap-palled Ádám.[19]

Ambivalent Remains

At the same time, the House of Terror's aesthetics and marketing also produce the amusement and ironic enjoyment familiar from nostalgia and other attempts to tame socialism's remains. The museum's gift shop, much like that of the Statue Park Museum, offers an array of communist kitsch that includes candles in the shapes of busts of Stalin and Lenin, blank arrest warrants, and retro-themed mousepads. The stylish midcentury aesthetic of the museum's interiors—its bookstore, coffee shop, and lounges—similarly reveal a more ambivalent fasci-nation with the visual and material culture of an era that the museum otherwise denounces.

Of course, the responses these kitsch objects and aesthetics inspire are distinct from those of nostalgia, and the inconsistency between the exhibit and these other spaces may simply reveal the desire to condemn the past era and also profit from it. As with its representation of the Holocaust, the House of Terror thus simulta-neously minimizes and appropriates competing memories of the recent past. But just as nostalgia promises its consumers that they can hold onto fond memories of the past while still being successful under postsocialism, here the House of Ter-ror may offer the perhaps even more appealing possibility that its subjects can laugh at the past and yet still lay claim to being victimized by it. By arguing that socialism's remains continue to endanger postsocialist life, the museum enables its visitors to connect contemporary party politics to a longer history of national suffering—and thus to extend the moral legitimacy of having been victims of "terror" into the present.

Europe and the Memory of Totalitarianism

Despite what would ultimately be Fidesz's highly contested loss in the 2002 elec-tions, the House of Terror's warning of the threatened return of communism's remains would continue to influence political life and public discussion over the following years. Unlike the Statue Park Museum, whose visitor numbers declined soon after its opening, the House of Terror has proved enduringly popular with locals and international tourists who visit what has now become a genre of museums devoted to remembering communist oppression across the former Soviet bloc.[20] The House of Terror would also serve as both a symbolic and physical rallying point for the reenergized right wing led by Fidesz, which in the years after its 2002 defeat used the museum's exterior as a site for demonstrations and political speeches. And since returning to power in 2010, Fidesz has enshrined the museum's narrative of "double occupation" by both fascists and communists in Hungary's new constitution.

Moreover, the museum's implicit deployment of the theory of totalitarianism has proved to be the first of many postsocialist attempts on both the state and international levels to institutionalize a narrative of totalitarianism that explicitly draws equivalence between the victims of fascism and communism. Estonia's Museum of Occupations and Freedom opened in 2003, and in 2008, an international conference in Prague on "European Conscience and Communism" produced a declaration that called for an institute devoted to researching Europe's totalitarian past, as well as a day of remembrance for its victims. With backing from right-wing politicians and scholars and from former dissidents such as Václav Havel, the European Parliament voted in favor of both proposals in 2009. The institute—now an EU educational project titled "Platform of European Memory and Conscience"—has called on the European Parliament to hold a tribunal for the crimes of communism. Its president also signed an agreement to produce a European museum of totalitarianism, as part of a ceremony held at the House of Terror to commemorate the Day of Remembrance for Victims of Totalitarianism in 2012. These efforts to institutionalize the narrative of totalitarianism have thus succeeded in producing a cosmopolitan countermemory to rival the prevailing transnational discourse that insists on the uniqueness of the Holocaust and the centrality of "negative remembrance" for European identity.

Meanwhile, the House of Terror has become one of the most popular museums in Budapest. Since the museum opened, I have been making periodic visits to it along with other sites of memory, and I have never failed to find the House of Terror packed with visitors, even on days when other museums devoted to Hungary's twentieth-century history (such as the Statue Park Museum or the Holocaust Memorial Center opened in 2004) were nearly empty. A 2012 analysis of high school visits to the House of Terror by Domonkos Sik argues that the crowds of visitors and density of experiential cues in the museum are so overwhelming that little of the museum's intended historical narrative or ideological message is legible to its visitors (2012, 29–50).[21] But as Aniko Szucs observes, such semiotic instability may be the key to the museum's appeal: its ability to draw multiple audiences as "a historical exhibition of Nazism and communism, a collection of artefacts featuring post-communist nostalgia, a theme park of communism, and a shrine that commemorates the victims of terror" (2014, 240).

Regardless of the success or failure of its exhibition strategies, the creation of the House of Terror nonetheless helped Fidesz to inaugurate a successful shift in conceptualizing the problem of socialist remains from a discourse of mastery to one of ongoing victimization. As we shall see, the events that followed the opening of the House of Terror and the 2002 election campaign would confirm Hungary's entrance into a postnostalgia moment, in which simple acts of distancing, disavowal, or recuperation no longer offered sufficient response to the challenges of memory posed by socialism's troubling remains. The substance of remains thus also shifted: from intrusive materialities and canonized histories to hidden perpetrators of terror, secrets, and lies who required exposure lest their crimes go misrecognized, overlooked, or forgotten. And although Fidesz attempted to deploy the threat of such remains to attack their political enemies, this new conceptualization of the socialist past as posing a hidden danger that demanded exposure would soon exceed the boundaries of party politics. Instead, the search for remains would reveal troubling secrets on both sides of the political spectrum—and at the heart of the national family.

SECRETS, INHERITANCE, AND A GENERATION'S REMAINS

In late January 2006 the historian András Gervai published an article in the weekly journal *Life and Literature* (*Élet és Irodalom*) that identified the film director István Szabó as having informed on his colleagues as a young film student between 1957 and 1963 (Gervai 2006). What made this revelation so shattering was Szabó's iconic status as a symbol of Hungarian cultural prestige and artistic moral authority both domestically and internationally. The only Hungarian filmmaker to win an Academy Award in the United States (for *Mephisto* in 1981), Szabó had often spoken out about the narrative and moral challenges facing artists before and after the fall of socialism. In fact, many of Szabó's films had examined the very dilemma he was now forced to confront: the relationship of the individual to larger structures of power, and the moral compromises that can result in the pursuit of artistic or personal self-interest.[1]

Szabó responded aggressively to this revelation. Although one of his colleagues, Zsolt Kézdi-Kovács, soon also publicly admitted that he had been recruited as an informer while a film student, this potential scandal was quickly resolved by his expression of regret and contrition. Kézdi-Kovács acknowledged his past participation and explained, "I was never very brave, but here bravery would have been in vain. I knew that I wouldn't be able to withstand being beaten or giving up what I had finally achieved: college, filmmaking" (Kézdi-Kovács 2006). In contrast, Szabó refused to apologize, instead declaring that his actions were heroic. Warned in advance of the article that revealed his involvement, he responded the day of its publication with an interview in the daily newspaper *Népszabadság*.

Szabó claimed to be planning a film on this topic, which he hoped would act as "a medicine to many people, and show a clearer picture of the period between 1957 and 1960" (*Népszabadság* 2006a).[2] Moreover, he said that he was proud of his activity as an informer, which he argued enabled him to save a schoolmate (the late fellow film director Pál Gábor) who had participated in the events of 1956 (*Népszabadság* 2006b).

Szabó's attempt to portray his past activity in a noble light drew support from many of his colleagues and members of the public, as well as strong criticism from others for not having admitted his activity as an informer earlier. The criticism that received the most attention—and inspired a controversy of its own—was that of a thirty-year-old graduate student, Balázs Bodó, in an article the following week (Bodó 2006). Bodó challenged not the act of informing, but Szabó's failure to admit or apologize for it, arguing that Szabó's silence and lack of remorse represented the older generation's betrayal of its cultural children. "You are stealing the past, my past, and you are stealing the present as well," he declared, arguing that Szabó's cowardly self-interest had kept the crimes of the past alive in the present, thus victimizing the youth who were to inherit this legacy. Like Ádám, who had debated his mother Vera's account of the quotidian realities of life under late socialism, Bodó claimed the older generation's experience under the past regime as a trauma of his own, in order to expel such remains of socialism from the heart of the national family.

In this chapter, I examine the Szabó case, which was one of the most contentious of a series of scandals that emerged after legal changes in 2002 provided greater access to the files of the former communist state security. The Fidesz government's creation of the House of Terror had reconceptualized remains in terms of communist crimes and their perpetrators who threatened to continue Hungary's victimization into the present. The museum thus helped to mobilize political sympathies for Fidesz's narrowly unsuccessful 2002 reelection campaign by reviving the danger of communism and dividing the nation into right-wing victims and left-wing persecutors. With the informer scandals, however, this dichotomous moral division collapsed. Now, remains took the form not of newly visible histories of terror, but of the shocking unveiling of unexpected secrets: hidden, intimate betrayals whose perpetrators could be found across the political spectrum. The discovery and exposure of these remains thus represented the return of a far more equivocal and obdurate past, in which each political side not only struggled to lay claim to the moral high ground but also faced internal contestation: torn among demands for justice, sympathy for those forced into informing, and worries that their own informer pasts or those of their political allies might be revealed. The revelations of the past regime's informers thus revived the ambiguities of the socialist era and its ethical choices in ways that resisted easy exorcism through the election process, challenging the way people and political parties sought to lay claim to the moral authority of victimization.

The charged idiom of family and generational conflict would be one of the key ways in which the debates about the informer revelations took shape, whether that entailed betrayal by one's cultural elders (as in the Szabó case) or by one's actual parent (as I discuss using the work of the novelist Péter Esterházy). By phrasing the call to accountability as a matter of generational inheritance—the passing down of knowledge from one generation to the next—these cultural "children" reconceptualized the problem of socialism's remains as not only the challenge of banishing the past but also the danger of reproducing it in the future. The revelations of past informers from across the political spectrum would demonstrate that the specter of communism, once summoned, could unleash unwanted effects: shattering national fantasies of family unity and generational continuity.

Background

Efforts at transitional justice faced several challenges in the years following the end of state socialism in Hungary. Because the change of system was bloodless and lawful, negotiated from above between the reform communist government and its democratic opposition, the old communist elite was not prosecuted after democratic elections removed them from office. Moreover, the new government led by the conservative MDF (Hungarian Democratic Forum) had little impetus to make the files of the former state security publicly available, since during the MDF's time as an opposition movement in the final years of socialism, it had been infiltrated by the state security (Nalepa 2010, 79–80). Miklós Németh, the last communist prime minister, was known to have given his postsocialist successor, József Antall, a secret list of previous informers still active in public life, with the understanding that these individuals would not be exposed. Antall was rumored to have used this information to exert political pressure on members of his coalition as well as his opponents, by handing them envelopes containing incriminating information (Hack 2003, 69–70, quoted in Kiss 2006, 930).

In 1990, the SZDSZ (the Alliance of Free Democrats) proposed a bill to make the state security files publicly accessible, but this motion was defeated by the governing coalition (Kiss 2006, 930).[3] Another bill that would amend the criminal code by suspending the statute of limitations for unpunished communist-era crimes such as treason or murder was passed by Parliament in 1991 but was struck down by the Constitutional Court soon afterward. It was not until shortly before the national elections in 1994 that a bill was finally passed that legislated accountability for acts undertaken during the previous regime. This Screening Act, which threatened former agents and informers with disclosure if they did not voluntarily resign from public or civil positions, was presumably intended to threaten the MDF coalition's greatest rival, the MSZP (Hungarian Socialist Party), who nonetheless won the election. The Constitutional Court rejected much of the 1994 law as unconstitutional; it was amended in 1996 by the MSZP-led coalition government, and again in 2000 under Fidesz (Kiss 2006, 930–933).[4]

Overall, while most Hungarians generally supported the principle of full access to the files, these laws and the moral issues they raised were not topics of sustained public discussion or debate during the first decade of postsocialism. There were several reasons for this. First, although the total number of informers in Hungary is likely to have been similar to numbers elsewhere in the Soviet bloc,[5] during my interviews in Budapest and the village, my interlocutors usually assumed that this number was much smaller—a misconception that helped preserve the Kádár-era fantasy of a private life untouched by communist authority. (As one recalled, in a perhaps deliberate disavowal of the very nature of domestic surveillance programs, "We all knew there were informers, but I certainly never encountered one.") Second, in the early years of postsocialism, most Hungarians were satisfied with the peaceful handover of power and were impatient to move forward rather than dwell on past injustice. Third, the politicization of the informer question when it did emerge meant that many viewed the informer revelations as political weapons rather than part of a broader national process of transitional justice. Hungary thus entered the second decade of state socialism with access to the files still very limited—and with little public incentive to change this situation.

The Medgyessy Case

When Fidesz lost its bid for reelection in 2002, its supporters warned that the victory of their left-wing opponents represented the return of the communist past. The university student Ádám, whom we met in chapters 2 and 4, thus complained to me in an email the following morning that "The past has begun"—a sadly ironic play on a Fidesz campaign slogan that celebrated its accomplishments by trumpeting "The future has begun!" For Fidesz supporters like Ádám, the fear that the remains of the previous era had returned to public life appeared to be confirmed just weeks later, when the right-wing newspaper *Magyar Nemzet* revealed that the newly elected prime minister Péter Medgyessy had been a secret officer (*szigorúan titkos állományú tiszt*) for the state socialist regime, by acting as a member of the III/II counterintelligence service in the 1970s.

Within days, Fidesz organized demonstrations that called for Medgyessy's resignation. The revelation of Medgyessy's past also inspired debate within the MSZP–SZDSZ coalition. Medgyessy's position as a counterintelligence officer did not legally prevent him from holding office, and although the specifics of his activities were still protected as a state secret, most people did not consider counterintelligence work to be as morally offensive as being an "informer" (*besúgó*) who reported on family, friends, and colleagues. Nonetheless, members of the left-liberal SZDSZ, which had long called for lustration in Hungarian politics, criticized Medgyessy's dishonesty for not having publicly disclosed his past, and they insisted that he should step down (Kiss 2006, 934). (Meanwhile, as the MSZP struggled to hold onto its political legitimacy, counterrevelations appeared in the media that ultimately implicated public figures across the political spectrum for having been informers under the previous regime, including the father of the Fidesz party chairman and House leader, Zoltán Pokorni.)[6]

But Medgyessy refused his challengers on both the right and left, arguing that he had chosen to work with counterintelligence to help prepare Hungary to join the International Monetary Fund without Moscow's knowledge. Moreover, the SZDSZ feared that political upheaval might force a new election and help Fidesz to victory (Kiss 2006, 935). After fierce internal negotiations, Medgyessy was thus able to win a vote of confidence from his coalition.[7] The public debates, demonstrations, and subsequent revelations his scandal inspired would nonetheless ultimately help to inspire legal changes that would make the question of the past regime's informers and collaborators increasingly urgent in the second decade of postsocialism.

In 2003 a new law was passed that offered greater access to the informer files.[8] It redefined information about high-ranking public officials as public data, and it also reorganized the former Historical Institute that had guarded these documents into a Historical Archive of the State Security Services. In the following months, approximately seven hundred scholars and journalists were permitted to do research in the archive (Deák 2006). With the scope of this new law continuing to be limited by issues of constitutionality and data protection, however, many considered its revisions to existing legislation to be inadequate, arguing that without the full release of informer names, the issue would only become further politicized.[9] Such fears appeared to be realized in the ensuing months and years, as revelations about the secret pasts of still more political or cultural figures became dependable media events: more volleys in the ever-escalating moral battle between Hungary's left and right-wings, in which each side sought to discredit the other by uncovering additional informers among them. These scandals implicated politicians and cultural figures across the political spectrum, including even those such as Szabó who had previously spoken out passionately against the past system and the moral compromises it had demanded.

But such revelations did not necessarily lead to justice or moral clarity. Instead, by expanding access to the files and redefining some information as public data, the 2003 law made the morality of exposure even murkier. The screening law it replaced was intended to find public officials who were given the chance to either admit their involvement publicly or quietly resign. But what would be the consequences for the popular art critics, sports figures, and other cultural personalities whose names were now unearthed by the historians and journalists in the archive? These revelations, many of which were publicized in the pages of the weekly literature and culture journal, *Élet és Irodalom*, ranged from church leaders to the rock singer Gyula Vikidál to the famous soccer player and coach Dezső Novák. Were these individuals merely collaborators with the previous regime? Or were they just as victimized as those whose confidences they betrayed?

The emergence of the "informer" and his or her secrets to characterize the problem of socialist remains thus problematized the previously established forms of identity through which Hungarians had narrated their experiences of state socialism. The House of Terror functioned as a moralizing discourse, drawing an experiential continuum from murder and torture to cultural consumption and thus dividing the national community into the moral categories of victims and perpetrators. In contrast, the informer scandals offered an image of prominent Hungarians as simultaneously victims of an unjust system that often blackmailed its informers into participation and perpetrators whose actions nonetheless threatened the livelihoods (and, in some cases, lives) of their families, friends, and colleagues. As a result, reactions to revelations from the state security files were often ambivalent. Some rushed to condemnation, whereas others were hesitant to pass judgment on the difficult moral choices the informers had faced.

Fallen Heroes

Szabó's decision to claim that his actions had helped save the life of a colleague met with divided reactions. For many of his peers, his strategy was successful. Well-known intellectuals, artists, and public figures (such as the former president of Hungary, Árpád Göncz, and the acclaimed filmmaker Miklós Jancsó, who had been the target of one of Szabó's reports) rushed to support him in the form of an open list of signatures published the following day in *Népszabadság* (2006c). Others defended Szabó by arguing that this revelation had been timed to disrupt the annual Hungarian Film Week, during which his film *Relatives* (*Rokonok*), an adaptation of a novel by Zsigmond Móricz, was scheduled to premier (Janisch 2006; Ragályi 2006).

Meanwhile, some readers of *Élet és Irodalom* wrote to protest and cancel their subscriptions, terming Szabó's actions the "slip" of a young man who had not harmed anyone, and had even already done his penance by working through similar issues in his films. Questioning the motives of the historian who revealed him, they argued that the research reflected professional jealousy (Arató 2006), and thus threw into question the moral legitimacy of the entire project of uncovering past informers. Some argued that it was historians like Gervai who deserved condemnation, for failing to put individual acts of betrayal into the broader context of a regime that had forced these difficult moral choices (Lánczos 2006). Exposing past actions, these defenders maintained, now merely repeated the informer's victimization by the former regime, in light of which the very decision to inform might even be viewed—as Szabó controversially insisted—as a kind of heroism. Also at stake was the very definition of "public personality" that allowed such negative discoveries to be made public in the first place. As the historian István Deák asked, in an evenhanded analysis of the informer debates, "Is it fair to label a young cleric or a student a public personality just because he later became a cardinal or a world-famous film director? And is it right to expose their names in connection with acts committed thirty or forty years ago which were not then punishable by law and are not punishable today?" (2006).[10]

Others, however, were less convinced by Szabó's portrayal of his past actions. They questioned the ability of young film school students to outwit the state security (Munkácsy 2006, 4), and challenged the assumption that Szabó had no choice but to collaborate with them.[11] Moreover, the outpouring of public support for Szabó raised the question of why the actions of an unrepentant informer were applauded while other artists guilty of similar involvement had been condemned. Some critical responses mentioned the case of the late novelist Sándor Tar, who unlike Szabó did not ultimately enjoy support from the same intellectuals after it was revealed in 1999 that he had written reports on some of his colleagues (Darvasi 2006), and who died in shame and isolation some years afterward.[12] Was Szabó to be forgiven merely because his art had won Hungary great prestige? How were his self-serving justifications in the past and present to be reconciled with the demands for moral accountability made in his films? And if he was so proud of his past activities, why had he not publicized them in 1990, when the man he had claimed to save was still alive?

Under pressure from this controversy, Szabó would soon be forced to modify his initial defense. In a television interview several days after the original revelation, he admitted that although he did not think he had harmed anyone through his actions, he had acted primarily out of self-protection because he feared being expelled from film school if he refused to cooperate.[13] Szabó apparently failed to realize, however, that it was not the act of informing per se that many of his critics found morally objectionable. After all, as many people told me, it is difficult to judge another's behavior when you do not know how you yourself might act in a similar situation. Nor did they consider Szábó's past actions necessarily to be of public importance or interest; instead, they saw the matter as only relevant to the small circle of intellectuals who argued on the pages of Hungary's newspapers and cultural weeklies.

What did anger and disappoint Szabó's critics was his reaction to the revelations, particularly in light of his celebrity, prestige, and moral status—his "cowardly" refusal to apologize, and his efforts to "turn shame into glory," as my friend Katalin, a freelance video producer then in her mid-thirties who told me she had followed the scandals avidly, described Szabó's explanation. Even more upsetting, Katalin argued, were those defenders of Szabó who demonized the historians as informers and argued that uncovering the past was hurtful because it caused trouble for what one letter writer termed "benevolent" people (Pál 2006). In Katalin's view, equating historical research to informing relativized the entire informer problem, turning perpetrators not only into victims of the previous system but also into heroes.

Szabó's defiant self-aggrandizement—and the public support he nonetheless enjoyed—also rejected the affective norms that had increasingly governed the public revelations of informers in postsocialist Hungary, whereby apology had become the precondition for public forgiveness.[14] That is, given the general disinclination to condemn the informer's past actions, people instead exercised moral judgment by evaluating the informer's affect in the present via an "ethics of sincerity" (Morris 2004, 226) that called for the public display of remorse and contrition. As the article's author Gervai himself argued, in an interview about the book that later resulted from his research on the film industry (Gervai 2010), "Forgiveness can only be given to those who request it [*Bocsánatot csak annak lehet adni, aki bocsánatot kér*]" (Magyari 2010).

This expectation that informers express regret for their past actions returns us to the problem of remains. We can interpret the demand for apology as a demand for an act of self-distancing: a gesture that would transform present-day secrets into the remains of a now-disavowed past, and thus performatively enact the temporal break between then and now. In contrast, Szabó's silence and subsequent bravado represented, to his critics, an alarming continuity with the previous regime. By presenting his informer past as a tale of heroism rather than a remain of socialism to be rejected and atoned for, Szabó's actions suggested that the break from the past system was still incomplete.

"You Are Stealing the Past"

This perspective was expressed most vehemently by the graduate student, Balázs Bodó, in his article published the following week (Bodó 2006). Titled "Csóko-lom" (literally, "I kiss your hand": a deferential greeting used by young people toward their elders), Bodó's article began with the declaration, "I don't know if you've noticed, but meanwhile a generation has grown up that has hardly any (or literally no) direct memory of before 1989. We are your children." Rather than question the act of informing itself, Bodó challenged the morality of not admitting and apologizing for it, arguing that what was at stake was not the long-dead past, but the nature of the present that Bodó and his generation were to inherit. He then proceeded to accuse his cultural parents of sabotaging the goals of the informer laws so as to perpetuate a silence that only served their self-interests. In his eyes, the older generation was accountable not only to those they had informed on. Also at stake, he argued, was the betrayal of the younger generations by their elders, who "while silently enjoying the manifestations of unsuspecting respect" given to them, "act as if nothing happened back then."

> Because your silence is a lie, an unforgivable and hateful crime, worse than what you committed long ago. Because today nobody can force you into either collaboration or silence. Because no jail or execution threatens you. There is no other excuse for your silence than your own crimes, your own comfort, or those particular benefits that you would lose by speaking out, and which accordingly you enjoy undeservedly and un-justly. Because with your silence you are collaborators today as well, because you strenuously protect the very system which made you into betrayers, whether through blackmail, or money, or by appealing to your patriotic enthusiasm. This system does not deserve protection, but with your silence you don't, either.

By arguing that the silence of the older generation reproduced the very regime of lies that had coerced them into informing, Bodó thus challenged the narratives of victimization—and, in Szabó's case, heroism—through which these activities had previously been narrated. Regardless of what happened during the socialist era—"whether you were gay or a counter-revolutionary . . . whether you believed in communism during your twenties"—what mattered, he argued, was the pub-lic accounting after socialism's demise. "There would have been an opportunity in the past decade and a half to stand up and say, 'Sorry.'"

> Your silence steals my past from me. . . . There wasn't any Arrow Cross here, or ÁVH [Államvédelmi Hatóság; State Protection Authority], there

weren't informers, there is no late Kádár party elite that retained its power; here everyone is merely a victim, and now you too step into this line. You are stealing the past, my past, and you are stealing the present as well; you are producing anew this century's entire neurotic, cowardly, opportunistic lie, and for this there is no excuse.

Personal cowardice and self-interest perpetuated past injustice in the present, victimizing the youth who were to inherit this legacy.

Bodó's polemic attempted to shift the tenor of the debate from one focused on past moral choices and contemporary political expediency to one entangled in an even more intricate web of familial loyalty, inheritance, and obligation. This struck a chord with some of my interviewees who, like Bodó, were then in their twenties or thirties and who thus had only childhood memories of the past regime. Like those of the transitional generation (who were five to ten years older), this cohort was often uncomfortable with the idea of passing judgment on the actions of the older generation and the difficult choices they had faced. The silence that surrounded this issue for much of the first decade and a half of postsocialism thus appeared to be not just in their parents' interest but also in their own.

What made Bodó's article so refreshing for people like Katalin was that he both rejected his generation's silence concerning the past and asserted his right to judge the older generation's handling of it in the present. Accusing these cultural parents of stealing the past—and thus the present—from their children, Bodó challenged the narratives of heroism and victimization that structured the way public figures like Szabó spoke of their actions under the state socialist regime. His article thus sparked several letters of protest that drew on the familial idiom he had invoked in order to scold him as an errant child and reject the moral authority he claimed. One letter writer listed all the sacrifices contemporary Hungarian parents endure to provide for their selfish children: an apartment, a fashionable car, a college education. Criticizing Bodó as "inconsiderate, haughty, cruel, and lacking style," she told him, "You don't know anything, only to make demands and pass judgment, oh and to accept material goods graciously. . . . [I hope you] get back with interest this rigidity from your children, if you even have any" (Albert 2006). (Ironically, this seemingly self-evident logic, in which Hungary's youth owes its parents obedience and gratitude in exchange for material support, echoed the conditions of political citizenship in the paternalist state of late socialism.)

Another letter writer, who identified himself as being in his early fifties, responded with scorn rather than anger, mocking Bodó's rhetoric as if it were the frustrated shrieks of a toddler:

> Dear little Balázs, age 30! Well, how was it with that past? Since your past practically has just begun. Concretely, what did they steal from you? . . .

> At 30 years old, you don't have anything better to do than to fret about an age in which you didn't even live? . . . I have two sons just a couple of years younger than you. They live in the present, they plan for tomorrow—about the Kádár era, though, they mostly don't give a shit. I'll tell you why, since you would never figure it out yourself: because they're normal. It's that simple. (G. Kovács, "Give It Back," 2006)

Whereas Bodó located cultural pathology in the current silence and lack of remorse that colluded with the lies and blackmail of the past, his critics instead argued that such concern for the past was itself unhealthy. The task of members of the new generation was to occupy themselves with the present and future, and they owed their elders gratitude rather than criticism for giving them the material means to do so.

Even some of those who supported Gervai's exposé of Szabó's past were nonetheless critical of Bodó's position and the moral inflexibility they assumed it implied. Gyuri, an artist then in his mid-fifties, knew Gervai socially, and commented on the irony that Szabó—with his fame, personal charisma, and imposing patrician appearance—looked the part of a hero much more than Gervai did. "But Szabó is a coward and what [Gervai] did was very brave," he insisted. At the same time, however, Gyuri criticized Bodó for his youthful "black and white" view of the past, arguing that Bodó's outrage merely demonstrated his ignorance of the difficult moral choices faced by those who were adults during the socialist era. "He doesn't understand *anything*," Gyuri told me heatedly, when I asked whether he agreed with Bodó's article. "He acts as if he would have been braver and would have refused to be an informer, when he doesn't know." Moreover, Gyuri went on, there were many nuanced distinctions that Bodó failed to consider: between those who informed out of ideological conviction and those who were blackmailed; and between those who agreed to inform during the harsh years of post-1956 repression and those who consented in the more politically lenient years of late socialism. "Just because one person was able to refuse to inform doesn't mean that everyone could."

In July 2009 I met with Bodó at a coffee shop near one of Buda's shopping malls.[14] Bodó was then finishing a graduate degree at Eötvös Lóránd University, and he also taught courses at another university in Budapest. Given his own research focus on digital preservation and copyright piracy, Bodó characterized himself as someone who did not usually directly involve himself in current affairs or Hungarian politics, and he told me he had been surprised that his article aroused so much controversy. "It was more like personal therapy," he told me, explaining that its impetus came out of research he had conducted on political dissidence in the underground art movement under socialism. "What I saw there was a history full of very strong personal tragedies. People denied the chance for a normal life, people being intimidated, forced abroad, forced into suicide, alcoholism." The contrast between the suffering he saw among members of this community and the current "denial, normalization, and then heroization" of Szabó triggered a "very sudden and very sharp emotional reaction" that he was not prepared for. "I was angry that the moral elites of Hungarian culture were behaving so badly."

Bodó thus chose the title of his piece, "I Kiss Your Hand," to echo the demonstrations of respect that children given their elders.

> This was my moment of growing up and becoming disillusioned with the adult world—with those individuals and that society which I thought had many problems but nonetheless were governed by certain ideals or rationality or moral standing. I didn't want to make it a generational issue; I just wanted to signal that—and this is because I teach at the university and every day I meet with people who were born after '89—there is a whole new generation who is untainted by this whole world, and who were raised by the Cartoon Network, speak English very well, read foreign news sources, use the internet, and for them it's a completely different world. And if you don't make transparent what those issues were that made you make the decision of working with the secret service, then you maintain those very structures that you were the victims of.

Bodó was thus dismayed by most of the reactions to his article: the way people on both the left and right used it support their political agendas (including a popular television personality, Sándor Fábri, who handed out photocopies of the article on the opening night of the annual film festival) and response articles like the ones in *Élet és Irodalom* that he felt misunderstood and misrepresented his critique. "I was not casting a judgment on what Szabó did 30 years ago," he insisted with clear frustration. "I was criticizing his lack of judgment now."

> People missed this distinction. I was really asking what justifies his current actions. I'm not judging anyone's past actions. I can understand that there is a very wide variety of decisions to be made in such pressing situations.
>
> But not doing that now, and not coming out now, and not trying to help us now, there is no excuse, there is no such force that it can be founded on. This is the whole point. If we're really not living in a dictatorship then you have to clean this mess up. And this I remember was part of the reasoning, so if you now are defending those who fucked you up in the past, you're continuing their legacy.

Bodó thus contrasted Szabó's attempts at concealment and self-justification with the reactions his article received in the underground scene. Szabó had nothing to lose except his reputation, he argued, whereas his subjects—"the ones who were kicked out of the country in the seventies or the eighties, or went into internal exile"—were very scared for Bodó. "They were warning me I was dead." Others were afraid to show public support for Bodó in written form but only congratulated him in private. Such fears of repercussion—and the implication that the former regime's informers were less at risk than those who criticized or exposed them—seemed to suggest that the socialist past still determined the present in ways that the younger generation was not equipped to recognize and the older generation was unwilling to acknowledge. "And if we don't talk about the situation," Bodó concluded, "we are doomed to repeat it."

Revolution or Reproduction? The Politics of Youth

Bodó's claim that his parents' generation was "stealing my past" is reminiscent of a statement made by the Fidesz leader Viktor Orbán, who was one of the speakers at Imre Nagy's reburial in 1989. Fidesz would later reinvent itself as a center-right conservative party after 1994 (and then shift to right-wing populism in 2010), but it entered the political scene in 1988 as a liberal youth movement that explicitly rejected the older generations' perceived moral compromises with state socialism. During the first elections in 1990, it offered voters a party of blue-jeaned young intellectuals who were presumably untainted by any association with the previous regime and who claimed moral authority based on their refusal to admit anyone over the age of thirty-five.

Speaking at Nagy's reburial on behalf of his generation, Orbán attacked the reconciliatory efforts of the reform communists by accusing their party of stealing the future of Hungary's youth. Referring to the empty sixth coffin, which was dedicated to the "unknown freedom-fighters," Orbán said:

> We know that the victims of the Revolution and the repression were in their majority youths of our age and condition. But that is not the only reason to regard the sixth coffin as ours. . . . Truly, the Hungarian Socialist Workers' Party robbed today's youth of its future in 1956. Thus, the sixth coffin contains not just a murdered youth but also the next twenty—or who can say how many?—years of our lives. (Litván 1996, xiii)

Nearly twenty years later, Bodó's polemic similarly condemned the older generations by drawing on the moral authority of youth: now symbolically uncorrupted
by the experience of state socialism as well as by the negotiated nature of the political transformation itself. But by reversing this temporality—arguing that what had
been stolen was not the uncertain time to come, but rather the status of what had
gone before—Bodó complicated the long-standing association of youth with futurity and national renewal. Instead, he conceptualized youth as caught between two
countervailing forces: either to reject the past or to reproduce it.

Such metaphors of generational conflict and upheaval have long had great res-
onance in Hungary. Typically, the concept of generation is understood not
merely in terms of life cycle or cohort, but as a specific place within—and thus
relationship to—history (Mannheim 1952, 290–291). Generational divisions have
thus been a particularly powerful source of horizontal affiliation in countries such
as Hungary whose turbulent twentieth-century history has resulted in different
age groups with very different historical subjectivities. (Times of historical transformation are marked by the acceleration of the sense of historicity, in which
only a few years is enough to mark a specific generation and place it in competition with others.) At the same time, however, it is important to note that such
generational identifications are never simply the function of chronological age
but also represent strategic moral positionings. After all, a number of Szabó's peers
condemned him, and certainly not all members of Bodó's age group shared his
outrage. Rather than treat generational belonging as a self-evident fact, I instead
regard it as a specific moral claim to historical disjuncture that, combined with
the modern association of youth with moral purity and futurity, gave Bodó's arguments particular force.

Bodó's observation that his students appeared to be untouched by the socialist past reflected a common logic in the way older generations regarded younger
ones. Many people insisted to me that the younger generations experienced postsocialist Hungary in a very different way than their parents did, who were still
burdened by the physical and metaphorical remains of the previous era. "They
know computers, study languages, go abroad," said Ágnes, the Budapest schoolteacher whom we met in chapter 2, told me in an interview. Ágnes was divorced
and one of her two children was autistic. She picked up tutoring jobs on the side
that helped to pay for his therapies, most of which she complained were not covered by the state. She explained that the older generations like herself found the
withdrawal of state services and the economic uncertainties of postsocialist life
to be traumatic after growing up with the promise of lifetime security. "But the
young people seem so much more calm, more open. . . . For them, I think
Hungary is more like the West." In Ágnes's eyes, the socialist past was irrelevant

to Hungary's youth given their focus on their current personal tasks of university study, building their careers, and finding partners. This perspective echoed that of one of Bodó's critics, whose letter argued that Hungary's youth had already entered the future: "They live in the present, they plan for tomorrow—about the Kádár era, though, they mostly don't give a shit."

Yet many young adults insisted to me that starting out in life was much more challenging for them than it had been for those even a decade older. The market economy demanded that they be flexible and entrepreneurial in their approach to their careers, yet they faced limited opportunities that forced many of them to seek work abroad. Such expressions of frustration stood in contrast to the older generation's envious assumption that this generation enjoyed both an unburdened past and a promising future. (Indeed, one reason that Bodó's declaration that "You are stealing my past" may have resonated so greatly is because many young people perceived the greed and corruption of Hungary's political elites to have stolen the younger generation's economic future as well.) Even Bodó himself told me that his career had suffered due to "being born at the wrong time." He noted that because members of the transitional generation, who were five to ten years older than him, entered adulthood at the time the regime ended, they had benefited disproportionately from the social and professional disruption of the system change: quickly moving into jobs and positions that would prevent later cohorts from enjoying the same accelerated upward professional mobility. "Because so many young people took key positions, the normal channels of career [for my generation] were a bit blocked because the people in the key positions were not people fifteen to twenty years older than us, but five to ten. So a lot of my friends have gone abroad. There's nothing for them here."

Moreover, it was not necessary for the younger generations to have experienced state socialism to be affected by it. As we saw in the case of Ádám whom we met in chapter 4, young people grew up in a condition of what Marianne Hirsch terms "postmemory": surrounded by remains of socialism and embedded within family histories greatly shaped by the socialist past, but with limited or no concrete memories of that era themselves and little official knowledge about the past (2012). Lacking public consensus on the past and the common ground of shared generational experiences of the socialist era (whether positive or negative), many postsocialist teenagers and young adults formed their understanding of state socialism from family memories that might range from longing for the material security of Kádárism to bitter recountings of political persecution to—most commonly of all—personalized reminiscences that discarded broader commentary on the socialist era altogether. Others, like Ádám, constructed their own histories of the socialist era determined by their political affiliations, even if some of their family who lived through that era challenged their assumptions.

As a result, alongside fantasies of youth untroubled by the remains of the socialist past lay the fear that children were condemned to reproduce the past of their parents. In interviews I conducted in the mid- to late 2000s, for example, some members of the transitional generation (who were now parents entering early middle age) voiced the anxiety that long after the regime had ended, a new generation of their children's classmates was being taught to be nostalgic for the security and entitlements of the past era. They warned that without a broader critical context for these recollections, their parents' relationship to the past risked being reproduced in the younger generation—producing a new generation of Kádárist subjects. Bodó's article thus called attention to the lies and omissions that made such generational reproduction possible. Without true knowledge of their parents' past, he argued, Hungary's youth would see no harm in reproducing it and would thus unwittingly perpetuate its injustices.

The Family Romance of Postsocialism

Freud's concept of the "family romance" describes how children, as they become aware of the faults and limitations of their once-omnipotent parents, fantasize that their parents are not their own and that they are instead descended from noble birth (1959, 237–239). This fantasy of new lineage not only offers a way to understand individual psychological development in the context of the social order but also helps to characterize the way societies "collectively imagine . . . the operation of power" (Hunt 1992, 8), since narratives of family are central to the constitution of political authority.[15] Scholars such as Lynn Hunt (1992) and John Borneman (2004) have thus examined the way political revolutions are often figured in terms of the demise of parental authority, whereby the family romance becomes an idiom through which to imagine new political relations and a transformed social order.

Elsewhere the "death of the father" has been crucial to revolutionary politics, and even Hungary's own bloodless political transformation was narrated as a coming-of-age story in which the nation reached adulthood and threw off the paternalism of late socialist rule. But ambivalence about cultural parentage—the tension between revolution and reproduction discussed above—was already a well-established cultural trope in Hungary during the twentieth century. The history of Hungarian film, for example, reveals an enduring anxiety about paternal authority, caught between the longing for absent fathers and dissatisfaction with those who remained: from the fathers who died in World War II, to the "great generation" who were imprisoned or fled in 1956, to the laughable, impotent figures of authority in films made during the 1970s and 1980s, during which the perceived absurdity and corruption of socialist rule was mapped onto its parental figures.[16] By the time of the system change, the very legitimacy of paternal authority was in crisis, as many unfairly portrayed the older generation not only as bumbling and incapable of transformation from *Homo Sovieticus* to the new capitalist entrepreneur but also as corrupted by the past regime by the sheer fact of having survived it.

Hungary's entrance into democracy moved the problem of cultural parentage into a mythic register, by foregrounding the problem of origins and the need for a new national lineage that could distance the recent past and project a new postsocialist future that would build Hungary anew. The reburials and political battles to define a new national pantheon in the early years of postsocialism thus constituted attempts to replace now-discredited socialist "forefathers" with a new set of heroes. Yet, at the same time, representations of the recent socialist past itself tended to evade the threat of generational conflict via their wholesale disavowal and rejection of state socialism as inauthentic to the Hungarian nation: whether by demonizing the previous era as one composed solely of Soviet oppressors and Hungarian victims or by evading ideological concerns entirely through discourses of everyday life and nostalgia for the soft dictatorship of Kádárism.

The narratives of betrayal and complicity that emerged from the communist state security files in the second decade of postsocialism challenged these existing strategies for making sense of the past era. Problematizing the established categories of hero, victim, and oppressor with the ambiguous figure of the informer, these revelations foregrounded questions about individual participation in the past regime that had largely been absent from Hungarian public discourse after the end of socialism. If, as Hunt argues, nations are "families writ large" (1992, xiv), the family romance of the Szabó case offered a new way to reimagine the moral orders of postsocialism, through Bodó's demand for a new cultural lineage defined not by his elders' past choices but by a politics of remorse in the present, in which a truthful accounting of the past might yet redeem cultural parents in the eyes of their children. Arguing that the past was a possession that had been stolen by the lies and betrayal of the informers and the passivity of those who supported them, Bodó thus challenged the older generation's assertion of parental authority to deal with their own past as they saw fit.

Bodó's critique of Szabó and his defenders thus complicated the dichotomy of victims and perpetrators that had already come to characterize the problems of remains in the 2000s. By declaring that the past belonged to those who represent the future, he shifted the claim of victimization from those who suffered under socialist rule to a younger generation denied full knowledge of the past's injustices. And in arguing that the older generation had condemned their children to unwittingly reproduce the silences and lies of the past era, Bodó rephrased the fear of a future polluted by socialism's remains as a problem of corrupted inheritance. If Hungary's elders did not pass down the truth of their past, their cultural children would be unable to break from it.

I now want to examine another, slightly earlier example of the informer scandals as family romance. In 2002 (the same year that Medgyessy was under attack for his past involvement in counterintelligence services), one of Hungary's most celebrated writers, the postmodern novelist and essayist Péter Esterházy, published a book about his recent discovery of the informer activities of his beloved late father, Mátyás. Esterházy (who was fifty-two in 2002) represented an older generation that had an experience of the socialist era different from Bodó's; moreover, the intimacy of Esterházy's father's betrayal made Esterházy's reaction more anguished—and ultimately more ambivalent—than that expressed by Bodó. As a result, Esterházy's painful exploration of both the files and his experience of reading them offers another approach for understanding inheritance and working through the experience of generational betrayal: no longer torn between truth and lies, revolution and reproduction, a stolen past and a returned one.

Death of the Father

> My father must not be spoken of. To speak well of him almost always amounts
> to flattery. To speak ill of him is fraught with danger if he is alive, while it is an
> act of cowardice if he is dead.
>
> —Esterházy, *Celestial Harmonies*, 56

In 2000 Esterházy published a work of imaginative tribute to his ancestors, one of the leading noble families of Hungary. Titled *Harmonia Caelestis* (*Celestial Harmonies*—the title of a piece written by Haydn when he was part of the Esterházy court), the book examines both the Esterházy family mythologies and the narrative generativity that Esterházy views as intrinsic to the very notions of father and family inheritance.

The novel is divided into two books: "Numbered Sentences from the Lives of the Esterházy Family" and "Confessions of an Esterházy Family." The first is a free-wheeling exploration of all that accrues to the name of "my father" (literally, "my dear father" [*édesapám*], a term of greater affection and respect), which Esterházy uses to refer both to his own parent and as a generic term to encompass his entire lineage. Mixing personal history, historical fact, Esterházy's own artistic invention, and credited and uncredited excerpts from writers ranging from James Joyce to Italo Calvino to Donald Barthelme, Esterházy spins fantastic—and often contradictory—tales about the countless generations that preceded him, in a series of 371 numbered sections. In contrast, the second half mostly abandons this intertextual play, instead detailing the fortunes of Esterházy's own father, Mátyás Esterházy, who was exiled from Budapest and forced to work in a series of menial jobs after the communist takeover. A study of both the iniquities of the communist system and what Esterházy perceived to be his father's unwavering dignity in the face of such oppression, the second half thus presents a catalog of twentieth-century loss that stands in stark counterpoint to the imaginative abundance of the presocialist past.

Taken together, the two halves of the book function as a work of filial tribute to Esterházy's aristocratic and personal heritage as well as the notion of paternity and all that inheres in it. For Esterházy, "my father" is the progenitor of both personal and cultural mythology. Indeed, given the extent to which the fortunes of the Esterházy line and the Hungarian nation intersected, the figure of the father—its historical triumphs, its debasement under communism—functions as an allegory for the Hungarian nation itself. As one reviewer noted, the flattened temporality of the first book, in which countless Esterházys are all subsumed under the same address, highlights not only the simultaneity with which any person encounters the past but also how thoroughly this past in its variegated glory has become lost to the author as its inheritor. In this light, Esterházy's fabulistic invention and textual borrowings from other sources do not represent mere formal play, but an attempt to fill in lost gaps and re-create his proud family history: a cultural inheritance that was stolen by the communist regime (Györffy 2000, 114).

Celestial Harmonies met with critical acclaim domestically and internationally, winning the Hungarian Literature Prize and the Sándor Márai prize in Hungary, the Premio Circeo in Italy, and the Herder Prize in Germany. Yet at the very time that the book was being prepared for publication, Esterházy discovered one of the missing pieces in his family history. He had asked the Historical Office for access to any files that might involve his family, assuming he would find reports that others had written about his family's activities. Instead, he discovered that his father himself had informed for the domestic security services from 1957 to 1980, and although initially unwilling, had ultimately executed his task so well that in the 1970s he was promoted to "secret agent" (*titkos megbízott*).

This revelation of his father's past as an informer imperiled the family romance that inspired Esterházy's previous novel and had been a guiding theme throughout his work. As Miklós Györffy argues,

> What Esterházy learned within days of finishing his big novel in certain respects immediately put the validity of that work in question, indeed,

put a question mark on his entire oeuvre to date, because his writings have been based in no small measure on the fiction that, for all the stumbles and frailties, the moral right of father and family alike was incorruptible, and that the first person narrator loves his father, mother, grandparents, and their forebears, loves the very idea of being an Esterházy, and, ultimately, loves his native land, the world he regards as his home, not in any nationalistic but in an almost religious sense. The fact that his father was a snitch, no different from those who put him in this dishonourable position, and that this vileness managed to infiltrate even places where decency had every right to consider it was protected—this shattered the image, undermined the love. (Györffy 2002, 131–132)

In the months that followed, as *Celestial Harmonies* was released to great acclaim, Esterházy secretly began writing a follow-up book that would expose this family history, and thus throw the very status of *Celestial Harmonies* into question.

Released in 2002, *Revised Edition: An Appendix to Celestial Harmonies* (*Javított kiadás: melléklet a Harmonia caelestishez*) takes the form of a series of nested conversations with the father found in the informer files: a figure whom Esterházy found impossible to reconcile with his own memories. Structured as a set of diaries that chronicle Esterházy's experience of discovering the existence of the files and reading them, the book quotes excerpts from his father's reports as well as Esterházy's own initial reactions to them and his reflections from later readings. In addition, as if to compensate for his father's dishonesty—and his own celebration of what he now realizes was a false image of his father—throughout the book Esterházy also carefully lays bare his own emotional and physical reactions: tears, self-pity, and even the pain medication necessitated by the stress of this emotional and physical labor. As he explains in the preface, "I watched myself, like an animal, curious to see how I would conduct myself in this situation, how I would react to things, and how things would act on me" ("Preface to *Revised Edition*," 144).[17]

Esterházy's painstaking exploration of the files and his "revision" of the family romance of his earlier work thus narrows the expansive imaginative scope of *Celestial Harmonies* into a meticulous effort toward factual and emotional comprehensiveness. This anxious attempt at transparency throws into question not only the thematic territory of his previous novels but also the very genre of *Revised Edition*. Esterházy begins *Celestial Harmonies* with the declaration that "it is deucedly difficult to tell a lie when you don't know the truth" (*Celestial Harmonies*, 5), and he mitigates even the avowedly confessional tone of the second half of the book with a note warning that the characters described are fictitious (*Celestial Harmonies*, 395). With *Revised Edition*, however, Esterházy declares himself forced to abandon the fictional constructs invented to fill the gaps of a heritage denied to him. (As he writes, "My God, how *good* it would be if I had merely made this up!" [*Revised Edition*, 96]). Although the book does not fall easily into the non-fiction genre of biography (or autobiography), it thus does not follow Esterházy's usual playful prose style, which deliberately blurs the lines between fiction and reality, "the who-is-who, face as mask, roleplay and citationality" (*Revised Edition*, 19). Esterházy even decides to turn back to *Celestial Harmonies* and re-interpret it "in 'relation' to new facts," taking sections and sentences and trying to remember what inspired them, "as if I were reading a family memory of my father, and not a novel" (*Revised Edition*, 33).

Esterházy does not undertake this performance of transparency merely out of the desire to "correct" the depiction of his father in *Celestial Harmonies* and to provide a more accurate retelling of his family's history—that is, to replace one past with another.[18] After all, as he notes in the preface, his original goal in requesting the files was not to "clarify" the past, but "to show a certain attentiveness towards it" ("Preface to *Revised Edition*," 137). Esterházy soon discovers that the anguished task of "attending" to the contents of the files and their impact on him only entangles him further in his father's guilty past, unmaking not only his previous literary oeuvre but himself as well. As Aniko Szucs observes in her analysis of the book as a performance-event, over the course of Esterházy's painfully close engagement with his father's files, his disgust with his father's actions battles with his dismay about the similarity of his own labor: the diligence of his efforts, the physical discomfort of writing, the furtive attempts to hide the news from others, and the guilt and paranoia his own behavior produces (2016, 74). He internalizes his father's position: the "I" blurs into "we" (Szucs 2016, 104). In so doing, Esterházy comes to recognize the ways in which the shame and secrecy of his father's betrayal have already influenced his childhood and the memories he recounts in *Celestial Harmonies*. Even the closing image of *Celestial Harmonies*, which portrays Esterházy's father hard at work at his typewriter, now takes on new sinister meaning: "Let's not prevaricate: it's a beautiful scene, one of the most beautiful endings that a novel could have—ambiguous, painful, and elevating. It's just: an informer writing his report" (*Revised Edition*, 112; Szucs 2016, 115–116).

If the imaginative reconstruction of Esterházy's noble family history in *Celestial Harmonies* constituted a family romance, in *Revised Edition* Esterházy is forced to surrender his longing for uncorrupted origins in both his family and himself. He realizes that the secret of his father's guilty past has not been "stolen" from him (to return to Bodó's formulation) but rather, as Szucs argues, it has been in his possession, affectively and somatically, all along (2016, 120–121). Esterházy's relationship to his father's informer past is thus not one of revelation or discovery, but of bringing into consciousness a knowledge that has always already been there.

Yet even as Esterházy attempts to understand and reveal the ways in which he was already aware of his father's betrayal without realizing it, his attempts at writerly and filial honesty are also challenged by all that he cannot ever know. As his translator Judith Sollosy points out, what Esterházy finds in the files produces more questions than answers because the information he gains is limited and incomplete: whether that be his father's reasons for compliance, why the regime worked so hard to recruit him, or what use the state security made of the material he provided them (2009, 134). Moreover, the knowledge Esterházy does acquire also entails loss: loss of the innocence of his childhood memories, loss of the image of his incorruptible father, and the loss of his own identity as proud son and heir. If *Celestial Harmonies* represented Eszterházy's attempt to fill in the gaps of a heritage denied to him, in *Revised Edition* he must come to terms with all that an unwanted inheritance takes away.

Inherited Remains

In *Specters of Marx*, Jacques Derrida argues that inheritance does not represent a simple transmission to be embraced or discarded. Rather, the act of claiming something as inheritance is always inherently interpretative and transformative: "If the readability of a legacy were given, natural, transparent, univocal, if it did not call for and at the same time defy interpretation, we would never have anything to inherit from it. We would be affected by it as by a cause—natural or genetic" (1994, 16). As Nicole Pepperell goes on to explain:

> Inheritance is not comprised of the contents of some transparent communication from the dead, and therefore heirs cannot be distinguished from one another by their authenticity or accurate possession of what has been bequeathed. Inheritance is not a form of passive reception, but rather something actively enacted—a performative act—one that takes place through interpretations that selectively appropriate what will, and what will not, be inherited. The dead do not bury themselves—and so they, least of all, are safe from the actions of those who would inherit them: *inheritance interprets the past in a way that intrinsically transforms it*. (2009, 225, emphasis added)

Derrida uses this understanding of inheritance as transformative enactment to reject forms of critique that seek to distinguish proper inheritances from corrupted or inauthentic ones. Such approaches are grounded in a logic of presence that denies what he terms "spectrality": "destabilizing potentials that haunt any possible present" (Pepperell 2009, 225). In contrast, Derrida argues that the task of inheritance is to "commune with the dead" by reckoning with the ways in which the present is always already haunted and out of joint (225). Rather than lay the past to rest, he thus enacts an "impure" inheritance of Marx that identifies the spectralizing forces at work in Marx's thought (231).

Derrida's argument in *Specters of Marx* relies upon a conceptual framework of unfinished burial and revenants that I do not want to apply to my own analysis of remains. Moreover, neither Bodó nor Esterházy share Derrida's critique of inheritance as a problem of truth-seeking; instead, the identities of informers, the fact of their actions, and the personal and cultural betrayal their choices represent are paramount. Nonetheless, Derrida's formulation of inheritance helps to complicate our understanding of the work inheritance does in the present, by troubling the fantasy of a clean break—and thus uncorrupted future—that often grounds the desire to locate and banish the remains of the past era.

For the sake of comparison (and with apologies to Bodó for simplifying his more complex argument), we could characterize Bodó's approach to the problem of the past regime's informers as one that posits inheritance as a project of knowledge, in which an older generation confesses its guilty secrets so that its cultural children can know—and break free from—the lies of the past. This logic of revelation and catharsis is familiar in the postsocialist context as well as in other postauthoritarian and postconflict societies that have made the public exposure of hidden crimes and secrets the very condition for "working through" painful collective pasts.

In turn, Esterházy's struggle to make sense of the unwanted inheritance of his father's guilty secrets demonstrates the limits of this fantasy of wholeness: the longing for a past that can be fully known (and thus overcome). *Revised Edition* represents Esterházy's laborious attempt to inherit his father's past as thoroughly and honestly as possible—an interpretive task that extends past analyzing the information in the files to encompass even his own emotional and physical reactions to his father's secrets. But while the facts of his father's actions are known, determining their significance—and thus their legacy—is less clear, whether that be his father's motivations in the past or the judgment his betrayal merits in the present and future. Indeed, rather than enable Esterházy to break free of the socialist past, the process of inheriting enacted through the writing of *Revised Edition* ultimately only highlights the disruptive potential at the heart of any inheritance. As we have seen, the more Esterházy attempts to learn from the files, the more he discovers himself already entangled in their logic: inheritance is both transformed by and transformative of its inheritor. Moreover, this revelation is not only the ground for knowledge, but it also unsettles what he thought he knew, and what indeed may be knowable—for inheritance itself entails loss.

Foremost among the losses of inheritance is the potential loss of the love that Esterházy feels for his father, and throughout the book he struggles with the question of whether he must in fact relinquish it. Beyond Esterházy's personal, filial anguish, what makes this question so important is that in Esterházy's work, the fate of his father has long served as a stand-in for the fate of the Hungarian nation. As Esterházy gives up the fantasy of his father's essential morality and incorruptibility in the face of political turmoil and hardship, he must also contend with what this means for his understanding of how Hungary has lived through and remembered its history. Ultimately, he concludes the book by deciding that coming to terms with his father's actions does not mean that he has to give up loving him.

> We can't forgive my father—we, people: those he betrayed and those he did not—because he didn't admit his actions to us and didn't regret them, didn't mind, that the darker half of his soul was beating him. So you can pity him, you can hate him, and you can ignore him. Spit on him or dismiss him as unimportant: this is the fate of my father.
>
> In addition to the above options (which I also accept), I still love him: the man, whose first-born child I am. (*Revised Edition*, 280)

In refusing the false choice between condemning and loving his father, Esterházy is not suggesting that Hungary embrace its informers or that everyone bears equal guilt for the crimes and betrayals perpetrated under state socialism. Nor is Esterházy absolving his father of his duplicity. Rather, by making peace with his own ambivalence and with the ambivalent figure that has replaced the heroic father of his previous books, Esterházy suggests that his compatriots must also acknowledge the ambivalence of the recent past, and thus relinquish the pervasive logic that divides Hungary's population into "those evil people who sow injustice" and "the poor sufferers" (a dichotomy which he characterizes as a "great, living national self-deception" [*Revised Edition*, 77]). "It's not a matter of 'others,' it's not a separate game of vicious commies and vicious snitches [*szemét téglák*], but it belongs to all of us, even while not all of us were (vicious) commies and snitches" (*Revised Edition*, 122–123).

Esterházy uses these insights not to deny the importance of knowing his father's actions, but to offer another way to understand the inheritance of socialist remains across generations. The logic of nostalgia—symbolized in chapter 3 in the well-loved quote from *The Witness*, "But it's ours!"—suggested that one could break from the past without losing it: a fantasy in which everything changes, but nothing is lost. At the beginning of the second book of *Celestial Harmonies*, Esterházy appears to express a similar desire for painless historical rupture when he declares, "What's the big deal if there's a traitor in the family or not? In the past. The past belongs to us not because it is glorious, but because it is ours" (*Celestial Harmonies*, 52). In *Revised Edition*, Esterházy discards the levity and sense of historical mastery that drove both of these arguments. But he does so without invoking a family romance that would simply condemn his father and reject his father's past actions as simply alien remains. Instead, by continuing to understand this past as both his father's and his own ("ours" rather than "his" or "mine"), Esterházy suggests that the task posed by socialism's remains may entail "communing" with the past (Pepperell 2009, 25), rather than exorcizing it: learning to live with both dreaded loss and unwanted knowledge.

The Task of Inheritance

In this chapter, I have examined how the family romance of the informer scandals enables an understanding of socialism's remains a form of inheritance and thus, as Derrida reminds us, a task for the future (1994, 54). The different approaches to this task offered by Bodó and Esterházy reflect their different generational positions as well as their different degrees of social distance from those whom they perceived to have betrayed them. Nonetheless, in both cases the reception of their work was controversial: if Bodó was attacked as an ungrateful and uncomprehending child who saw everything in black and white, Esterházy's book had a mixed critical reception based on its ambiguous relationship to genre (fiction versus autobiography) and his ambivalent approach to his father, which conservative commentators condemned as excusing moral responsibility for the crimes of the past.[19]

In the years that followed the Szabó scandal and Bodó's critique of his present-day behavior, revelations from the informer files would continue—as would repeated demands that the files be fully opened. Moreover, the fraught idiom of family relations would continue to be one of the key ways that other writers and artists would grapple with the legacies of the past regime's informers.[20] But their continued insights into how the family romance of postsocialism influenced the challenge of socialism's remains would not significantly shift a public discussion of the past already overdetermined by a discourse of victims and perpetrators. Instead, as Hungary neared its third decade of postsocialism, political and economic upheaval would only accelerate demands to expunge the remains of the past from a present in crisis.

A PAST RETURNED,
A FUTURE DEFERRED

In September 2006, four years after my initial fieldwork ended, I returned to Hungary for a brief visit to continue tracking the fates of Hungary's remains of socialism. The MSZP–SZDSZ (Hungarian Socialist Party–Alliance of Free Democrats) coalition that had ousted Fidesz from power in 2002 was reelected that past spring, and I was curious to learn how this coalition government would be commemorating the fiftieth anniversary of 1956 the following month. After the MSZP's controversial attempt to portray its members as Imre Nagy's inheritors during the anniversary commemorations of 1996, the party had withdrawn from engaging in national historical politics, ceding this important symbolic terrain to the right wing. As a result, although public debates over the fate of the communist past continued in the years after the MSZP coalition took office (such as the Szabó controversy earlier in 2006), such battles over Hungary's recent history had become relatively subdued in the political sphere. Now, however, the MSZP was tasked with officially celebrating a historical event that it had been unable to exploit as political capital, and whose memory also risked inspiring unwelcome parallels between the past regime and the MSZP's own status as one of the successors to the communist party.

As I soon discovered, the MSZP's solution was to portray the 1956 revolution as uncontroversially as possible. Rather than use the memory of national resistance to communist oppression to fuel conflict with its political rivals, it instead attempted to represent the revolution as a shared national heritage that would overcome party divisions and the fragmentation of memory that had begun more than a decade before. The new monuments, television spots, and exhibitions that the government initiated or sponsored thus avoided offering a specific narrative of the revolutionary events that might provoke opposition. Instead, many of these sites of memory invited engagement with the past in the form of immersion in its styles and relics, such as open-air exhibits of civilian and military vehicles and weapons, staffed by actors dressed in clothes from that era. For example, my first afternoon back in Budapest, I visited the Petőfi Csarnok, a concert hall and cultural center, in order to attend a city government-funded exhibit dedicated to everyday life during the time of the 1956 revolution. The exhibition presented fenced-off tableaux of the kitchens and living spaces of that era, as well as a gallery of posters providing historical context and information. The majority of the space, however, was devoted to a 1950s-style café, with a band playing jazz standards sung in English. Above the café stood a platform featuring mannequins of Stalin, Rákosi, and (anachronistically) Kádár, smiling beatifically at the visitors beneath a banner praising the "eternal friendship" of the Hungarian and Soviet alliance.[1]

FIGURE 6.1 Exhibition at the Petőfi Csarnok commemorating everyday life during 1956. From left to right, the banners read "Working peasants! With good spring work and excellent results in animal husbandry, forward with accomplishing the Five Year plan, peace, and the better life of our people!" and "Let the most important token of our peace and independence grow stronger and flourish: the eternal friendship of the Hungarian and Soviet people and their unbreakable brotherly alliance." Personal photograph, 2006.

In contrast to the House of Terror's attempt to criminalize everyday life and the informer scandals that had revealed some of what remained unsaid in nostalgic recollection, the exhibition strategy at the Petőfi Csarnok suggested that the recent past could now be entirely defanged. The former polarization between painful memories of state oppression and the depoliticized affection for socialist-era domesticity appeared to vanish, as the divisive emotions once summoned by the memory of the past were reduced to a shared appreciation of form and style. As I wandered through the poster gallery, contrasting the exhibit's representational strategies to those found in the House of Terror, I began to wonder if my own research interest in remains was itself another relic of an anachronistic temporality—a now outdated era in Hungary's decade and a half of postsocialism.

I returned to my hotel room that night and turned on the television news. The main story announced the leak of an audio recording of a private speech given by the MSZP prime minister Ferenc Gyurcsány (who had replaced Péter Medgyessy after a party reorganization in 2004), shortly after his party had won a second term in office in spring 2006. Speaking to a party conference that past May, in a talk littered with obscenities and self-recrimination, Gyurcsány attempted to convince a reluctant party faction of the necessity of undertaking painful and unpopular economic reforms. Declaring that his government had lied to the country about its ailing economic situation for the past "one and a half to two years" in order to be elected, and that it had accomplished nothing during its previous term, Gyurcsány called on party members to put aside their own political interests and take action to "change this fucking country [*kurva ország*], because otherwise who else will?" (Gyurcsány 2006). His remarks were secretly recorded, and now, several months later on September 17, they were anonymously released and publicized on Hungarian radio.

Although some interpreted Gyurcsány's speech as a passionate call for reform, many others condemned it as the expression of a cynical and power-hungry politician. By the next evening, peaceful demonstrations and calls for Gyurcsány's resignation had already turned into violent protests outside Parliament that would last for several days, with protestors breaking into the Hungarian public television (*Magyar Televízió*) building and setting cars on fire. These demonstrations would revive a month later on October 23, to mark the fiftieth anniversary of the beginning of the 1956 revolution. They again erupted in vandalism, retaliatory police violence, and—in an unexpectedly literal evocation of 1956—the theft of a tank from an open-air exhibition. (The man drove it 150 meters through the crowd toward the lines of riot police before he stopped the tank and was arrested [Plankó 2011]).

For some, these protests represented an honorable revival of national revolt against Soviet rule. Others viewed the protestors as a drunken mob of soccer hooligans manipulated by the right wing. There was much debate concerning who was responsible for releasing the recording; when Fidesz became aware of the tape and how it had prepared for its revelation; to what extent Fidesz had orchestrated the protests; and the scope and severity of the retaliatory police violence.[2] What nonetheless united these diverging perspectives was the sudden reanimation of socialism's remains, whether that took the form of a past that refused to stay past—the communists who never left power—or the perceived inability of Hungary's political transformation to have produced both democratic governance and a peaceful democratic citizenry. Regardless of which interpretation they embraced, many people I spoke with would view these demonstrations as evidence of the failures of transition: whether they placed the blame on Gyurcsány and his government, the demonstrators, Fidesz, or the previously marginal extreme-right radical nationalist party (Jobbik) that emerged in the aftermath of these demonstrations to become an important—and, in the eyes of many, dangerous—political force in Hungary.

The revelations from the state security files had generated public debate that warned that the work of breaking from the socialist past was still incomplete. These scandals revealed the socialist remains lurking at the heart of the national family and inspired the fear that without their exposure, the younger generation would be condemned to unwittingly reproduce the secrecy and lies of their elders. With the 2006 political events and the later experience of the global financial crisis in 2008, which hit Hungary with disproportionate force, the very success of transition was increasingly thrown into question. Complaints about the ways in which remains of socialism polluted both politics and everyday life—from corruption among political and economic elites to incivility and mistrust in daily interactions—now took on new vehemence and urgency. As Hungary neared the twentieth anniversary of the demise of state socialism, the memory of 1989 would not inspire celebration. Instead, the persistence of socialism's remains became evidence of transition's failure to enter the promised future.

"Communism Never Ended"

The MSZP's victory in the spring 2006 elections had been the first reelection of an incumbent political party in Hungary since 1990. It thus represented the first active endorsement of the MSZP's reinvention as a democratic socialist party, whose pursuit of neoliberal policies made it both ideologically and practically opposed to communist principles.[3] But in September, the revelation of Gyurcsány's private acknowledgment of lies and manipulation now suggested alarming continuities with the past regime. For the protestors and their supporters, Gyurcsány's refusal to step down or allow new elections to be called only seemed to reinforce the perception that what was at stake was not merely popular will versus autocracy—the breaking of the democratic political contract between an elected government and its citizens—but the traumatic return of communist rule.[4] The MSZP's victory in 2002 and reelection in 2006 now threatened the achievements of Hungary's postsocialist transformations—or worse, suggest that these changes had never succeeded in the first place. In this right-wing perspective, 1989 and 1990 no longer represented the end of socialism, but merely a new era in which former communist oppressors now pretended to be democratic. Even some of those who deplored the protests nonetheless argued that the problem with the system change (rendszerváltás) in 1990 was that it did not also change the system's elites (elitváltás). "Some say that the entire thing was planned and orchestrated to just pass on state wealth to the nomenklatura," Ágnes the schoolteacher from chapter 5 told me. "This isn't true, of course—but I can understand why they see it that way."

What made this perception of trauma distinct from earlier claims to victimhood was that outrage about the traumatic repetition of "communist lies" now inspired the possibility of reparative mastery. For some, the demonstrations offered the opportunity to reenact the end of socialism in 1989 and 1990, now with all the popular fervor and participation absent from the political transformation. At the time of the system change, most Hungarians had taken pride in their peaceful and bureaucratic political transformation, which represented a welcome divergence from the upheavals of Hungary's twentieth-century history. Over the years, however, the negotiated nature of the transition became one of the main complaints of those on the right, who argued that it had failed to eradicate communists from political life. Now 1989 represented a missed revolution: the failure to truly end the previous system. And 2006 offered the opportunity to rectify it; as one protestor told me, "We waited sixteen years for this!"

To repair the "missed revolution" of 1989, protestors returned to the memory of 1956 that had been so central to its symbolic politics. The historical slogans and iconography that had been reduced to retro style at the Petőfi Csarnok exhibition now became models for political action, and the revolution's key figures were no longer the martyred prime minister and his associates, but the Budapest street fighters. Protestors thus re-enacted key scenes and tropes of the 1956 revolution, including taking over the national television station building in order to deliberately evoke the 1956 demonstrators' attempt to broadcast their demands at the Hungarian Radio (Magyar Rádió).[5] In so doing, their actions declared war on the memory work of the previous decade, arguing that if the transition had failed to eliminate remains of socialism and thus lay the foundation for a successful future, it had equally failed to honor and fulfill the promises of Hungary's revolutionary history.

Such attempts to claim the legacy of 1956 did not necessarily reflect a growing consensus on the meaning of the revolution and its implications for the future, and nor did the protestors' attempts to write themselves into history as the revolution's inheritors go unchallenged. Most people I spoke with readily identified the ways that the protestors were self-consciously attempting to evoke the memory of 1956, although few considered these historical parallels to be legitimate. But others did not possess the historical vocabulary to recognize these references; for example, one teenager who supported the demonstrators and described his political sympathies as being on the far right displayed the growing lack of knowledge of 1956 discussed in chapter 2 when he argued to me that the choice of the centrally located Hungarian Television building was merely coincidental. "It could have been *RTL Klub* [a German-owned commercial television station]," he told me, "but it's too far from the city center." (He then produced a map to show me the location of both buildings.)

Moreover, because the significance of the events of 1956 was freely acknowledged but—as we saw in chapter 2—its historical interpretation was highly contested, its memory could be deployed simultaneously for a number of practically and ideologically inconsistent ends. After all, even the speech of Gyurcsány that sparked this protest invoked the memory of 1956. His admission that "we lied morning, night, and evening [*hazudtunk reggel, éjjel, meg este*]" (Gyurcsány 2006), echoed words commonly attributed to the writer István Örkény in a state broadcast on October 31, 1956: "We lied in the night, we lied in the day, we lied on every wavelength! [*Hazudtunk éjjel, hazudtunk nappal, hazudtunk minden hullámhosszon*]" (*Népszabadság* 2007). The potency of 1956 thus remained in Hungarian public culture, but primarily as a stockpile of decontextualized events and symbols, in which references to the revolution functioned as signs of a generalized temporal depth, historical precedent, and present-day outrage—rather than specific narratives or political content.

The memory of 1956—once expected to represent the shared foundation of a new postsocialist national identity and then fragmented by party politics—thus refused to become a finished past. And in the case of the sixty-five-year-old protestor who briefly commandeered an old tank that had been part of an open-air exhibit on the 1956 revolution, even the very periodization of past, present, and future was thrown into question. On the one hand, the protestor subverted the tank as an important motif in 1956 iconography, in which it functions as a symbol not of popular rebellion but of Soviet oppression (or—when depicted with a Hungarian coat of arms—a symbol of when the army changed sides to support the protestors). But on the other hand, what made this tank an effective political tool for this protestor and those who helped and cheered him on was his refusal to treat the tank solely in symbolic terms: an anachronistic historical relic to be either abandoned or recontextualized in terms of its potential educational, historical, and museological value. Instead, by returning the tank to its original function as a weapon, he used this museum object precisely as its producers intended, and in a way none of its current owners could have anticipated. Although the protester himself explained his actions as being "caught by the winds of nostalgia" (*Index* 2006b), ironically his actions thus appropriated the history the tank was intended to symbolize in a far more literal way.[6]

But such attempts to transform remains of the socialist past into tools of a revolutionary present could only go so far. As I discuss below, most people did not view the demonstrations as a revival of revolution, but rather as a crisis of political and urban civility. As Seleny notes, although actions such as the attack on the post–World War II Soviet liberation memorial—in which protestors removed the memorial's Soviet insignia and threw it into the Danube—may have reminded some of the similar removal of the Soviet coat of arms from the memorial in 1956, for others, it stirred up memories of the fascist Arrow Cross party's execution of Jews along the Danube river bank in 1944 and 1945 (2014, 48–49). Even for those who participated in the demonstrations, it may have been "1956 for ten minutes," as the protestor who took over the tank recalled (Plankó 2011), but he then turned off the ignition and exited the vehicle.

In years to come, the right wing would remember 2006 not as a revival of the 1956 revolution, but in terms of the excessive police violence that had ensued in response to these protests: the victimization of the contemporary right wing by the violent agents of an illegitimate regime. Ultimately, the events of fall 2006 would fuel the rise of the right wing (including both Fidesz and the extreme-right Jobbik party) and the fragmentation and decline of the left.[7] Fidesz would later return to power in 2010, winning the elections with a super-majority that Orbán called a "revolution in the polling booth" that claimed to finally accomplish the work of transition.

Trauma and the Problem of Transition

Given this political context, it would be easy to dismiss complaints about traumatic repetition in 2006 as mere right-wing political rhetoric, in which the claim of "communist return" was used to demonize the MSZP for quintessentially postsocialist offenses: not only lies to win an election, but corrupt privatization, economic mismanagement, the failure of lustration, and the lack of democratic transparency, among others. And indeed, critics of this logic (whether supporters of the

MSZP or merely those who decried the polarization of present-day political discourse) argued that the rhetoric of anticommunism was merely a crude political weapon that prevented insight into the contemporary political and economic problems Hungary faced.

But laments about traumatic repetition were not limited to the right wing's attempt to label its political opponents as communist criminals. Instead, they were symptomatic of a temporal logic shared by my interlocutors across the political spectrum in response to the 2006 events and the experience of the global financial crisis that followed in 2008. I thus want to take the perception of traumatic repetition seriously, because regardless of its truth value, its claims about the temporalities of the present day help us further understand what was at stake for socialism's remains at the time of these various crises.

Trauma, in its psychoanalytic formulation, is fundamentally a problem of temporality: it is the outcome of an event so sudden, unexpected, and overwhelming that it exceeds the subject's capacity for comprehension. It thus represents a challenge to both knowledge and self-consistency; trauma is what has been experienced but cannot (yet) be known. This inability to be fully present to the event produces traumatic repetition, in which the subject repeats past experience in an attempt at reparative mastery that ultimately only reenacts the past wound. For this reason, trauma is a temporality of belatedness, in which the event can never be known in its originary state, but only in its repetition. This repetition thus does not represent the return of the past as *past*, but rather functions as an attempt to master and integrate a past event that is experienced as an endless *present*. As such, the structure of trauma forecloses the possibility of true futurity, by projecting the future as merely the perpetual reiteration of a present that, in turn, only repeats the past.[8]

Following this logic, we could argue that the rhetoric of anticommunism was not about the return of the past, but rather about insisting that the past had never ended in the first place, in order to inspire renewed attempts to eliminate socialism's remains. I want to take my analysis in a different direction, however, by focusing upon the ways that such complaints about traumatic repetition were as much about the experience of "transition" as they were about Hungary's four decades of state socialism—and thus as much about the future as the past.[9]

Of course, in the early 1990s, most Hungarians did not view the end of communism as traumatic. In both everyday life and political rhetoric, the change of system instead represented the *end* to a trauma narrated variously in terms of Soviet occupation, lack of political freedoms, and a lower standard of living than that found in the West. But the experience of later disappointment—the notion of transition as a promise that was never realized—retrospectively renarrated the end of state socialism as traumatic in a structural sense, as an event that constantly intrudes into the present-day, demanding to understand and interpret why this promise of the future went unfulfilled. This rhetoric of traumatic repetition mourned the now-failed future of the past, as well as the hopes of a present whose capacity to move forward was now experienced as continually deferred. As we have seen, some responded to this perception of traumatic return by attempting to re-enact and master the originary break. The protestors' invocation of 1956 thus represented an attempt not only to justify their actions through reference to an honored past, but to repair the "missed revolution" of 1989 that had similarly drawn on the memory of 1956 for legitimacy in order to make a new future possible. But for others, the very fact of the violent protests themselves was a sign of transition's failure. A colleague who was a university student in 2006 later told me that she remembered feeling empty and "frozen" as she watched the protests on television. For her, the future appeared threateningly devoid of possibility. "I couldn't see how we could continue on from this. I couldn't see the future."

As a result, people I interviewed during the 2006 political crisis (and later, during the 2008–2009 economic crisis) would express the discourse of remains in two distinct but mutually reinforcing ways. On the one hand, remains took the form of the presence of an unwanted past that was painfully evident in politics, the economy, and everyday experiences of frustration, disappointment, and corruption. On the other hand, what made these experiences difficult to bear was the disjuncture between the present day and the past's lost fantasy of what the present was supposed to look like. That is, the disappointments of the present meant that the past's dreams of the future were also becoming obsolete remains.

I now want to investigate in more detail the key idioms through which the people I spoke with mourned these lost futures and their frustrated expectations of a better life: laments for a "normal" existence that they felt they should already enjoy and anxieties concerning the "crises" that prevented these dreams of normality from coming to fruition.

Normality and the Remains of a Lost Future

Despite the worldwide media attention on the protests and the revival of a revolutionary history that insisted that democracy was yet to be attained in Hungary, during the two weeks I spent there in September 2006, Budapest did not feel like a city under siege. With its sense of eventfulness mediated through spectacles staged by the protestors for newspapers and television reports, the space of the city itself often felt benign, with locals strolling in the end-of-summer evenings or seated in outdoor restaurants only a block or two away from the demonstrations at Parliament. Many visited the protests with their cell phones and cameras ready, viewing their own participation as a form of tourism rather than political dissent. (In turn, food stands and tables selling souvenirs and nationalist memorabilia soon appeared outside Parliament.)

Although some of my interlocutors were able to shrug off both the scandal and the protests, for many others the seemingly casual acceptance of political dishonesty and urban unrest only deepened the general sense of alarm. They condemned Gyurcsány's speech and the protests themselves as well as the failure of transition these phenomena seemed to represent: the failure of both Hungary's institutions and its individuals to reinvent themselves as moral democratic subjects. This "ethical crisis" (erkölcsi válság) of the government and its citizens made visible the loss of a democratic urban civility that perhaps had never been fully attained in the first place. "Of course they're setting things on fire," an architect then in her early forties complained to me. "This is a city where people buy expensive dogs and expensive pet food, but no one cleans up after their dog on the streets. People are selfish—there's no civic pride."

Miklós, the early member of Fidesz who now owned his own business, agreed with this assessment. He went on to argue that the public's indifference to its own collective well-being, as materialized in the space of the city, was ultimately the fault of a political elite who lacked morality and did not even have the savvy that politicians possess in the West. "Sure, all politicians lie," he complained, "but they aren't stupid enough to be caught." Even the state of the water cannons on the riot vehicles was evidence that Hungary was becoming "a third-world country," he argued, noting that the vehicles did not look as if they had ever been serviced since the peaceful demonstrations held during the political transformations sixteen years earlier. One of the water cannons was so weak that it produced more like a gentle spray, he told me, and the other broke down so that the police abandoned it, and the demonstrators had to help the operator inside leave the vehicle before they could then set it on fire. "It's embarrassing," Miklós concluded. "Such things don't happen in normal countries!"

This lament—"it's not normal!" (normális)—echoed throughout the days of the demonstrations, whether aimed at the venality of Gyurcsány's government, the crudity of the protestors, the inadequacy of infrastructure, the violence of the police response, or, more broadly, the perceived failure of Hungary's postsocialist transformation itself, fifty years after 1956 and sixteen years after the democratic elections that were supposed to sweep the communists from power. More was at stake in these complaints about dirty streets and broken-down equipment than simply the lack of bourgeois respectability. Complaints about the failure of "normal life" brought the mass-mediated political crisis into everyday interactions and experience through a preestablished idiom of complaint. Like Ádám's argument with his mother about the purpose of the string bag under socialism, such complaints represented the private life of public feeling, which Kathleen Stewart has described as "ordinary affects": "feelings that begin and end in broad circulation, but they're also the stuff that [seemingly] intimate lives are made of" (2007, 13).

There is a rich literature on the "normal" as the standard by which citizens across former state socialist societies have evaluated the experience of both late socialism and postsocialism.[10] Krisztina Fehérváry, whose analysis of the discourse of the "normal" in 1990s Hungary shapes my discussion here (2002, 2013), observes that this Western loanword shares the English connotations of health (the absence of disease) and typicality (the ways things usually are). But the meaning of "normal" in socialist and postsocialist societies goes beyond the traditional sense of the term to extend to connotations of humaneness, respectability, and livability that are primarily measured not vis-à-vis individual behavior but general living standards (Fehérváry 2013, 40–42).

This understanding of normality is a legacy of state socialism, whose desire to remake not only society but human nature itself was broadly perceived as unnatural and abnormal, and whose living standards were experienced as inferior in relation to the capitalist West (Fehérváry 2013, 40). Fantasies of a "normal" life determined by the perceived living and consumption standards of the West thus informed socialist citizens' critiques of the regime, by replacing the workers' utopia of socialist ideology with the values of a bourgeois middle-class existence (42). Yet despite the often oppositional nature of such fantasies and aspirations, they were themselves inculcated as part of state socialism's modernizing project of creating socialist laborers and consumers (Fehérváry 2002, 385, 2013; see also Bren 2010 and Rausing 2002).

As we have seen, Hungarians welcomed the political transformation in 1989 and 1990 as the chance to finally enter the world of Western normality defined as a certain standard of living and entitlements: professional mobility, access to Western goods, comfortable and humane living spaces, and the ability to travel abroad, among many other aspects. By the mid-2000s, however, the disappointments of postsocialism would shift the rhetorical use of the "normal" from imagining possible futures back to critiquing the failures of present-day Hungary to meet standards idealized as everyday practice elsewhere. Of course, what actually constituted a "normal" standard of living changed in different contexts; as Marysia Galbraith (2003, 2) notes, the term functions as a shifter. For some of the pensioners I spoke with after the 2006 austerity budget cuts, the lack of normality in their lives was visible in the fact that they were challenged to find enough money to pay for food and heating bills. On the other hand, for some middle-class professionals, the lack of the normal meant having to cut down visits to the psychotherapist from twice a week to once.

But what both these understandings of abnormality shared was the self-reflexive perception of not living in a "normal" place where things can be taken for granted as safe, secure, trustworthy, and predictable. In both cases, individuals felt entitled to more than they were getting: in their eyes, their demands were unexceptional and the abnormality of their situation stemmed from the difficulty of attaining what were truly humble goals (Fehérváry 2013, 27). In the words of Ferenc, an urban planning student in his late twenties in 2006, attaining "normality" would mean that he did not have to always be fighting just for the basics of life (regardless of how these basics are defined), but that he would have time to engage with "things of higher [personal] value" as well. "To be honest," he told me, "I don't really feel like there's a possibility of a normal life here."

The concept of the normal might seem merely to substitute for the utopian impulses that have otherwise been thoroughly discredited by the experience of communism. Yet the difference is that now to desire a better life for oneself was not phrased as a beautiful collective dream that only radical social, political, and/ or economic transformation could accomplish. Rather, my interlocutors viewed this better life as a preexisting individual entitlement to something experienced as customary elsewhere, but difficult to attain in the "abnormal" circumstances of present-day Hungary. Indeed, what made the use of term "normal" so powerful in describing these expectations was the way it simultaneously referenced what was "typical" and what "should be" (in the words of Janine Wedel, who first noticed the discourse of the normal in socialist Poland [1986, 151]). By enabling its users to narrate their material desires as entitlements that ought to be taken for granted, it allowed them to reframe what would otherwise be considered conspicuous consumption as merely "average" in the West (Fehérváry 2002, 370). My interlocutors thus blamed their inability to achieve a normal life on the failures of transition, rather than question the nature of this aspiration itself. (At the same time, however, some also renarrated the experience of socialism as more safely predictable than the current moment: as the elderly pop star Uhrin Benedek complained to me in the early 2000s, "The problem with the system change [rendszerváltás] is that now there isn't even a system [nincs is rendszer].")[11] This accounts for why I sometimes found it difficult to balance my explanations of social and economic inequalities in the United States with what my friends and colleagues assumed typical experiences to be, because my counterexamples were explained as simple divergence from a commonly experienced norm.

But the term "normal" speaks not only to material aspiration and entitlement. "Normality" in the postsocialist context also contains a disciplinary component that subjects citizens to regimes of normalization that are broadly experienced as moral and rational (Greenberg 2011). That is, the desire for normality also reflects the longing for a specific relationship between the state and its citizens defined in terms of values and ethical structure. The lack of normality became a way to mourn not only postsocialism's standard of living, but also the new national subjectivity the political transformation was supposed to produce. It explained the perceived inability of Hungarians to attain the individual and institutional transformations in morality, transparency, and public civility that they had anticipated after the end of communism.

Several days after the demonstrations began, I left Budapest to visit my friend Vera and her family in a village to which I had traveled for research since 1999. The quiet village, with its historic church just steps away from the town center's few small shops, initially appeared to me unchanged save the flag of the European Union that now waved alongside the Hungarian tricolor from municipal buildings. But as Vera explained, both the economy and the population of the village were beginning to transform. A new inn had opened to encourage village tourism, and, with the local youth continuing to leave in order to seek employment in Budapest and abroad, the village's aging population was being supplemented by Western European retirees, who had started to buy up property to take advantage of the village's sleepy beauty and relative proximity to both Budapest and another regional city.

Later, we sat around the kitchen table with the county newspaper, comparing its account of the demonstrations to my experience of the events and the stories Vera and her husband Iván had gathered from friends, family, and the media over the past days. Like those I had spoken with in Budapest, Vera was suspicious of the protestors' attempts to link themselves to the revolutionaries of 1956. For her, as for many others, what had made the political transformation in 1989 and 1990 so radical was not the experience of popular revolution, but rather its absence: the peaceful, negotiated handover of power. In her eyes, the protests not only violated norms of urban civility, but they were also an affront to the very idea of democracy. They represented merely an outbreak of football hooligans and neo-Nazis using Gyurcsány's exposure as a pretext for mayhem. "It's terrible that such things are happening," Vera declared. "It's not normal."

But what was normal, I asked? "In everyday life or politics?" Vera asked. "In everyday life, it means being able to work and have enough money to eat, to live, and to rest as well—to go on vacation two weeks every year and go somewhere, even if only within Hungary!" Normality in politics, she continued, meant being honest. "It means speaking so even a street sweeper might understand," her husband Iván chimed in.[12]

I was struck by this definition that linked political honesty and clarity to quality of life on the individual level. What seemed to be at stake was not merely good governance—the idea that material security is the self-evident result of a transparent and well-functioning government. But rather such political honesty and communicational clarity was the enabling factor for normal lives (Fehérváry 2013, 42)—lives as moral subjects in which there is work and this work is compensated adequately, where one pays taxes and in return one gets public services, in which the chance to go on vacation and rest is not merely an individual entitlement, but, as under Kádárism, this entitlement is the very evidence of a social contract that works. What connected these two themes of material comfort and political transparency was the notion that dishonesty itself was a form of property theft. As one placard at Parliament insisted. "Whoever lies, steals as well [*Aki hazudik, az lop is*]. To lie and cheat is an MSZP/SZDSZ [the ruling coalition] thing." As I traveled back to my apartment from the train station a day later, a taxi driver similarly told me that only in dictatorships do politicians remain in power when people do not want them. "It's as if you took money from a neighbor, but then didn't give it back and acted as if nothing was wrong." "After 2006, people lost faith in politicians," Ágnes later recalled in 2008. "If the prime minister starts lying, everyone can. It degrades life here."

Moreover, as many people expressed to me, living in an environment of dishonesty only encourages everyday lies, immorality, and corruption. "It's so hard getting people to pay their bills," Miklós told me. "There's no sense of personal responsibility here—none at all." In his eyes, the irrationality of the current system—exemplified in a convoluted tax code that he argued discouraged entrepreneurship or business expansion—made criminals out of honest Hungarians. "Sure, there are other places with high tax rates," he argued, "but you get something for it. Here, we pay high taxes, but we don't see any of it. It just goes into the pockets of politicians and the people who don't want to work at all." Another friend later pointed to a piece of graffiti on a street near his apartment that read "Never work!" (*Sose dolgozz!*) and I suspected he had chosen our route deliberately to illustrate his argument. "See?" he said. "We work just to support all the people who are lazy."

Many of my interlocutors thus experienced the pain of not being "normal" in terms of both everyday material insecurity and the perceived impossibility of being good subjects within an ethical disciplinary regime (Fehérváry 2013, 231; Greenberg 2011, 95). That is, not only did they worry about not measuring up to established norms, but also they were concerned that there may no longer even be agreed-upon ethical norms to measure up to. Attempts to act normally in an abnormal state could prove catastrophic; as several interviewees insisted, if anyone actually tried to follow the tax laws, they would go out of business the next day. This dilemma complicated the question of personal responsibility and agency: the idea that being a citizen requires a sense of public citizenship. Instead, as Violetta

Zentai argues in her study of "winners" and "losers" in the early years of post-socialism, "civic virtues" risked becoming conflated with "civic vices" (1999, 19): if cheating is what you have to do to get by, then choosing not to cheat or lie is to put yourself and your family in danger. Moreover, as the complaints above make clear, the frustration produced by navigating such quandaries not only alienated individuals from regimes of power but also threatened the very possibility of sociality. The anger, mistrust, and disillusionment with which people regarded the state could thus also easily extend to each other.[13]

Crisis and the Loss of the West

In 2009, I met Miklós again at a fashionable restaurant near Andrássy Avenue, the elegant boulevard that also includes the controversial House of Terror. The previous fall, the global financial crisis had disproportionately jeopardized Hungary's economic solvency and political stability, due to structural problems that included the country's heavy reliance on foreign debt, overburdened pension system, and the corruption and ineffective policies of the MSZP. Gyurcsány was forced to step down in March 2009 and was replaced in his party by a young economist-technocrat, Gordon Bajnai. Only with the help of the International Monetary Fund (the first-ever such bailout of a European Union country) and Bajnai's unpopular austerity measures was Hungary's economy able to recover from the brink of bankruptcy. But although Bajnai was able to improve confidence in Hungary's economic stability internationally, his government was unable to win back domestic credibility: even in the eyes of many long-term supporters, Hungary's political left was corrupt and inept.[14]

Miklós barely sat down before he began a litany of grievances about the abnormality of life in contemporary Budapest. He pointed to the "dog shit" on the sidewalk, called my attention to a nearby inexpensive Chinese restaurant (büfé) (which he felt brought down the tone of its surroundings), and noted the number of homeless people he saw each morning as he walked to his office a few blocks away. He contrasted these observations with what he considered to be everyday and "normal" in North America and Western Europe, whether that was political civility, care for the economically marginalized, or bourgeois standards of living and consumption in the cities' most expensive districts.

When I pointed out to Miklós that in New York City (to which he had traveled many times), there is a lot of dog shit on the sidewalks as well, he agreed with me but rejected the broader comparison. "Yes," he said, "but in New York there is quality: the best of everything. The best and the worst—that makes it worthwhile." He paused for a moment to reflect. "You know, it's funny, I was in Sicily last summer and I was surprised that all the dirt and chaos didn't bother me. Then I realized it was because Sicily was an honest mess. It didn't pretend to be anything it wasn't. But Budapest acts as if it's normal, but it isn't."

By now, these complaints about Hungary's hypocrisy and lack of normality were familiar to me as both descriptive complaints and ritual cultural performances (Ries 1997) that sought to convince the listener that life was not as it should be. But at a time when the notion of living in a global financial "crisis" (*válság*) was entering both local and international circulation, such complaints about the "dishonest mess" of postsocialism were becoming increasingly urgent. Media reports and everyday conversation represented Hungary's economic crisis as pathological and exceptional—as indeed, all crises are. A claim to crisis is a claim to a situation outside the normal order of things: a state of disruption that demands some form of resolution. But at the same time, many of my interlocutors in Hungary also greeted the experience of the country's financial crisis as confirmation of the preexisting laments of returned communists and shattered futures that already permeated public life and everyday discourse. These established idioms of complaint enabled the people I spoke with to interpret the unexpected experience of global economic instability in ways that identified the specifically national dimensions of the crisis—as something wrong with Hungary and its experience of transition itself.

As Véra's husband Iván told me later that week, "We Hungarians, we know how to make good out of bad. But better out of good we can't do. Instead we just degenerate back down into bad." His son Ádám, now working in information technology, similarly insisted that the financial crisis in Hungary was "95 percent" due to local causes, and only "5 percent" due to the global crisis. After all, he pointed out, none of Hungary's neighbors had sunk as low economically as Hungary had, and even though in the early years of postsocialism Hungary had been expected to triumphantly lead the region in economic development, now "even Slovakia" had gone to the euro before Hungary.

This perception of the national exceptionality that made crisis possible—as well the failure to remain ahead of one's neighbors and attain the anticipated future—was perhaps best summed up in a widely quoted Gallup survey conducted in early 2009. It revealed that among 120 polled countries, only the residents of Zimbabwe, which had recently experienced violent upheaval in the aftermath of its 2008 elections, viewed their present status and future possibility more negatively. Hungary occupied the second-to-last spot, alongside Haiti and Burundi (Gallup 2009). This bleak result reflected Hungary's current experience of economic instability, which included rising unemployment, deepening social disparities, and a decline in quality of life due to the need to reduce expenses. It also indicated fearful anxieties about the future, whether they concerned the difficulty of saving money to defend against further setbacks or the alarming warnings in the media that that Hungary might "become the next Iceland" (which had experienced a massive financial crisis after the collapse of its three main banks in 2008).

But without dismissing these ways the economic impact of the crisis was experienced in both everyday life and structures of expectation, the hyperbole of this poll result also suggests the need to take seriously the work performed by the concept of "crisis" as a specific interpretive frame. Like claims to historical victimhood and martyrdom, the insistence on the particularly lamentable status of Hungary also represented a declaration of uniqueness. The many people who told me that the 2006 protests made them "ashamed to be Hungarian" or emphasized the ways that the current crisis represented a specifically national ignominy thus offered the flip side of the ironic pride to be found in the celebration of socialist nostalgia as a prosaic form of cultural heritage. And the fetish of statistics—evident in the great amount of media coverage the Gallup poll received—made visible both the external expectation that things should be better and the internal shame about not measuring up, in which national exceptionality could only be assessed in negative terms.

Moreover, the disinclination to interpret the experience of crisis as the failure of the global system Hungary had sought for so long to enter (or, perhaps, even more threateningly, as evidence of the effective functioning of a system that is structured by cycles of boom and bust) did not only represent a condemnation of Hungary's current political and economic elites. Rather, by shifting responsibility for global problems to national actors, complaints of crisis also offered an implicit critique of the facelessness of the global economy itself (in which, as Katherine Verdery observes, "the visible hand of the state [was] replaced by the invisible hand of the market" [1996, 219])—as well as the hope that a solution to its challenges might be found in local hands.

Crucially, however, these complaints of crisis and the longing for an idealized standard of "normal" life elsewhere did not necessarily reproduce existing hierarchies between "West" and "East." Initially, I wondered during these conversations what drove my interlocutors to reinforce so vehemently their inferior position within global regimes of cultural value—particularly at a moment when "crisis" rather than normality was beginning to define a new epoch in neoliberalism in the West as well.[15] Was it only my own presence as a mixed-race researcher from the United States that encouraged such self-presentation? (As one friend commented, using scare quotes and heavy irony, "Of course they would say all this to you, Maya: you're from the '*civilized world*.'")[16] But I soon realized that they used such complaints not merely to contrast the "dishonest mess" of Hungary with the normality experienced elsewhere, but to express disillusionment with their own past expectations about what the future of transition would bring.

In other words, it was the remains of the lost future of postsocialism, and not the present-day reality of Hungary's Western neighbors, that such references to the "normal" ultimately mourned. (Indeed, as Anna Seleny observes, it was Hungary's entrance into the European Union and the middle class's ability to participate in some of "the very trends that had raised Hungarians' standard of living . . . [such as] mortgages denominated in Swiss francs or other foreign currencies" that had now thrown the lives of some of my interlocutors into financial uncertainty [2014, 55].)

Friends and colleagues now mocked as naive their hopes of the early years of postsocialism, in which entrance into a European future of prosperity seemed not only assured, but imminent. These critiques went beyond the disenchantment with Western consumerism that had earlier fueled practices of socialist nostalgia. For example, Szonja, whom we met in chapter 2, recalled not only the fantasy of quickly attaining a Western standard of living and consumption, but also the assumption that she would retain the security and predictability of state socialism. Szonja had attended university during the final years of the regime with the assumption that she would find an academic position and "have a job for the rest of my life." She remembered visiting family in Canada in 1989, and being shocked to learn that "people could lose their houses" if they became ill. "It was a very strange feeling: okay, Canada is nice, but somehow it's not safe here. My cousin's husband was unemployed and it caused all kinds of problems. I felt there was no safety net."

Szonja smiled wryly across the desk from me in her office. Her academic career never materialized, but she told me that she enjoyed her current job in higher education administration. Nonetheless, she noted how hard it was to support two daughters as a single mother who paid 80 percent of her salary just to cover her mortgage and utilities. "Now, of course, looking back and comparing what is here in Hungary currently, Canada has a safety net. We're the ones who don't have it anymore." But Szonja's disenchantment with both late 1980s Canada and 2009 Hungary did not mean that she had any desire to return to the state socialist past. Rather, she had bittersweet memories of a moment of optimism that better alternatives could be found. "We thought that of course there would be difficulties," she told me, "but everything would work out."

As Hungary neared the twentieth anniversary of its democratic transformation, the desire for normality in the face of political and economic crises thus no longer necessarily indexed future expectation. Instead, it marked the space of loss, in which even the fulfillment of long-held hopes, such as Hungary's entrance into the European Union in 2004, was the source of new disenchantments. Over the years, polls have consistently shown that popular support for EU membership is high in Hungary (Medvegy 2019), but the experience of the EU's various political, economic, and administrative demands has helped to highlight that "normality" is not merely an internal aspiration but also an external demand to "be like the West!" (Krastev and Holmes 2018, 117). In this context, "Europe" represents not only the ambition for a better life but also the experience of being subject to what are often experienced as unjust and irrational regimes of normativity: impossible standards that demand dishonesty and thus prohibit the possibility of ethical action.[17]

More generally, then, perhaps the real challenge of the normal at Hungary's times of crisis was the anxiety that there may no longer be a normal to aspire to. The "normal" now no longer represented a model for future action: a stage to be reached in a triumphant linear transition from state socialism in which starting off ahead of its neighbors meant that Hungary would always outpace them. Rather, like the desire to banish socialism's remains, mourning the lost dream of "normal" life emblematized the temporal anxieties of transition: the fear of moving backward, the fear of not keeping up, and the fear that the longed-for future would never be realized.

Such concerns would help the right-wing Fidesz coalition to return to power in 2010. By declaring that its victory represented the success of a transition that should have happened twenty years earlier, the party would thus claim to have enabled the project of pursuing normality to begin anew. But, as I discuss further in the conclusion to this book, in so doing Fidesz reversed the Western hierarchy that constructed Hungary and its former Soviet bloc neighbors as "backward": always in the process of trying to imitate and catch up to the West rather than being accepted as coeval. Instead, Fidesz would argue that its increasingly illiberal policies represented the normative model to which all of Europe should aspire.

The End of Socialist Nostalgia

Since 2008, proclamations of crisis—whether economic, climactic, political, or social—have dominated public discourse across the globe.[18] "Crisis" offers both a description and a diagnosis; it makes visible the experience of economic and political instability as well as the increasing skepticism about the neoliberal order that produced this precariousness. Moreover, it renarrates these experiences of disempowerment and disappointment—whether spectacular or everyday— as pathological and exceptional. (After all, the term "crisis" originates as a medical term for a turning point that results in either life or death [Shevchenko 2009, 3].)[19] By casting the stakes of the present situation in such stark terms, declarations of crisis offer the opportunity to argue for the necessity—and indeed the imperative—of change.

Rather than treat "crisis" as only a self-evident term of description, I have been interested in what enabled "crisis" and the lack of "normality" as cultural rhetorics in Hungary—and what, in turn, these rhetorics enabled, given the way many people I spoke with experienced the events of 2006 and 2008 as confirmation of an ongoing crisis in Hungary's transition from socialism. In so doing, I do not mean to deny the specificity and historicity of the ways my interlocutors experienced these crises. Nor do I want to explain away the rhetoric of crisis as merely the product of local politics or global mass media, or—on the other hand—merely the repetition of Hungary's long-standing discourses of martyrdom, pessimism, and persecution, in which the present is always worse than everything that came before. Rather, what characterized the experiences of political and economic crisis in Hungary two decades after the end of state socialism was the perception of a doubled temporal loss: a future that is endlessly deferred and a past that refuses to stay past. That is, to live in crisis was to live in a state of what Claudio Lomnitz has called present saturation, in which the present never moves forward and the past always threatens to return (2003, 132). "Crisis" offered an interpretive frame and an affective mode of encountering and narrating the world: a way to narrate historical experience in which the cultural landscape was not only littered with the past's remains, but these remains threw time itself—past, present, and future—into disarray.

At stake in this experience of stalled temporality was the perceived success of the political transition. Although Hungary's former Soviet bloc neighbors may have greeted 2009 as the twentieth anniversary of the demise of communist rule, during my research trip that summer, such commemorations were muted in Hungary. As with the fiftieth anniversary of 1956 in 2006, the MSZP-led coalition government wanted to avoid the uncomfortable questions (or accusations of appropriation) raised by such anniversary celebrations, and it instead attempted to portray the legacy of 1989 as one of cooperation between the government and the opposition—an interpretation that Fidesz and Jobbik vehemently rejected (Seleny 2014, 47). (The October 23 commemorations were similarly polarized.) And no one I spoke with saw anything to celebrate anyway (*nincs mit ünnepelni*). For what had changed, my interviewees asked me rhetorically? The "communists" were still in power, and even those who resisted the conflation of the MSZP with the former regime argued that there were more continuities than breaks with the socialist past. Balázs Bodó, whose critique of István Szabó demonstrated that he appreciated the symbolic power of temporal divides in other contexts, sighed heavily during our interview when I asked him whether he found the twentieth anniversary significant. He replied:

I don't think that anything can happen on a single day, and for me the last 20 years is the perfect demonstration that 20 years ago didn't mean anything because the transition process still very much underway. The key tasks are still unsolved, so I don't think it makes sense to . . . it's very counterproductive to say that 20 years ago, this day, transition has happened. Because then we just obfuscate the fact that there have not been complete changes.

This argument that transition was yet to be fully accomplished was also visible in the reception of the book *Retro Dictionary*, released in 2008 just months before the global financial crisis took hold. A collection of keywords from World War II up until the end of the communist era, *Retro Dictionary* was—like many previous attempts to capture the lost knowledge of the previous era—accompanied by news articles and television interviews. Yet, unlike *Rainbow Department Store* and other earlier publications, *Retro Dictionary* was explicitly concerned not with capturing the collective and personal reminiscences of the socialist past, but with providing a dictionary of terms that might serve as a reference for those who lived through state socialism and for the younger generations who were curious about it.

This transformation from the idiosyncracy of personal recollection to the claim of official status as "dictionary" would seem to imply an easy linear progression from unruly memory to established history, or what Jan Assmann calls from "communicative memory" to "cultural memory" (1995). Yet, although the book did offer a representative selection of the unique concepts and terminology of the past era (from Sparrow cigarettes and the soft drink Bambi to the Peace Loan [*békekölcsön*)] and China's Cultural Revolution), one reviewer argued that the book's function as a historical archive was undermined by the disturbing continuities it unintentionally revealed between past and present. "The phenomena are the same and the structures haven't changed," he argued, writing in the liberal political and cultural journal *Beszélő*. "Only the name [is different]." He described these similarities in terms of both party politics and the cultural landscape of postsocialism. What is so different, he asked, between the communist party hagiographies of the past and the public relations campaigns of contemporary politicians, or between the socialist state's public service announcements and the current government funding a commercial television station to promote the European Union on one of its soap operas? "Even retro," the title of his piece argued, "is no longer retro" (Szerbhorváth 2008).

As we have seen, consumers of socialist nostalgia a decade earlier found pleasure in remembering the gray but cozy world of late socialism, as a way of both asserting the cultural value of this shared heritage and reinforcing the superiority of their present-day circumstances. Now the experiences of crisis and the loss of the dream of achieving normality drew the past too painfully near to comfortably redeem remains of socialism as mere nostalgia. And with the inability to feel distant and superior to one's previous selves, the triumphalism that pervaded these earlier practices of nostalgia also disappeared, along with the fantasy of mastering both the present and past that it once made visible. Thus, although we might expect that the experience of economic and political upheaval would only fuel nostalgic longing, it instead overturned the very conditions for its possibility.

At a time of postcrisis austerity, the concept of "nostalgia" now became stigmatized as a socially divisive idiom of entitlement that deprives and burdens others. In 2009 and 2010, many of my interviewees only used the term when they wanted to describe the older generation's longing for the security and stability of the previous era. Such "selfish" nostalgia for government entitlements, they argued, was a threat to Hungary today. "These people want what they had under socialism," Ágnes told me, "but they don't realize times have changed." Use of the term "nostalgia" in this context thus shifted from a "reflective" practice that insists on the irretrievability of the past era to the accusation of a desire for "restoration" that seeks the past's return (Boym 2001, 49)—but without giving up any of the advantages of the present. In this logic, nostalgic aspirations for a better life became the very proof of a *lack* of normality, an inability to surrender past entitlements to present-day reality. My interlocutors thus redefined—and delegitimized— nostalgia in explicitly political terms: no longer proof of the mastery of Hungary's transition, but rather as yet another remain of socialism that stood as an obstacle to attaining it.

CONCLUSION

In this book, I have conceptualized remains not as a fixed set of objects or sites, but as a logic that seeks to master the challenges of the present by locating them in a pathologized past. The battles to define specific remains and determine their fate thus also represent opportunities to imagine dreaded or desired futures—and in so doing, to address the anxieties produced by encounters with a Western hierarchy that has tended to view those on its political peripheries as burdened by dangerous historical legacies. Over the first two decades of postsocialism, this logic of remains shifted significantly. Initially, remains took the form of concrete and intrusive embodiments of the past regime's ideology (whether statues, official historical narratives, or the material culture of everyday life) that enabled Hungarians to fantasize quickly overcoming the experience of political, economic, and structural inferiority, through acts of mastery that ranged from banishment to replacement to ironic recuperation via nostalgia. But with the growing disillusionments of postsocialism, the discourse on the past in both public life and everyday conversation changed from triumph to victimization. Now remains represented hidden acts of persecution, betrayal, dishonesty, and corruption that continued to endanger the present and frustrate any attempt to move forward. By the twentieth anniversary of 1989 and 1990, many people regarded the memory of transition not as the beginning of a desired future but as a missed opportunity, as we saw poignantly illustrated in the case of Marxim in the opening pages of this book. The restaurant, which opened in 1991, once represented the optimism of triumphing over—and capitalizing on—the recent past. Twenty years after 1989, however, Marxim's faded, dusty furnishings merely evoked the similarly out-dated fantasy of a clean break, in which everything changes but nothing is lost because all can be redeemed through commodification.

But although the memory work of sites like Marxim is no longer effective, this does not mean that everyday life in Hungary is now empty of the objects and iconography of the communist past. To the contrary, as Hungary finishes its third decade of postsocialism, products and shops that declare themselves to be "retro" or that are drawn from or reference Hungary's decades of state socialism continue to be popular. Even new communist-themed pubs can be found in some of Budapest's most touristy thoroughfares. However, neither consumers nor local commentators interpret such practices as linked to the personal or cultural memory of the socialist past, whether transition's triumphalism or the bittersweet recollection of nostalgia.

As Krisztina Fehérváry has argued, many of these practices represent a new form of "retro" that does not seek to redeem the socialist past but rather renarrates its objects as embedded in an alternative national history "that was never cut off by an 'iron curtain' from the regimes of value in the modern world" (2015, 1). That is, the revival of brands such as Tisza sneakers—Hungary's socialist answer to Adidas—is not about recuperating the material culture of what the earlier wave of nostalgia viewed as the backward and limited but cozy world of late socialism. Instead, Fehérváry demonstrates, the popularity of Tisza sneakers makes visible an argument for coeval modernity, in which Hungary never needed to catch up with the West in the first place because its own consumer culture evolved alongside that of capitalist countries (2015, 7). Unlike nostalgia in its myriad forms, this logic of "retro" thus enables a pride in national achievement that does not need to justify or reject its relationship to the political regime that produced these products. No defensive disavowal of ideological content is now necessary because these practices dismiss the historical context of state socialism as irrelevant. The narrative of retro is thus not premised on the notion of temporal break that defines the logic of remains—rather it posits a seamless line of continuity that extends from the past into the present day.

It thus might seem that the logic of "remains" is no longer relevant in Hungary, at a time when even the adjective "postsocialist" may be outdated. And if the socialist past no longer appears to provide a relevant point of orientation, the fate of the future seems equally fraught in the global "postcrisis" moment, in which neoliberalism's narratives of progress increasingly appear empty of possibility. Yet alongside these laments for a lost future and what Fehérváry calls the "material nationalism" of retro (2015, 7), other discourses continue to insist that the socialist past is still with us. They have primarily separated along a right/left social and political divide, insofar as such polarization has only increased over the past decade. A summary of this broader context is thus necessary to put the continued salience of remains into perspective.

Fidesz and the Future of Europe

In the 2010 elections, Hungarian voters overwhelmingly rejected the MSZP (Hungarian Socialist Party) government out of disgust with its scandals and the state of Hungary's postcrisis economy. The now populist right-wing party Fidesz, in coalition with the KDNP (Christian Democratic People's Party), returned to power with a super-majority under the promise that it would finally accomplish the work of transition. Under the banner of a "revolution in the ballot boxes," Fidesz soon enacted sweeping legal and constitutional changes that many critics argued have threatened the democratic achievements of the first two decades of postsocialism. These changes have included a new constitution that removed many checks on the government's political power; the centralization (and corruption) of government bureaucracy; the weakening of the judiciary; the nationalization of education; the creation of new research institutions to help canonize Fidesz's narrative of twentieth-century history; and tight control of the media and the staffing of head positions in culture and the arts with Fidesz loyalists. In addition, new electoral laws, along with the creation of a reliable voting bloc by extending citizenship to ethnic Hungarians living in neighboring countries, have made it very difficult to remove Fidesz from office.[1] As a result of both its own efforts and the fragmentation (and, in some cases, disintegration) of its political opposition,[2] Fidesz was reelected in both 2014 and 2018 in coalition with KDNP. Fidesz has used this opportunity to further centralize its power and, among other initiatives, it has brought more and more institutions under control (from mass media to academia to arts and literature) to curtail independent criticism and dissent.

In its first years back in power, the government launched new efforts to eliminate remains of socialism and bring the postsocialist period to a close. In keeping with the argument that only Fidesz's reelection in 2010 finally accomplished Hungary's transition from communism twenty years earlier, the city government changed the name of one of Buda's central transportation hubs from "Moscow Square" to its pre-1951 name of "Kálmán Széll Square."[3] And as part of its rehabilitation of the controversial memory of Hungary's interwar period, the government removed every statue erected since 1944 in the area surrounding Parliament. By thus restoring (or re-creating) the monumental landscape of that period, Fidesz thus attempted to draw a direct line of continuity to the interwar era and thus excise the memory of all that elapsed in the intervening years: as if the experiences of fascism, state socialism, and twenty years of postsocialist transition were irrelevant.

But although Fidesz's fierce antipathy to communism drove its rhetoric during its years out of power, the decline of the MSZP and the fragmentation of the political opposition more generally has opened a symbolic vacuum to be filled by a new enemy: the European Union and the danger it purportedly presents to Hungary's national sovereignty. That is, if once the Nazis and Soviets attempted to push Hungary off its "proper" course of history, now the EU is preventing Hungary's return to national authenticity (Hann 2015b, 905). Taking inspiration from Russia's Putin and Turkey's Erdoğan, Orbán now argues that Western liberal values such as religious and ethnic tolerance and openness to immigration have doomed Europe's future. His government thus made Western headlines in 2015 for its harsh treatment of asylum seekers from the Middle East, culminating in the creation of a border fence to limit these refugees' ability to transit Hungary on their way to Western Europe. For Orbán, such battles with "Brussels" are part of an ongoing populist struggle to preserve Hungary's self-determination against an interlinked web of hostile others that include both "illegal immigrants" and the EU policies that allegedly support them.[4] During the migration crisis, he justified his antirefugee stance on the international stage by presenting Hungary as a Christian bulwark against the "Muslim invasion" of Europe, and he defended himself against criticism of his domestic policies by portraying his government as the sole party capable of protecting the nation from falling into either communism (his left-wing opponents) or fascism (Jobbik, which in recent years has moved more towards the center).

In line with this logic, Orbán now also regards institutions of civil society as a national threat, arguing that since the representatives of such organizations attempt to interfere in politics and public life without having been elected to office, their activism represents an assault on popular sovereignty. A key target of Orbán's rhetoric has been the financier and philanthropist George Soros, who has promoted open society in Hungary by opening an institution of higher education in Budapest (Central European University; CEU) and funding numerous civil organizations and initiatives that have been some of Hungary's most vigorous defenders of refugee rights and proponents of independent political criticism.[5] In 2017 the government passed laws that ultimately prevented CEU from operating U.S.-accredited programs in Hungary,[6] and it also enacted legislation to require nongovernmental organizations (NGOs) that receive funding from international sources to register as "foreign-funded" organizations. With the success of these efforts, Fidesz then turned its attention to eliminating or bringing under the government's direct control other realms of independent thought and potential criticism. A "culture war" in summer 2018 ultimately replaced the leadership of the country's main literary museum in order to ensure that the museum's exhibitions and activities serve the government's interests. And in the spring and summer of 2019, the Fidesz government built on earlier efforts to restrict academic autonomy (such as introducing government-appointed chancellors into university administration) by effectively shutting down the 1956 Institute and taking over the Hungarian Academy of Sciences' network of research institutes in order to eliminate independent academic oversight of the Academy's work and funding.[7]

Orbán's attacks on both the values and institutions of the EU have increasingly strained Hungary's position within it, as well as Fidesz's membership in the center-right European People's Party organization, which suspended Fidesz's membership in March 2019. (Due to Hungary's anti-NGO legislation, the European Commission is currently pursuing infringement proceedings against Hungary at the Court of Justice of the European Union.) But much like the similar PiS (Law and Justice) party in Poland, Orbán's claim to be acting in the Christian interests of all of Europe have also won him support among other anti-migrant populist constituencies in the EU and have made him one of the continent's most prominent politicians. Rather than try to "catch up" or be recognized by the West, Orbán is now positioning himself as Europe's new vanguard: rescuing democracy in a new illiberal form, by abandoning "political correctness" and reflecting what he claims to be the true will of the people.

Many of Fidesz's critics insist that the transformations enacted by Fidesz have revived the communist past under the guise of eliminating it. The perceived similarities between the Fidesz regime and the communist past (whether the harsh oppression under Mátyás Rákosi [Hungary's Stalin] in the 1950s or the soft dictatorship of Kádárism) have inspired comparisons that I have heard repeatedly from interlocutors on both the left and oppositional right wing (Jobbik) during my trips since 2010. They decry Orbán's seemingly authoritarian ambitions, the suppression of oppositional media, and the blatant corruption of Fidesz and its cronies. They also mourn the ways these transformations have affected their own professional lives, as they tell me they now feel cautious about expressing political opinions and must curry favor with the Fidesz loyalists who staff many prominent positions. "I can say whatever I want and I won't go to jail," one friend told me, lowering her voice so that others would not overhear. "But I could get fired the next day." A colleague who works in the arts similarly observed that his interactions with some of his colleagues had become much more guarded, and that in his work at institutions that have increasingly come under the direct control of the state, he sometimes felt forced to give preference to those whose friends or partners were currently in favor with the regime.

What is crucial about these complaints that "we have returned to Kádárism" is that they do not merely critique Fidesz's policies, but they also reflect transformations that my interlocutors perceive the government to have wrought in everyday life and in my subjects themselves. Over the years, there have been several significant waves of protest against the Fidesz government, including demonstrations in 2011 and 2012 organized by the Milla social movement; the 2017 and 2018 large-scale protests against the closing of CEU; demonstrations in the days following the 2018 election that called on Orbán to resign;[8] and, most recently, rallies in December 2018 and January 2019 to protest a "slave law" that would enable employers to require overtime work of up to four hundred hours a year and delay payment for up to three years. Each time, these protests appeared to invigorate Fidesz's popular opposition. ("People are rediscovering that they have to fight for democracy," one former dissident told me in 2011, excited by the large crowds that attended Milla protests.) But thus far, the hopes that these protests might accomplish political change were dashed, and the opposition parties failed to effectively collaborate or otherwise capitalize on voter dissatisfaction to push Fidesz out of power during the 2014 and 2018 elections. (As this book goes to press in fall 2019, however, coordination among these opposition parties resulted in non-Fidesz candidates winning key positions in recent local elections, including that of the mayor of Budapest. This has inspired optimism among Fidesz's opposition and its supporters that future collaboration among these parties can tap into voters' growing dissatisfaction with Fidesz in the 2022 national election.)

During my summer research trips over the past several years, many of those I spoke with who oppose the Fidesz regime described themselves as disillusioned and increasingly apathetic, resigned to the impossibility of a strong political opposition or personally being able to effect political change. Some with marketable skills were seeking work abroad, as part of a general labor drain that has created a significant shortage within Hungary. Others self-consciously chose a form of internal exile, telling me that they had retreated into their domestic, private concerns, just as Hungarians did as subjects of state socialism a generation ago. Some did so with a shrug—such as Miklós, the early member of Fidesz who no longer agrees with some of its policies but has not found a compelling alternative among the new parties that emerged in the wake of the MSZP's 2010 electoral failure. "But as long as I can go where I like and do the kind of work I want to do," he told me, "I'm not too worried about Hungary—this is still a democracy, after all." Others, however, viewed the situation much more catastrophically; in the words of one colleague, "This is a return to the old regime [*rendszervisszaváltás*]. Kádár broke our spines, and I didn't think that we would return this quickly to the old ways of thinking."

But although over the years since its return to power, Fidesz's popular support has fluctuated, its policies and rhetoric have nonetheless found significant support among Hungary's voting electorate. A poll after the 2018 elections revealed that the main reason voters supported Fidesz was its stance on the refugee issue. (Other key factors included party loyalty and an improvement in living conditions [Dull 2018]). This result helps remind us that economic hardship is far from the only thing driving people to right-wing populism. Hungary is economically stable and relatively prosperous, thanks in part to the significant funding that it receives as an EU member.[9] And although wealth inequality in Hungary continues to grow (G. Kovács, "How Much Are They Really Worth?" 2019)—the upper-middle-class population in Budapest benefits while villages in the countryside are increasingly impoverished—many of those who do continue to be hard-hit economically do not blame the Fidesz government for their predicament. With local media now largely limited to progovernment publications,[10] and with Fidesz enacting populist measures such as introducing employment in public works and giving food vouchers to pensioners before the elections, these Fidesz supporters target their anger at migrants, Roma, and the purported threat to national self-determination posed by the EU.[11] Much as in Poland, the ruling elite has thus been able to pacify potential class resentment by transforming anger about economic issues into a problem of identity politics (Ost 2005, 179), in which nationalist rhetoric is both the response and the solution to the perception of structural inferiority vis-à-vis Western Europe.[12] In addition, Fidesz supporters also praise what they consider to be the party's commitment to protecting Hungarian families, whether that be the defense of conservative Christian values (such as the condemnation of gay marriage) or the enactment of government policies that include housing subsidies for families with three or more children. (Such social welfare measures may seem socialist in intention, but since they primarily benefit the upwardly mobile middle class, they ultimately have the effect of increasing rather than ameliorating social inequality [Szikra 2014].)

In my conversations with Fidesz supporters both in Budapest and the countryside, they tend to regard criticism warning of Fidesz's danger to democracy as hyperbolic and ill-intentioned. Although they do not defend every one of Fidesz's measures, they are inclined to agree with Fidesz's equating of the nation with its governing party, whereby criticism of Fidesz is criticism of Hungary as a whole, and thus only voiced by those who seek to divide and weaken the national polity. "I don't need to pay attention to every little thing," a lawyer in his early fifties told me in 2017. "I know I can trust them to do what's right." He criticized the ongoing demonstrations and media coverage in support of CEU at the time as unnecessary politicizing of what was simply a legal matter: CEU failed to comply with the law, and now it needed to do so. The fact that Fidesz had written that law to force CEU out of Hungary was thus, to him, less relevant than the fact that Fidesz has almost always remained within the realm of law and procedural correctness. Moreover, he and other supporters had only to point to the corruption and mismanagement by the previous MSZP coalition to justify their assertion that the alternative would be much worse: in their eyes, the parties on the left were hopelessly incompetent and morally corrupt.

This narrative of left-wing perfidy was echoed by Béla Aba, the graphic artist who produced the 1990 "National spring cleaning!" Hungarian Democratic Forum (MDF) campaign poster whose image opens this book. In a conversation in summer 2018, he explained that the inspiration for this and the MDF's other posters that he designed were the product of brainstorming within the campaign rather than his own invention. (He was also hired by Fidesz, he told me, to create its famous orange logo.) Although he was proud of the image, he now regarded its hopes of sweeping away the remains of socialism to be overly optimistic, and he blamed his disappointments on a left wing that endangered the nation economically and morally. Aba explained that he was loyal to the former MDF[13] and did not vote for Fidesz because he considered himself to be more traditionally conservative. Nonetheless, he argued that having Fidesz in power to protect Hungary's national sovereignty served as a bulwark against the threat of left-wing parties as well as the misrepresentations of a Western media that condemn any expression of Hungarian national pride as dangerous and antisemitic. "I'm not a Fidesz supporter," he concluded, "but I am satisfied with them."

Remains of Transition

Fidesz's 2018 reelection campaign was the first in which the rhetoric of anticommunism did not play a prominent role. But although its political discourse no longer emphasizes the danger of communist return, it continues to engage or rework the various remains of socialism in the paradoxical ways similar to those discussed in this book: whether the government's ongoing financial support of the House of Terror, whose narrative of continuous foreign occupation from the Nazis through the Soviets is now enshrined in the preamble of Hungary's new constitution; its obstruction of legislation that would enable greater access to the state security files; or even Orbán's public celebration of the twenty-fifth anniversary of Fidesz's founding with a bottle of the socialist-era soda, Bambi (*HVG. hu* 2013). Orbán presumably chose the orange soda to match the party's official color, but his public consumption of Bambi nonetheless reflected the current political decontextualization of the past regime's products as "retro," rather than either socialist nostalgia or—as the House of Terror's permanent exhibition argues—dangerous propaganda from the communist regime.

Fidesz and its representatives also continue the battle to determine the legacy of 1956 and claim it as their own. The party has discarded the *polgári* narrative discussed in chapter 2, in which the 1956 revolution was a civic uprising of Hungary's emerging middle class. Now it focuses on the young men who fought in street battles (*pesti srácok*), narrating the revolution as a battle for national sovereignty against an encroaching foreign power, much like Hungary's current struggle against the EU. To support this historical interpretation, official commemorations have increasingly marginalized the role of Imre Nagy in the revolution. As part of the government's ongoing renovation of the squares near Parliament, in 2019 it removed and relocated the statue of Imre Nagy erected in Martyrs' Square by the MSZP in 1996. (In its place, the government has reinstated a pre-1945 monument commemorating another set of "national martyrs": the victims of the 1919 red terror.) In so doing, Fidesz thus eliminated the Nagy statue not merely as a remain of socialism, but a remain of a now-discredited moment in Hungary's postsocialist transition as well.

The ironies of this attempt to banish the Nagy statue as a "remain of transition" became vivid on the thirtieth anniversary of Nagy's reburial on June 16, 1989, which represented perhaps the most major event of Hungary's system change. The Fidesz government marked this anniversary with a rock concert dedicated to "thirty years of freedom," and it displaced the memory of Nagy himself with a celebration of Orbán's role during the reburial, during which he, like some of the other speakers, called on Soviet troops to leave Hungary. The memory of 1956 and its political rehabilitation, which had been so crucial in 1989, now receded from view; and, in keeping with Fidesz's claim that the transition in 1989 and 1990 was corrupted and incomplete, so too did the understanding of Nagy's reburial as the beginning of a new thirty-year era in Hungary's history that decisively broke with an unjust past.

As a result, it was thus irrelevant that in the months and weeks before the event, the government had removed Nagy's statue from its original location, effectively shut down the 1956 Institute, and decided to include among the concert's lineup of performers a musician (Gyula Vikadál) who had been publicly exposed as an informer a decade before. Instead, Fidesz celebrated 1989 in terms of Orbán's heroism: the moment that Fidesz entered the national stage to fight for a freedom that would only fully be achieved in 2010. That is, rather than represent the end of communism, 1989 ultimately was important because it symbolically represented the beginning of Fidesz. (A group led by some former dissidents and children of 1956 participants held a silent protest against the falsification of 1989 at the concert.)

Farewell to the Future That Once Was

Over the years, many opposition parties have struggled to capture the political imagination of Hungary's electorate, but apart from their anti-Fidesz stances, each has found difficulty in articulating a clear and compelling vision of Hungary's future to rival Orbán's narrative of a nation fighting invaders from both East and West. As both Zsuzsa Gille and David Ost have argued, during the 1980s, Eastern European oppositional political movements and civic initiatives were actively engaged in reimagining progressive politics and democratic theory (Gille 2010, 21; Ost 2005, 191–192). But when the regimes ended, the cost of "entering Europe" was submission to established Western values, institutional practices, and politics of recognition: whether that meant embracing neoliberalism as the only way to build democracy and civil society (Ost 2005, 192) or abandoning attachments to ethnonational identities in favor of becoming multicultural and postnational (Gille 2010, 24). This lack of opportunity to build and participate in an indigenous public sphere has led to an impoverished political discourse in Hungary (Gille 2010, 29), in which the left's vision of a European future is one that many regard as already disenchanted or discredited. (Moreover, few of these parties have directly challenged Fidesz's anti-migrant position, which is now broadly held across much of society.)

In contrast, what has perhaps made Fidesz's politics so persuasive to its supporters is that it has declared war not only on the socialist past, but on "transition" itself. As we saw in the chapters of this book, the argument that Hungary's postsocialist transformation was handled incorrectly and failed to achieve its promises is a familiar one. But Orbán's rejection of European liberalism as both a political and economic project has taken this critique a significant step further. Instead of mourning transition's lost future, Orbán has cast it aside in order to present a new vision in which Hungary no longer needs to catch up to Europe but instead leads the way. In his eyes, Hungary is now more European than an ailing West weakened by liberalism, political correctness, and migration—and Fidesz's policies provide a model for the rest of Europe on how to protect national sovereignty from foreign invasion and to resist bureaucratic threats to national autonomy from the EU.

For Fidesz's left-wing critics, however, neither the past of communism nor the first two decades of transition are fully past. They continue to defend liberal values of tolerance, openness, and freedom of expression. And their comparison of their current predicament to the experience of Kádárism has helped to make their warnings of encroaching authoritarianism more urgent, as well as to breed new forms of nostalgia as political critique, in which some complain that, ironically, it was easier to live a "normal," honest life under late socialism than it is now.

Of course, there are both political and historical limitations to interpreting the present-day experience of Fidesz's "illiberal democracy" through the lens of Kádárism. While my interviewees worry about Fidesz's tendencies towards authoritarianism, few evince concern that it will return in its twentieth-century form. Instead, their anxieties concern living in a country where the formal existence of democracy is used to cloak the centralization of power and muffling of organized dissent. I nonetheless want to take this complaint of Kádárism's return seriously as a form of historical argumentation, in which the absence of a desired future—and the challenge of formulating an alternative one—means that the disavowed past is providing one of the few useful remaining points of navigation.

In the final pages of this book, I have focused on the ways in which party and political alignments have overdetermined how remains of the socialist past are currently conceptualized. But there are also memories of the past that cross party boundaries in significant ways. In 2019, for example, a public opinion poll revealed that of those who expressed a preference, a relative majority of Hungarians perceive the Kádár era more positively than 1990–2010 or the period since Fidesz returned to power in 2010 (Szurovecz 2019).[14] Without overstating the significance of one set of polling data, such results appear to be in keeping with general trends in both Hungary and the former Soviet bloc (Pap 2017; R. Tóth 2016). As we have seen, disavowing attachments to the stigmatized past has been the very condition for entering Europe, as both a political and administrative unit and a modernist fantasy of progress and future prosperity. And the threat of socialism's return—what Chelcea and Druta term "zombie socialism"—has proven to be remarkably effective in the service of postsocialist neoliberal policies that include reduced wages and social spending (2016, 537). As a result, since the end of state socialism, there have not been sustained opportunities in political or public discourse to address positive evaluations of the previous era in ways that avoid either depoliticized nostalgia or outraged condemnation. Instead, each attempt to locate the socialist past in an unpalatable remain to be expelled has also represented an attempt to wrestle with the challenge of remembering the Kádár era, torn between memories of material security and the system's political oppression. These contradictions and incommensurabilities of the Kádárist experience have continually renewed the generativity of remains, at once "too much" and "not enough" for the cultural work demanded of them.

Now, at a moment when the frustrations of the East/West hierarchy have become visible in different ways on both the political right and left in Hungary, there may be an opportunity to address and reevaluate the ambivalent legacies of what had to be discarded in order for Hungary to belong to Europe. Otherwise, even three decades after the demise of state socialism in Eastern Europe, remains may continue as both an enduring problem and the site of cultural productivity: demanding as well as frustrating the desire for historical mastery.

Notes

INTRODUCTION

1. Founded in 1988 as a liberal youth party, Fidesz was originally named the Alliance of Young Democrats (Fiatal Demokraták Szövetsége). In 1995, as part of its ideological shift to the center right, the party changed its name to the Fidesz—Hungarian Civic Party (Fidesz—Magyar Polgári Párt), and it changed again in 2003 to the Fidesz—Hungarian Civic Union (Fidesz—Magyar Polgári Szövetség). Since the party's return to power in 2010, it has embraced right-wing populism. For the sake of simplicity, I refer to all of these names as "Fidesz" in the text.

2. For examples of analyses that draw on tropes of an unmastered past, see Alexander Etkind's *Warped Mourning* (2013) and Ann Laura Stoler's edited collection, *Imperial Debris* (2013).

3. Although it is important to recognize the significance of the Holocaust for memory studies, Jeffrey Olick, Vered Vinitzky-Seroussi, and Daniel Levy warn against deterministic accounts that assume that its traumatic impact was solely what inspired the twentieth-century boom in memory as both a cultural practice and sphere of academic inquiry. (2011, 34–35).

4. Greenberg 2014, Oushakine 2009, and Shevchenko 2009 have similarly explored the productivities of discourses of disappointment, despair, and crisis, respectively. Anna Lowenhaupt Tsing's multisited ethnography of matsutake mushrooms also argues for the unexpected possibilities enabled by life in "capitalist ruins" (2015).

5. The fascination with ruins has a long history in modernity, as the inevitable counterpoint to its fetishes of novelty and temporal progress (Benjamin 1977; Simmel 1959). In the past decade, ruins have emerged as a governing metaphor through which to understand the financial, environmental, and industrial depredations of late capitalism. Images of ruinous decay stand as testament to the folly of modernity's fantasy of progress, but, as Andreas Huyssen argues, they also enable nostalgia for that fantasy, when hopes for a better future were still possible (2006, 8; see also DeSilvey and Edensor 2013 for a review of the current literature on ruins). As the following chapters demonstrate, however, although at specific moments the fate of remains may resemble that of ruins, the conceptual apparatus of "remains" enables us to treat the destinies of these cultural objects as the target of ethnographic inquiry, rather than assume their trajectories in advance.

6. My analysis builds on a previous generation of studies of postsocialist memory (for book-length works, see, for example, Berdahl 2009; Lemon 2000; Paxson 2005; Ten Dyke 2001; Verdery 1999; and Wanner 1998), as well as contributes a longitudinal perspective within a recent body of literature on how citizens of the region navigate the legacies of state socialism (including Bach 2017; Buyandelger 2013; and Pozniak 2014). For a review of the current trends in the study of postsocialist memory, see Głowacka-Grajper 2018.

7. The evolutionary paradigm embedded in the rhetoric of transition is of course not unfamiliar to people in the region, insofar as communism itself was an ideology of progress toward a predetermined end. See also Manduhai Buyandelgeriyn for an analysis of how the anthropological literature has challenged the social evolutionary approach of transitology and its "contemptuous belief that cultural identities, values, and systems are obstacles to progress" (2008, 236).

8. In my analysis, I deploy the term "transition" only when I want to invoke the ideologies embedded in the concept. Otherwise, I use the phrases "political transformation" or "system change" (*rendszerváltás*) in order to avoid the rhetoric of transitology.

9. Recent anthropological studies of the future include Appadurai 2013; Piot 2010; Rosenberg and Harding 2005; and Schielke 2015.

10. Lacan defines the *objet a* as "something from which the subject, in order to constitute itself, has separated itself off as organ. This serves as a symbol of the lack, that is to say, of the phallus, not as such, but in so far as it is lacking. It must, therefore, be an object that is, firstly, separable and, secondly, that has some relation to the lack" (1978, 103).

11. In *The Politics of Gender after Socialism*, Susan Gal and Gail Kligman varyingly describe the pre-1989 regimes of Eastern Europe as "communist," "socialist," and "state socialist," although they note their tendency to use "communism" to describe the negative aspects of the regime and "socialism" to denote its more positive characteristics (2000, 120). I observed this practice among my Hungarian interlocutors as well. Rather than choose one term, I thus follow Gal and Kligman's example in order to preserve the tension my interviewees experienced between the oppressive and progressive features of the past system.

12. Officially, the Hungarian name for the communist youth group was simply "Pioneers" (*Úttörők*), but I follow the conventional practice of translating the term as "Young Pioneers" so as to connect it to similar movements elsewhere in the Soviet bloc.

13. Yurchak warns against either demonizing the socialist past or romanticizing it, arguing instead that life under real existing socialism was characterized by "control, coercion, alienation, fear, and moral quandaries . . . irreducibly mixed with ideals, communal ethics, dignity, creativity, and care for the future" (2005, 10).

14. As with the word "transition," I do not use the "West" as a simple term of description: a monolithic and essentialized category that denies internal difference and contestation among those countries and populations currently labeled as "Western." Rather, I deploy the "West" as a local category that in its narrow sense represents the way Hungarians referred to Western Europe and the United States (Fehérváry 2006, 59), and more broadly constitutes a symbolic geography through which Hungarians have historically talked about the challenges of national identity on Western Europe's periphery. As Gal argues, the discursive tension between "East" and "West"—between maintaining Hungarian national distinctiveness and embracing European cosmopolitanism—has long informed the ways that Hungarians describe the present and imagine the future (1991, 442–447). (See Yurchak 2005 for a discussion of the "Imaginary West" in the USSR, and Galbraith 2014 for an examination of how Poles regard the European Union as both a set of ideals and a means to advance personal and collective interest [3].)

15. The tension between intimacy and alterity is exemplified in the psychoanalytic concept of the "uncanny," in which the unsettling sensations produced by ghosts, doubles, and other hauntings do not reflect the shock of an alien presence, but rather the unpleasant intrusion of that which the subject already knows and wants to deny. As Mladen Dolar explains, the uncanny represents "the anxiety of gaining something too much . . . a too-close presence of the object" (1991, 13; see also Freud 1963; Ivy 1995, 84–85). Remains thus do not represent loss but rather the *absence* of loss: the unwelcome persistence of what individuals and communities seek to forget.

16. As Claudio Lomnitz has observed, if the West has often condemned its Others as backward for "lacking" history, it has also interpreted an obsession with history as "a diagnostic sign of failed modernities" (Lomnitz 2008, 39; see also Dirks 1989).

17. Many scholars of the region have questioned the continued salience of the term "postsocialism," suggesting alternate formulations such as "post-postsocialism" (Sampson

2002, 298) or arguing for expanding the scope of our analysis to post–Cold War studies (Chari and Verdery 2009). Following Marianne Hirsch's formulation of "postmemory," I nonetheless use the term "postsocialism" to evoke the ways "postmodernism" and "post-structuralism" denote both continuity and rupture: a critical orientation, rather than simply a temporal or regional marker (Hirsch 2012, 5–6). (As Douglas Rogers notes, much of the scholarship produced under the rubric of "postsocialism" has critiqued, rather than simply affirmed, Western social science concepts and the periodization they imply [2010, 13].) Moreover, I also take inspiration from Didier Fassin's discussion of the term "post-apartheid," which he uses "in a thick sense rather than in its common use—the end of the past regime which however remains present beyond its disappearance, both in the lasting inequalities inherited from the apartheid era (the historical condition) and in the expression of frustrations systematically interpreted as related to the remnants of apartheid (the experience of history)" (Fassin 2008, 318).

18. The Soviets removed Rákosi from power again several months later, and replaced him with one of his close associates, Ernő Gerő.

19. I conducted long-term fieldwork in Hungary between 1997–1998 and 1999–2002, and I have returned nearly every summer since 2006.

20. A brief word about political affiliation is necessary here. During my fieldwork in Hungary, many of my interviewees and colleagues seemed scrupulously concerned that I speak to people who held opposing political positions, particularly since this form of diversity is often considered a shorthand for other, more durable forms of difference in Hungary (family history, class background, urban vs. rural upbringing, etc.). I thus sought out a range of political views, and because many of my initial contacts outside the village identified with the left-wing intelligentsia, I particularly pursued opportunities to speak with those who identified as right wing. But as powerful as the rhetoric of a divided Hungary has been over the past three decades, it is important to note that it obscures the ways many people's political loyalties may change over time—whether this reflects disenchantment with a particular political party, a shift in personal values, or simply the desire to remove whichever elite is currently in power. Moreover, this understanding of political affiliation as intrinsically linked to specific social and class positions (in which the distinction between left and right is structured along traditionally perceived divides such as cosmopolitan liberal [often identified as Jewish] urban middle classes in the capital versus their more conservative Christian counterparts in smaller cities, or the former workers of regional industrial centers versus the inhabitants of rural agricultural communities) tends to conceal the variety of political opinions within many families and friendship groups.

1. BANISHING REMAINS

1. In a complementary logic, Western journalistic accounts also portrayed the newly democratic Eastern Europe with photographs of decaying factories and images of backwardness (from horse-drawn carriages to shoddy and outdated goods to the smokestacks of earlier industrial modernity). These visual arguments represented the legacy of state socialism as a polluted and wasteful system that only the cleanliness of capitalism could remedy (Gille 2007, 1–3).

2. Two weeks before the election, an article published by a newspaper in the city of Szombathely in western Hungary reported that it had taken three months for one of its photojournalists to find a Lenin bust to use for a photo essay. Under the headline "Where did all the Lenins go?!" its investigation revealed that some of the small sculptures that once were found in every state office, school, factory, and house of culture were being sold by weight (100 forints per kilo), and others were assumed to have been taken home or purchased by Western collectors (Új Tér-Kép 1990).

3. As Bruce Grant notes, fallen monuments also became "a central idiom for explaining the fragilities of power, the changing of the guard, and a Soviet cultural project somehow gone awry" (2001, 332).

4. For a detailed history of the statue and its destruction, see Tóth 1995.

5. Musil considered the invisibility of the monument to be a "carefully crafted insult" to the figure or event commemorated (1995, 64); as James Young argues, the monument's temporal completion seems to discharge the community from an obligation to remember, and thus the very impulse to memorialize may "spring from an opposite and equal desire to forget" (1993, 5).

6. This anecdote appears in the guidebook for the Statue Park Museum (Réthly 2010, 32).

7. For a first-person account of the event, see Zutyu 2008.

8. Katalin Sinkó (1992) provides a detailed discussion of the raising and demolition of communist monuments in Hungary between 1945 and 1956.

9. Before the twentieth century, Budapest did not have a long history of either monuments or monumental architecture. The cultural and economic fervor surrounding the 1896 millennial anniversary of the conquest of Hungary produced much of the grandeur of the city's landscape, and most of its monuments as well. As the historian John Lukács notes, "Whereas during the forty-five years before 1896 twenty-six statues had been erected in Buda and Pest, of which more than half were of modest size, from 1896 to 1910 no fewer than thirty-seven appeared" (1988, 51–52).

10. December 5, 1991, meeting of the Budapest General Assembly

11. László Baán's presentation at the December 5, 1991, meeting of the Budapest General Assembly. According to the committee's written proposal, seven of the nineteen affected districts did not respond.

12. Interview with András Szilágyi, Budapest, Hungary, April 20, 1998.

13. Although the circumstances of Captain Ostapenko's death remain unclear, the Soviets claimed he was killed by German soldiers.

14. Géza Sáska (Fidesz), during the December 5, 1991, meeting of the Budapest General Assembly.

15. Twenty-nine voted in favor of removing the monument, seventeen voted against, and eight abstained.

16. Interview with Ákos Eleőd, Budapest, Hungary, May 11, 2001.

17. Interview with Ákos Réthly, Budapest, Hungary, September 23, 1997.

18. The park also received several bomb threats during its construction, including one on the day of its opening ceremony. Réthly dismissed these threats as being from disgruntled local residents who worried about the lights, traffic, and noise that the park (a former junkyard) might bring to their neighborhood. Once reassured by a visit from Budapest's then-mayor, Gábor Demszky, their complaints subsided. "There is nothing for them to complain about," Réthly joked. "My garden dwarfs are just bigger!"

2. THE HOLE IN THE FLAG

1. It is important to note, however, that Béla did not begin practicing law until after 1963, the year of amnesty for those imprisoned or convicted for their participation. He thus did not participate in the trials against those who fought in the uprising.

2. See Gal 1991 for a discussion of the Bartók reburial and Rév 2005 (44–45) for the Horthy reburial. Verdery 1999 provides a detailed analysis of the role of exhumations, funerals, and reburials in postsocialist political culture more generally.

3. For more detailed discussion of the 1956 revolution, see Békés, Byrne, and Rainer 2002; Gati 2006; Litván 1996b; and (in Hungarian) Rainer 2016. For further analysis of conflicts over the memory of 1956 during late socialism and the early years of the system change, see Gyáni 2006; Litván 1997; Nyyssönen 1999; Rainer 2002; and Rév 2005.

4. This political movement was known as the Petőfi Circle (Petőfi Kör), named after the Hungarian poet Sándor Petőfi, whose revolutionary poem "National Song" (*Nemzeti Dal*) helped to inspire the 1848 revolution.

5. The extent of societal "amnesia" concerning 1956 is still under debate; for example, the publication of a book that interpreted the official suppression of 1956 literally as a collective forgetting (Péter György's *Mute Tradition* [*Néma Hagyomány*], 2000) was countered by several articles in one of Hungary's leading weeklies, which argued for the various ways the memory of the events had indeed been kept alive outside of official discourse (Gyáni 2001, Litván 2001).

6. In 1988 these efforts united in the Committee for Historical Justice (Történelmi Igazságtétel Bizottság [TIB]), founded by Miklós Vásárhelyi, a former colleague of Nagy, in order to agitate for the full rehabilitation of the participants and victims of 1956.

7. Specifically, these activists sought to replace the holidays on April 4, May 1, and November 7 with March 15 to commemorate Hungary's revolution in 1848; June 16 to mark the execution of Nagy; and October 23 to mark the beginning of the 1956 revolution (Stokes 1993, 95).

8. For extended discussion of the "Pozsgay affair," see Dienstag 1996.

9. The earlier, less overtly politicized reburial of composer Béla Bartók in 1988 represented another attempt by the reformers to align themselves with the moral legitimacy embodied in historical figures (Gal 1991, 450).

10. Rév 2005 and Seleny 2014 offer detailed analysis of Nagy's reburial.

11. The failure of 1956 to unify postsocialist national memory has been noted by, for example, Gyáni 2006, 1201; György 2000, 338; Litván 1996a, 54 and 1997, 18; Nyyssönen 1999, 142–45; Seleny 2014, 38; Szalai and Gábor 1997, 27; Vágvölgyi 2001.

12. Over the years, other interpretations would also focus on Cardinal Mindszenty, an iconic figure of postwar anticommunism, or emphasize the role of the "Pest Lads" (*pesti srácok*)" street fighters. Similar right-wing considerations were behind the Parliament's decision to choose the pre-1945 coat of arms of the Hungarian Kingdom as Hungary's new state symbol, rather than the version called the "Kossuth coat of arms," which was used from 1946 to 1949 and revived during the 1956 revolution (Rainer 2002, 218).

13. The efforts to produce scholarship on 1956 would also polarize along political lines: when the center-right party Fidesz came into power in 1998, it created a new historical institute (Twentieth Century Institute [XX. Század Intézet]) to combat the perceived "liberal bias" of the 1956 Institute. After Fidesz was reelected into power in 2010, it stopped funding to the 1956 Institute, which was forced to close as a free-standing institution and became an affiliate of the National Széchényi Library. In 2019, as part of the Fidesz government's attempt to bring all sites of independent academic research under government supervision and control, the institute was folded into the right-wing Veritas Institute. As a result, all members of the 1956 Institute resigned.

14. For further discussion of different interpretations of 1956, see Kende 1993 and Litván 1997.

15. MDF's prime minister (József Antall) was a historian, as were the foreign minister, minister of defense, three of the deputy ministers, and the president of the Parliament (Deák 1994, 35).

16. In 1993 the more radical nationalist branch of the MDF that had supported the reburial split off from the party to form the far-right Hungarian Justice and Life Party (Magyar Igazság és Élet Pártja), led by István Csurka.

17. The SZDSZ's decision to join its former opponent was highly controversial. It justified its choice by arguing that it would be better able to keep tabs on the former communists by working with them, and that such a coalition was necessary to defeat what it viewed as the threat of antidemocratic nationalism on the right. Moreover,

despite the former antagonism between the parties, both endorsed neoliberal economic policies.

18. As Zoltán Csipke notes, by focusing on the reform communist tradition and not the anniversary of 1956 itself, the MSZP was able to avoid fully breaking with the past and endorsing the revolution more generally (2011, 107).

19. In a 2003 discussion of a poll on 1956 in public opinion, the sociologist Mária Vásárhelyi observed that although societal understandings of 1956 and its objectives were not as divided as political battles might suggest, there was nonetheless little consensus concerning the meaning of the revolution, apart from the fact that it was a battle for Hungary's independence. Moreover, as a consequence of the overpoliticization and subsequent "deheroization" of the revolution, there were no social strata—whether workers, university students, or others—for whom the legacy of 1956 represented an important part of their current identity (2003).

20. Béla, the retired public prosecutor who told me that he had attended demonstrations as a university student in 1956, took a similarly skeptical view of its use in postsocialist political rhetoric. "Those people who bask and beat their breasts in the present-day glory of '56 weren't even there. The people know that. That's why it doesn't interest them. It's possible that the people who beat their breasts nowadays spent '56 bathing at the Rudas thermal baths. Here everyone can say what they want—who can prove that they were there and they fought? No one. I can say that I'm a 56-er and meanwhile I didn't do anything except go to demonstrations."

21. This disinclination to link up personal experiences of 1956 to broader national narratives has held true over several decades; both Szalai and Gábor's research in 1992 (1997, 40) and Domonkos Sik's 2012 study revealed similar findings (2012, 91).

22. In the early 1990s, the 1956 Institute's Oral History archive collected interviews with veterans and their families that were published in volumes such as Bindorffer and Gyenes 1994 and Molnár, Kőrösi, and Keller 2006. Much like Ágnes's uncle, few of these veterans deliberately chose to become "revolutionaries," but instead became involved in the events through accidental circumstances. The interviews with children of victims of the 1956 reprisals in Kőrösi and Molnár 2003 also reveal similarities to the perspectives I encountered in my own interviews, particularly concerning their reluctance to bring painful family memories of 1956 into conversation with the contemporary political battles to claim the revolution's legacy (2003, 137).

23. Over the twentieth century, August 20 has been celebrated as a Catholic holiday celebrating Saint Stephen, the king who Christianized Hungary; Constitution Day and the celebration of the "new bread" during the communist era; and the founding of Hungarian statehood by Saint Stephen in 1000, as it is now officially commemorated.

24. An abundance of material is available to teach the revolution. In 2005, an article reported thirty-eight different kinds of teaching materials (textbooks, workbooks, collections of worksheets) available for students in the eighth grade, and fifty for those in the twelfth grade. However, most of these texts read as a dry recitation of facts that substitute chronology for analysis (D. Varga 2005).

25. By the time of the fiftieth anniversary of 1956 in 2006, several news sources would report on a study demonstrating that students had very little knowledge of or curiosity about 1956, and that initiatives such as computer games were attempting to kindle student interest by bringing seemingly distant events to life (Index 2006a, Múlt-kor 2006).

26. Szalai and Gábor found a similar logic among the adolescents they interviewed in 1992. These young people inherited from the older generation an interpretation of history that simultaneously "classified the actions of Kádár as 'unpatriotic' in making the Soviet intervention of 4 November possible, and . . . interpreted Soviet intervention as also

NOTES TO PAGES 69–82

contributing to an improvement of living conditions and the elimination of the seemingly endless poverty of the early years under communism" (1997, 32–33).

27. Fehérváry 2013 offers a detailed a discussion of the changing meanings of *polgár* (151–142 and 182–185). After Fidesz lost its reelection bid in 2002, the party again redefined itself as an "opposition movement" and modified its name to Fidesz—Hungarian Civic Union (Fidesz—Magyar Polgári Szövetség).

28. See I. Tóth 2001 for a summary of the Magyar Millennium activities and Fowler 2004 for a detailed analysis of its rhetoric of national revival.

29. Interview with Edit Kiss of the Country Image Center, March 13, 2001.

30. Kürti 2001 offers a critical analysis of the Country Image Center's efforts.

31. Fidesz represented these street fighters as heroic freedom fighters battling both Russia and communism, thus disregarding the diversity of political motives (from democratic socialism to staunch anticommunism) that characterized their actions.

32. Interview with Kiss, March 13, 2001.

33. Interview with Sándor Holbok, February 15, 2001.

34. The Magyar Millennium celebrations and the activities of the Country Image Center were the target of much criticism on the left, which questioned the amount spent to fund these activities, as well as the lack of transparency in how these funds were allocated. The MSZP also attempted to offer an alternate interpretation of the millennial anniversary that de-emphasized Saint Stephen's conversion to Christianity and instead celebrated the founding of Hungary's statehood as representing its entrance into Europe as a secular project of progress and modernization (Fowler 2004, 64–66).

3. NOSTALGIA AND THE REMAINS OF EVERYDAY LIFE

1. For studies of nostalgia in Hungary and other postsocialist contexts, see Bach 2002; Berdahl 1999, 2009; Boyer 2006; Boym 2001; Ghodsee 2004, 2010; Hann 2015a; Klumbytè 2010; Kurtovic 2011; Oushakine 2007; Petrović 2013a; Petrović and Sujecka 2004; Platt 2013; Ten Dyke 2000; Todorova and Gille 2010; and Velikonja 2009.

2. References to places distant in time and space were a popular theme in nightclubs and restaurants that were named after Alcatraz, Wall Street, and medieval Hungary, or that reflected the global fashion for Cuba in the early 2000s (Mojito, Buena Vista, and Castro).

3. According to urban legend, Bambi contained tar and was thus unhealthy. An article in 2017 investigated this rumor and discovered that the soda's infamous tar-like flavor was due to the terpenization of its artificial orange flavoring after it passed the expiration date (Tenczer 2017).

4. This is not to say that the regime had no use whatsoever for national tradition. Particularly in the early years of communist rule, authorities drew on carefully selected examples of revolutionary potential from Hungary's history (such as the 1848 revolution) in order to buttress the regime's own claims to national legitimacy. Overall, however, communist ideology emphatically faced the future, rather than the past.

5. At the same time, Hungarians also defined themselves as superior vis-à-vis the standards of production and consumption found elsewhere in Eastern Europe. Although the material benefits of "goulash communism" allowed many Hungarians to consume higher-quality goods than their socialist neighbors, this mythology was rarely actualized on the level of production, given the division of industrial production across the Soviet bloc. Nonetheless, a man who briefly worked in a canning factory during the 1980s told me that he was instructed to take far better care of the products intended for internal consumption than of those scheduled to be exported east to the USSR. This example demonstrates

not only the obvious resistance to Soviet occupation but also the perception that unlike Hungarians, people in the former Soviet Union would "consume anything."

6. As Fehérváry notes in her detailed analysis of *Dolly Birds* and its postsocialist appeal, the film's recuperation of socialist-era mass culture was particularly popular among young Hungarians frustrated by the Western stigma of being backward and unsophisticated consumers (2006, 55).

7. Films about the recent past included *6:3, or Play It Again, Tutti* (*6:3, avagy játszd újra Tutti*, 1999; also made by the director of *Dolly Birds*, Péter Timár), *Little Journey* (*Kis Utazás*, 2000), *Moscow Square* (*Moszkva tér*, 2001), *Csócsó, or Long Live May 1st* (*Csócsó, avagy éljen május elseje*, 2001), and *Forward* (*Előre*, 2002). The German films *Sunshine Alley* (*Sonnenallee*, 1999) and *Good Bye Lenin!* (2003), both of which were enthusiastically received in Hungary, also fall into this category.

8. Newsreels, advertisements, and propaganda films were also objects of nostalgia. The film director Gábor Zsigmond Papp, for example, collected such archival footage to create the popular documentary film series, *Budapest Retro 1* and *2* (1998, 2003), *Balaton Retró* (2007), and *Magyar Retró 1* and *2* (2010, 2014).

9. Both Adidas and McDonald's had opened up shops in Budapest by the mid-1980s.

10. Ironically, many local products were bought up by multinationals in the years following the system change. Nonetheless, in my early trips to Hungary, friends would introduce me to "classic" Hungarian products such as the Sport candy bar (*Sport szelet*) without mentioning (or perhaps realizing) that these brands were now foreign-owned.

11. As Karl Mannheim argues, cohorts share a "common location in the historical dimension of the social process" (1952, 290).

12. Some examples of socialist-era youth films are Gyula Gazdag's *The Whistling Cobblestone* (*Sipoló Macskakő*, 1971), Tamás Almási's *Final Exam* (*Ballagás*, 1981), and Péter Gothár's *Time Stands Still* (*Megáll az Idő*, 1982).

13. The party was established under the name of its predecessor (the Hungarian Socialist Workers' Party) in 1989, changed to the Workers' Party in 1993 (Munkáspárt), to the Hungarian Communist Workers' Party (Magyar Kommunista Munkáspárt) in 2005, and the Hungarian Workers' Party (Magyar Munkáspárt) in 2013. Despite the Hungarian Workers' Party's attempts to reinvent itself as a modern alternative to capitalism, it has never won the 5 percent electoral vote necessary to win representation in Parliament.

14. Interviews with Gyula Thürmer and Attila Vajnai, October 2, 2000.

15. Throughout the film, the cultural obscenity of this repressed memory is literalized in the form of a mysterious phallic object hidden in a box, which one of the male characters repeatedly urges the women he meets to open. At the end of the film, one of them finally removes the object from its box and caresses it lovingly, identifying the provocatively shaped object not as a sex toy or prank, but rather as the finger from the Stalin statue destroyed during the 1956 uprisings in Budapest.

16. Lacan uses the term "ágalma"—sometimes interchangeably with "objet petit a"— to denote the precious and mysterious object hidden in the Other that incites the subject's love. (See his chapter on ágalma in Lacan 2015).

17. Elsewhere, Olga Shevchenko and I analyze how similar nostalgic practices in Russia and Hungary have been mobilized to support very different political agendas (Nadkarni and Shevchenko 2004).

18. Boym also discusses the Eastern European nostalgia for a fantasy of Europe—a desire represented not in terms of "euros, but Eros"—but she focuses on the ideals of democracy and humanistic liberalism that characterized this dream for the region's intellectuals (2001, 222).

19. Fehérváry recounts a similar anecdote from her fieldwork in Hungary in the 1990s (2006, 56).

20. Marko Živković's analysis (2011) of the metaphors and narrative tropes that characterize postsocialist Serbia provides another comparative example of a national imaginary positioned between "East" and "West."

4. RECOVERING NATIONAL VICTIMHOOD AT THE HOUSE OF TERROR

1. Államvédelmi Osztály (State Protection Department) and Államvédelmi Hatóság (State Protection Authority).

2. The first year in which incumbents were reelected to office was 2006, with the victory of the MSZP. After Fidesz returned to power in 2010, it was also reelected to second and third terms.

3. No executions took place at 60 Andrássy Street, however (Szucs 2014, 243).

4. During my summer weekend visits since the House of Terror's opening, the museum continues to be crowded, although now with primarily foreign tourists rather than local visitors.

5. For example, because history in Hungarian high schools is taught chronologically, there is little time available to devote to twentieth-century history, whether that is the Holocaust, the 1956 revolution, or the history of state socialism.

6. Böhm 2002; Pittaway 2002; Seres 2002; K. Ungváry 2002 (and the debate sparked by this article on the letters page of the weekly *Magyar Narancs* in the weeks that followed); and L. Varga 2002. For extended scholarly analysis of the museum and its reception, see Frazon and Horváth 2002; Rév 2005; Sik 2012; and Szucs 2014. For a comparison of the different commemorative strategies in the House of Terror and the Statue Park Museum, see Réti 2017 and É. Kovács 2004.

7. Seres 2002 includes a summary of these criticisms.

8. The Holocaust Memorial Center ultimately opened two years later, in 2004.

9. This law, known as the Numerus Clausus, placed a quota on Jewish admittance to higher education.

10. In later years, the cellar was even used to hold meetings of the communist youth party (Sümegi 2002).

11. As E. Kovács argues, the House of Terror "attempts to question the uniqueness of the Shoah, and make communism appear like Nazism, and communists like Nazis. Moreover, it suggests that the perpetrators and victims were the same in both dictatorships" (2003).

12. Apart from this suggestion that the same people acted as persecutors under both regimes, the House of Terror thus does not address the question of how and why people came to work for the ÁVH. It makes no mention of the possibility that some communist perpetrators may have been earlier victims of fascist persecution (or family members of those victims), just as some victims of communist terror may have once been fascist perpetrators.

13. The Dohány Street "Memorial of the Hungarian Jewish Martyrs" supplemented communist-era memorial plaques to the victims of fascism in Budapest and the countryside, as well as a memorial to Jewish victims in the Jewish Kozma Street cemetery.

14. Hungary is unique among the countries of Eastern Europe in that a substantial population of primarily urban and assimilated Jewish Hungarians survived the Holocaust. (For this history, see Braham 2000; Deák 1982; and A. Kovács 1994. For recent analyses of Jewish life in postsocialist Hungary, see A. Kovács and Forrás-Biró 2011 and A. Kovács and Barna 2018.)

15. See Vásárhelyi (2010) for public opinion data demonstrating an increase in antisemitism in Hungary, and Braham (2014) for a review of antisemitic trends in Hungarian politics since the end of socialism.

16. For an example of internet debates concerning *Sunshine*'s representation of Hungary, see vangog 2000. More recently, the Oscar-winning film *Son of Saul* (*Saul fia*, 2015)

has similarly inspired complaints that the Holocaust in Hungary receives disproportionate international attention and that filmmakers only choose this topic in order to guarantee that their film will win prizes at festivals. (For a summary and critique of these position, see Puzsér 2015.)

17. The Fidesz government erected a controversial memorial to victims of World War II that represented the Hungarian nation as the archangel Gabriel attacked by a German imperial eagle. Critics considered this a denial of Hungarian responsibility and an appropriation of the experience of Jewish suffering. That year, the government also began planning a museum to the child victims and Hungarian rescuers of the Holocaust (the House of Fates), to be designed by the House of Terror's architect and run by its director, Mária Schmidt. While the construction was completed by 2015, the museum has not yet opened.

18. After 2006, Fidesz's primary challenge from the extreme right would be from Jobbik (Jobbik Movement for a Better Hungary [Jobbik Magyarországért Mozgalom]), led by Gábor Vona until 2018. The popularity of Jobbik would push Fidesz to move farther to the right and to become more forthright in its attempts to appeal to right-wing populist positions.

19. As both Apor and Rényi point out, the museum's focus on everyday objects rather than artifacts that might lay claim to historical authenticity also helps support its aim to produce affect in, rather than transmit information to, its visitors (Apor 2014, 329–331; Rényi 2003).

20. For example, there are museums established to remember the experience of communist oppression and Soviet occupation (whether alone or as part of a succession of twentieth-century foreign invasions) in Lithuania (Klumbytė, forthcoming), the Czech Republic, Estonia, and Latvia.

21. Réti shares similar findings in her 2017 analysis of interviews with teenaged visitors to the Statue Park Museum and the House of Terror.

5. SECRETS, INHERITANCE, AND A GENERATION'S REMAINS

1. For example, *Mephisto* (1981), *Colonel Redl* (1985), *Hanussen* (1988), and *Taking Sides* (2001).

2. As of 2019, Szabó has not made a film that addresses his informer past.

3. When the SZDSZ entered a ruling coalition with the former socialists in 1994 to defeat the right-wing coalition, one of its conditions was that these names would be released, but this promise was never fulfilled.

4. Act LXVII of 1996 narrowed the number of positions in politics or public life that required lustration. It also established an archive to preserve the records. Act XCIII of 2000 expanded the categories of people to be screened (Kiss 2006, 933). Csilla Kiss provides a detailed discussion of the obstacles to transitional justice in Hungary's first decade and a half of postsocialism (2006). See also Monika Nalepa's comparative study of transitional justice in Hungary, Poland, and the Czech Republic (2010).

5. At a conference in 2012 (Scientific Research on Collaboration and the Agent Question [*A kollaboráció és az ügynökkérdés tudományos kutatása*] at the Research Center for the Humanities of the Hungarian Academy of Sciences, October 9, 2012), the historian György Gyarmati, director of the archive that holds the state security files, estimated the total number of Hungary's informers to be approximately 200,000. This number covers a spectrum of activity that ranges from long-term informers to those who gave only one report. Other historians, however, have offered numbers as low as 40,000 (Gyáni 2012, 100).

6. Pokorni, who had spearheaded Fidesz's attack on Medgyessy, resigned in response, but insisted that he stepped down not out of a sense of generational guilt but as a protest against those who wanted to turn his family tragedy into a political tool (*Hungary Around*

the Clock, 2002). He reentered Hungarian politics as deputy House leader elected by his party's caucus two months later. Two weeks after Pokorni's news conference, an SZDSZ member of parliament, Mátyás Eörsi, also publicly revealed that his father had also been an informer (*Origo* 2006).

7. According to polls, the majority of voters also supported Medgyessy remaining in office (Gallup 2002).

8. Act III of 2003, On the Disclosure of the Secret Service Activities of the Communist Regime and on the Establishment of the Historical Archives of the Hungarian State Security.

9. In contrast, by the time of the Szabó revelations in 2006, Germany, Bulgaria, and Slovakia all offered full access to the files of the state security, and the Czech Republic would make its files fully available the following year (Gruodytė and Gervienė 2015, 156). For comparative perspectives on transitional justice and the afterlives of the communist state security archives, see for example, Apor, Horváth, and Mark 2017; Borneman 1997; Gökarıksel 2013; Poenaru 2017; and Szucs 2016. For analyses of the ways the communist state security services produced knowledge about their subjects, see Glaeser 2010, Vatulescu 2010, and Verdery 2014.

10. For further analysis of the Szabó affair and these debates, see Rév 2008.

11. The historian Krisztián Ungváry, whose research also exposed prominent informers (such as the cardinal László Paskai), rejected the notion that Hungarians were all equal victims under the socialist regime, arguing that those who were pressured to inform did have some degree of freedom of action, insofar as other prominent Hungarians had refused to inform without suffering severe repercussions: "The files contain countless stories that prove that there were not only traitors but courageous people under the dictatorship. . . . It is in the interest of Hungarian society that we recognize the perpetrators and the victims in these histories" (K. Ungváry 2006).

12. When Tar was revealed to have been an informer in 1999, he initially apologized for his actions, and his friends and colleagues publicly forgave him. In the following years, however, Tar's increasing embrace of the role of victim suggested a lack of remorse that changed his fellow writers' forgiveness to condemnation. Tar died in 2005 (Szucs 2016).

13. "Freedom of Speech [*A Szólás Szabadsága*]," MTV, January 29, 2006; quoted in *Népszabadság* 2006d.

14. Interview with Balázs Bodó, July 4, 2009.

15. See also McClintock 1993 for an analysis of how the nation has been imagined as a family and Schorske 1978 on the role of generations in cultural change.

16. Examples of this trope of absent, departed, and impotent fathers range from Géza Radványi's *Somewhere in Europe* (*Valahol Európában*, 1948) and István Szabó's own *Father* (*Apa*, 1966), to Péter Gothár's *Time Stands Still* (*Megáll az idő*, 1982) and Ferenc András's *The Great Generation* (*Nagy Generáció*, 1985), to Gyula Gazdag's *The Whistling Cobblestone* (*Sipoló Macskakő*, 1971) and Tamás Almási's *Final Exam* (*Ballagás*, 1980). The postsocialist nostalgia film genre also revived these narratives in films such as *We Never Die* (*Sose Halunk Meg*, 1993), *Dolly Birds* (*Csinibaba*, 1997), *Little Journey* (*Kis Utazás*, 2000), *Moscow Square* (*Moszkva tér*, 2001), and *Forward* (*Előre*, 2002).

17. Currently, only the preface of *Revised Edition* has been translated into English (Esterházy 2009); translations of quotations from elsewhere in the book are my own.

18. Although the extent to which *Revised Edition* simply represents a diaristic account versus a carefully crafted artistic expression was of importance to some of the book's reviewers, I agree with Szucs that drawing this distinction is not necessary in order to analyze how the book approaches the challenge of informer revelations (2016, 96–97).

19. See, for example, the critical review of the book in *Heti Valasz*, which was then a pro-Fidesz weekly (Alexa 2002). For a summary of the book's reception, see Szucs 2016, 77–78.

20. Examples include the films *Apaches* (*Apacsok*, 2010, directed by Ferenc Török who also directed *Moscow Sqaure*) and the book *No Live File Remains* (*Élő kötet nem marad*, 2015) by András Forgách.

6. A PAST RETURNED, A FUTURE DEFERRED

1. For more on the 2006 commemorations, see Csipke 2011 and Pribersky 2009.

2. József Debreczeni's best-selling 2012 analysis of the 2006 events presents three dominant interpretations: the right-wing narrative of the protests as spontaneous uprisings, the left-wing accusation that these demonstrations were orchestrated by Fidesz, and a middle-ground position that condemns both the antidemocratic violence of the protests and the unethical behavior of the government (Debreczeni 2012). The author, a former MDF member of parliament and current member of the leadership of a new political party headed by Gyurcsány (Democratic Coalition [Demokratikus Koalíció]), argues that the second interpretation was most accurate. While some reviews applauded his findings, others maintained that the book's narrative of the events only replaces Fidesz's conspiracy theory with another version (Tokfalvi 2013).

3. Although the MSZP also won in 1994 and 2002, many viewed these victories primarily as a rejection of the previous right-wing governments.

4. In early October, Gyurcsány called for a Parliamentary vote of confidence in his coalition government. He won with 207 votes (165 against).

5. As Andreas Pribersky notes in his detailed discussion of the references to 1956 in the 2006 protests, there was no practical purpose to invading the Hungarian television building, since the private station *Hír-TV*, which had close ties to the right-wing Fidesz, was already broadcasting nonstop television coverage that encouraged parallels to the 1956 revolutionaries (Pribersky 2009, 222).

6. Another example of this literalism and reanimation of long-settled remnants of the past was the vandals who raided the grave of Kádár the following year, leaving graffiti that branded him a communist murderer and traitor. Neither the perpetrators nor the skull and other bones were ever found (*Index* 2007).

7. For more on Jobbik's ideology and constituency, see A. Tóth and Grajczjár 2015.

8. The temporality of trauma is thus the opposite of monumental time: whereas the monument sacrifices the present to the triumphal past and destined future, the circularity of traumatic repetition collapses both past and future into the present-day frustration of failed historical mastery. (I draw my understanding of trauma from Caruth 1996.)

9. As always, I use "transition" in its ideological sense, denoting not only the political, economic, and social transformations of postsocialism but also the expectation that such changes would follow a unilinear, teleological model of progress from socialism into a future defined by democratic politics and a prosperous market economy.

10. For analyses of the "normal" in Hungary and other former Soviet bloc contexts, see, for example, Fehérváry 2002, 2013; Galbraith 2003; Greenberg 2011; Rausing 2002; and Wedel 1986.

11. Nadkarni 2007 discusses Uhrin's unexpected success as a popular musician in the early 2000s.

12. Gyurcsány's coarse language gave the appearance of forthrightness, but the fact that he only made his admissions in private made his language seem merely disrespectful rather than honestly blunt.

13. Fehérváry observed similar phenomena in Hungary in the mid-1990s (2013, 227–231).

14. SZDSZ left the government in May 2008, after a proposal to introduce modest tuition and health insurance fees was overwhelmingly rejected in a national referendum. It

failed to receive enough votes for parliamentary representation in 2010, and officially disbanded in 2013.

15. In a reversal of this logic of backwardness, Andrew Graan argues that the experiences of postsocialist precarity may only have anticipated the postcrisis West (2013). Dzenovska and Kurtović 2018 make a similar point about the rise of illiberalism in the East presaging its appearance in the West.

16. Greenberg reports a similar anecdote from her fieldwork, in which her interlocutor pretended to speak from her position as an outside observer in order to give full voice to his anger and disgust with conditions in Serbia (2011, 93).

17. Zsuzsa Gille's examination of the international protest against Hungarian foie gras production argues that there was no space within these debates to acknowledge Hungarian livestock producers as sovereign moral actors (2016, 62–63). See also Fehérváry 2013 (241–243).

18. See Roitman 2013 for a critical analysis of the narrative structure of crisis and the kinds of knowledge its conceptual apparatus enables.

19. Traditionally, "crisis" in the social science literature has followed this definition, conceptualizing social crisis as a discrete event that breaks with the everyday. Scholars such as Claudio Lomnitz (2003) and Shevchenko (2009) have refused this binary, arguing that crisis is not always a break from everyday life but at times the very condition of its existence.

CONCLUSION

1. For an English-language discussion of Fidesz's first term and the responses of the political and cultural opposition, see Krasztev and Van Til 2015.

2. Many new parties have entered the political stage over the past ten years: a phenomenon that Fidesz has encouraged in order to divide its opposition. The following have had parliamentary representation: Politics Can Be Different (Lehet Más a Politika, or LMP, a green party); the Democratic Coalition (Demokratikus Koalíció, a splinter party from the MSZP that is headed by the former prime minister Ferenc Gyurcsány); Dialogue for Hungary (Párbeszéd Magyarországért, a splinter group from LMP); Together—Party for a New Era (Együtt—A Korszakváltók Pártja, a centrist party headed by former prime minister Gordon Bajnai that disbanded in 2018); and Momentum Movement (Momentum Mozgalom, a centrist party that began as a social movement to protest Hungary's bid on the 2024 Olympics). Another important political party is the extreme-right Jobbik (Movement for a Better Hungary [Jobbik Magyarországért Mozgalom]), which was founded in 2003 but came to national attention following the 2006 demonstrations against Gyurcsány. Over time, as Fidesz has shifted farther right, Jobbik has moved toward the center. Its place on the extreme right was taken by a new party, Our Homeland Movement (Mi Hazánk Mozgalom), formed in 2018 by former Jobbik politicians.

3. Kálmán Széll was a prime minister in the late 1890s, but his historical status is relatively obscure and his name was thus not familiar to most contemporary Hungarians.

4. Fidesz's rhetoric does not distinguish between people with legal claims to asylum and economic migrants, in order to portray both groups as unwelcome invaders depriving European countries of their resources and ethnonational specificity.

5. Fidesz's critics often point out that Orbán himself was the recipient of a grant from the Soros foundation to study institutions of civil society as a young law student during the time of transition. More recently, Fidesz used the language of civic movements to characterize its activity as an opposition party between 2002 and 2010.

6. See Nadkarni 2018 for further discussion of Fidesz's attempt to close down CEU. As of the 2019–2020 school year, its U.S.-accredited programs have moved to Vienna.

7. The government put the 1956 Institute under the purview of its own right-wing Veritas Institute. Over the next weeks, all the members of the 1956 Institute resigned.

8. These demonstrators protested not only Fidesz's victory, but the laws Fidesz put in place to favor its incumbency. (Due to legislation Fidesz passed in 2013 that restructured how votes are translated into parliamentary mandates, it was able to claim a two-thirds mandate in 2018 despite receiving only 49.2 percent of the popular vote.) There have also been compelling allegations of fraud in the 2018 elections (Goat 2019).

9. Many argue that these funds have also enabled Orbán and his close associates to amass considerable personal wealth, a condition that has led the Hungarian sociologist Bálint Magyar to term Hungary's current regime of crony capitalism a "mafia state" (2016).

10. Media outlets that are not explicitly progovernment have struggled with financial solvency since Fidesz took power in 2010, as they are deprived of state advertisements and have problems finding sufficient advertisers willing to risk the government's displeasure. Many of the most important oppositional magazines and newspapers have thus found themselves unable to continue financially—and some were subsequently purchased by Fidesz allies in order to be shut down (such as *Népszabadság*) or transformed into another progovernment source (such as *Figyelő*).

11. Opinion polls show that Hungarians overwhelmingly support membership in the EU; in 2018 the proportion was a record 85 percent (Medvegy 2019). However, what they most value is the EU's financial support and the opportunity to work abroad (Pap 2019).

12. József Böröcz and Mahua Sarkar (2017) also point out that although Fidesz's antimigrant discourse is critical of EU policies, it also represents a bid for whiteness and European belonging by enabling Fidesz to distinguish nonwhite "invaders" from Hungary's own laboring populations in Western Europe.

13. After failing to win parliamentary representation in the 2010 elections, the MDF was dissolved and reformed under a new name and party platform the following year (Jólét és Szabadság Demokrata Közösség [Prosperity and Freedom Democratic Community]). Since then, it has not received sufficient votes to enter Parliament.

14. Respondents were asked to evaluate the three periods vis-à-vis the prosperity of the rural population, the situation of families, job opportunities, and pensions. Preference for Kádárism was highest among those over forty, but even among the younger respondents, the majority preferred either Kádárism or stated that they did not know. One important exception was the upper class and upper-middle class, who favored the period since Fidesz returned to power in 2010. Surprisingly, however, although Fidesz voters also prefer the post-2010 period to the Kádár era, this difference was narrow (37 percent versus 35 percent) (Szurovecz 2019).

References

Albert, Mária. 2006. "Bodó Balázsnak" [To Balázs Bodó]. *Élet és Irodalom* 50 (6), February 10.

Alexa, Károly. 2002. "Elrontott kiadás" [Spoiled edition]. *Heti Válasz*, July 26.

Anderson, Benedict. 1990. *Language and Power: Exploring Political Cultures in Indonesia.* Ithaca, NY: Cornell University Press.

Anderson, Benedict. 1998. *The Spectre of Comparisons: Politics, Culture, and the Nation.* London: Verso.

Apor, Péter. 2014. "An Epistemology of the Spectacle? Arcane Knowledge, Memory and Evidence in the Budapest House of Terror." *Rethinking History* 18 (3): 328–344.

Apor, Péter, Sándor Horváth, and James Mark, eds. 2017. *Secret Agents and the Memory of Everyday Collaboration in Communist Eastern Europe.* London: Anthem Press.

Appadurai, Arjun. 2013. *The Future as Cultural Fact: Essays on the Human Condition.* London: Verso.

Arató, Jenőné. 2006. "Irigység és mocskolódás" [Envy and abuse]. *Élet és Irodalom* 50 (5), February 3.

Assman, Aleida. 2007. "Europe: A Community of Memory?" *Bulletin of the German Historical Institute* 40 (spring): 11–25.

Assmann, Jan. 1995. "Collective Memory and Cultural Identity." *New German Critique*, no. 65: 125–133.

Bach, Jonathan. 2002. "'The Taste Remains': Consumption, (N)ostalgia, and the Production of East Germany." *Public Culture* 14 (3): 545–556.

Bach, Jonathan. 2017. *What Remains: Everyday Encounters with the Socialist Past in Germany.* New York: Columbia University Press.

Barta, Balázs. 2000. "Kis utazás: a '70-es, '80-as évek fesztiválja" [Little Journey: the 70s and 80s festival]. *Index*, October 19. http://index.hu/belfold/kisutaz/.

Beck, Ernest. 1992. "Creating Leninland." *Art News* 91 (November): 53–56.

Békés, Csaba, Malcolm Byrne, and János M. Rainer, eds. 2002. *The 1956 Hungarian Revolution: A History in Documents.* National Security Archive Cold War Readers. Budapest: Central European University Press.

Benjamin, Walter. 1968. "The Work of Art in the Age of Mechanical Reproduction." In *Illuminations*, edited by Hannah Arendt and translated by Harry Zohn, 217–251. New York: Harcourt Brace Jovanovich.

Benjamin, Walter. 2002. *The Arcades Project.* Translated by Howard Eiland and Kevin McLaughlin. Cambridge, MA: Harvard University Press.

Berdahl, Daphne. 1999. "'(N)Ostalgie' for the Present: Memory, Longing, and East German Things." *Ethnos* 64 (2): 192–211.

Berdahl, Daphne. 2009. *On the Social Life of Postsocialism: Memory, Consumption, Germany.* Edited by Matti Bunzl. Bloomington: Indiana University Press.

Bindorffer, Györgyi, and Pál Gyenes, eds. 1994. *Pesti utca–1956: Válogatás fegyveres felkelők visszaemlékezéseiből* [Pest street–1956: Selections from the recollections of armed uprisers]. Budapest: Századvég Kiadó; 1956-os Intézet.

Bodó, Balázs. 2006. "Csókolom" [I kiss your hand]. *Élet és Irodalom* 50 (5), February 3.

Böhm, Ágnes. 2002. "A Terror Háza csalódást okozott" [The House of Terror was a disappointment (interview with Holocaust historian Randolph L. Braham]. *HVG* 24 (17), April 27.

Boland, Vincent. 1993. "Stalinist Memorials Find an Undignified Resting Place." *Irish Times*, August 7.

Borneman, John. 1997. *Settling Accounts: Violence, Justice, and Accountability in Postsocialist Europe*. Princeton, NJ: Princeton University Press.

Borneman, John. 2004. "Introduction: Theorizing Regime Ends." In *Death of the Father: An Anthropology of the End in Political Authority*, edited by John Borneman, 1–31. New York: Berghahn Books.

Böröcz, József. 1992. "Dual Dependency and the Informalization of External Linkages: The Case of Hungary." *Research in Social Movements, Conflicts, and Change* 14: 189–209.

Böröcz, József, and Mahua Sarkar. 2017. "The Unbearable Whiteness of the Polish Plumber and the Hungarian Peacock Dance around 'Race.'" *Slavic Review* 76 (2): 307–314.

Boros, Géza. 1993. "A Lenin-kertektől a Tanú térig" [From the Lenin gardens to Witness Square]. *Kritika* 22 (8): 11–13.

Boyer, Dominic. 2006. "*Ostalgie* and the Politics of the Future in Eastern Germany." *Public Culture* 18 (2): 361–381.

Boyer, Dominic. 2010. "From Algos to Autonomos: Nostalgic Eastern Europe as Postimperial Mania." In Todorova and Gille, *Post-Communist Nostalgia*, 17–28.

Boym, Svetlana. 1994. *Common Places: Mythologies of Everyday Life in Russia*. Cambridge, MA: Harvard University Press.

Boym, Svetlana. 2001. *The Future of Nostalgia*. New York: Perseus Books.

Boynton, Robert. 1998. "Enjoy Your Žižek!: An Excitable Slovenian Philosopher Examines the Obscene Practices of Everyday Life—Including His Own." *Lingua Franca* 8 (7). http://linguafranca.mirror.theinfo.org/9810/zizek.html.

Braham, Randolph L. 2000. *The Politics of Genocide: The Holocaust in Hungary, Condensed Edition*. Detroit, MI: Wayne State University Press.

Braham, Randolph. 2014. "Hungary: The Assault on Historical Memory of the Holocaust." Opening remarks at conference on "The Holocaust in Hungary: 70 Years Later," United States Holocaust Memorial Museum. http://www.ushmm.org/m/pdfs/20140318-Holocaust-in-Hungary-Braham-Assault-on-Historical-Memory.pdf.

Bren, Paulina. 2010. *The Greengrocer and His TV: The Culture of Communism after the 1968 Prague Spring*. Ithaca, NY: Cornell University Press.

Buck-Morss, Susan. 1989. *The Dialectics of Seeing: Walter Benjamin and the Arcades Project*. Cambridge, MA: MIT Press.

Buck-Morss, Susan. 2000. *Dreamworld and Catastrophe: The Passing of Mass Utopia in East and West*. Cambridge, MA: MIT Press.

Budapest Sun. 2003. "30,000 Stage Museum Demo." February 27.

Burget, Lajos. 2008. *Retró Szótár: Korfestő szavak a második világháborútól a rendszerváltásig* [Retro Dictionary: Age-defining words from the second world war to the system change]. Budapest: Tinta Könyvkiadó.

Buroway, Michael, and János Lukács. 1992. *The Radiant Past: Ideology and Reality in Hungary's Road to Capitalism*. Chicago: University of Chicago Press.

Buyandelgeriyn, Manduhai. 2008. "Post-Post-Transition Theories: Walking on Multiple Paths." *Annual Review of Anthropology* 37: 235–250.

Buyandelger, Manduhai. 2013. *Tragic Spirits: Shamanism, Memory, and Gender in Contemporary Mongolia*. Chicago: University of Chicago Press.

Caruth, Cathy. 1996. *Unclaimed Experience: Trauma, Narrative, and History*. Baltimore: Johns Hopkins University Press.

Chari, Sharad, and Katherine Verdery. 2009. "Thinking between the Posts: Postcolonialism, Postsocialism, and Ethnography after the Cold War." *Comparative Studies in Society and History* 51 (1): 6–34.

Chelcea, Liviu and Oana Druta. 2016. "Zombie Socialism and the Rise of Neoliberalism in Post-Socialist Central and Eastern Europe." *Eurasian Geography and Economics* 57 (4–5): 521–544.

Courtois, Stéphane, Nicolas Werth, Jean-Louis Panné, Karel Bartosek, Jean-Louis Margolin, Andrzej Paczkowski. 2000. *A kommunizmus fekete könyve. Bűntény, terror, megtorlás* [The black book of communism: Crime, terror, retaliation]. Translated by János Benyhe. Budapest: Nagyvilág.

Creed, Gerald W. 2002. "(Consumer) Paradise Lost: Capitalist Dynamics and Disenchantment in Rural Bulgaria." *Anthropology of East Europe Review* 20 (2): 119–125. https://scholarworks.iu.edu/journals/index.php/aeer/article/view/465/571.

Csepeli, György, and Márton Medgyesi. 2001. "A forradalom főszereplőinek emléke a mai közvéleményben" [The memory of the main protagonists of 1956 in contemporary public opinion]. *Magyar Hírlap*, October 24.

Csipke, Zoltán. 2011. "The Changing Significance of the 1956 Revolution in Post-Communist Hungary." *Europe-Asia Studies* 63 (1): 99–128.

Darvasi, László. 2006. "Én csak az utóbbi tizenhat évről beszélek" [I am only talking about the last sixteen years]. *Élet és Irodalom* 50 (5), February 3.

Deák, István. 1982. "Could the Hungarian Jews Have Survived?" *New York Review of Books* 29 (1), February 4.

Deák, István. 1994. "Post-Post-Communist Hungary." *New York Review of Books* 41 (14), August 11.

Deák, István. 2006. "Scandal in Budapest." *New York Review of Books* 53 (16), October 19.

Debreczeni, József. 2012. *A 2006-os ősz* [The autumn of 2006]. Budapest, Hungary: De.hu Könyv.

Derrida, Jacques. 1994. *Specters of Marx: The State of the Debt, the Work of Mourning, and the New International*. London: Routledge.

DeSilvey, Caitlin, and Tim Edensor. 2013. "Reckoning with Ruins." *Progress in Human Geography* 37 (4): 465–485.

Dienstag, Joshua Foa. 1996. "'The Pozsgay Affair': Historical Memory and Political Legitimacy." *History and Memory* 8 (1): 51–66.

Dirks, Nicholas. 1989. "History as a Sign of the Modern." *Public Culture* 2 (2): 25–32.

Dolar, Mladen. 1991. "'I Shall Be with You on Your Wedding-Night': Lacan and the Uncanny." *October* 58 (fall): 5–23.

Dombrádi, Krisztián. 2000. "Megtalált emlékezet [Found memory]." *Magyar Nemzet*. June 24.

Dominguez, Virginia R. 1989. *People as Subject, People as Object: Selfhood and Peoplehood in Contemporary Israel*. Madison: University of Wisconsin Press.

Douglas, Mary. 2002. *Purity and Danger: An Analysis of Concepts of Pollution and Taboo*. London: Routledge.

Dull, Szabolcs. 2018. "Publicus: Az ország fele elégedetlen a választási eredménnyel" [Publicus: Half of the country is dissatisfied with the election result]. *Index*, April 30. https://index.hu/belfold/2018/04/30/publicus_az_orszag_fele_elegedetlen_a_valasztasi_eredmennyel/.

Dzenovska, Dace, and Larisa Kurtović. 2018. "Introduction: Lessons for Liberalism from the 'Illiberal East.'" *Fieldsights*. https://culanth.org/fieldsights/introduction -lessons-for-liberalism-from-the-illiberal-east.

Eleőd, Ákos. 1994. "Epilógus" [Epilogue]. *Magyar Építőművészet* 94 (2): 24.

Esbenshade, Richard S. 1995. "Remembering to Forget: Memory, History, National Identity in Postwar East-Central Europe." *Representations* 49: 72–95.

Esterházy, Péter. 2004 [2000]. *Celestial Harmonies*. Translated by Judith Sollosy. New York: Ecco/HarperCollins.

Esterházy, Péter. 2002. *Javított kiadás—melléklet a Harmonia caelestishez* [Revised edition—Appendix to Harmonia Caelestis]. Budapest: Magvető Kiadó.

Esterházy, Péter. 2009. "Preface to Revised Edition." In Kamicheril and Robinson, *Wall in My Head*. 136–144. Translated by Judith Sollosy.

Etkind, Alexander. 2013. *Warped Mourning: Stories of the Undead in the Land of the Unburied*. Stanford, CA: Stanford University Press.

Fabian, Johannes. 1983. *Time and the Other: How Anthropology Makes Its Object*. New York: Columbia University Press.

Farkas, Anikó. 2009. "Húsz, negyven . . ." [Twenty, forty . . .]. In *89–09: A rendszerváltás pillanatai* [89-09: The moments of the transition], edited by Norbert Lobenwein, 30. Budapest: Volt.

Fassin, Didier. 2008. "The Embodied Past: From Paranoid Style to Politics of Memory in South Africa." *Social Anthropology/Anthropologie Sociale* 16 (3): 312–328.

Fehérváry, Krisztina. 2002. "American Kitchens, Luxury Bathrooms, and the Search for a 'Normal' Life in Postsocialist Hungary." *Ethnos* 67 (3): 369–400.

Fehérváry, Krisztina. 2006. "Innocence Lost: Cinematic Representations of 1960s Consumption for 1990s Hungary." *Anthropology of East Europe Review* 24 (2): 54–61. https://scholarworks.iu.edu/journals/index.php/aeer/article/download/233 /310/0.

Fehérváry, Krisztina. 2013. *Politics in Color and Concrete: Socialist Materialities and the Middle Class in Hungary*. Bloomington: Indiana University Press.

Fehérváry, Krisztina. 2015. "Hungarian Retro Branding and the Re-Mattering of History." Paper presented at Balkan Kruzhok Workshop, Harriman Institute, Columbia University, October 23.

Ferguson, James. 2006. *Global Shadows: Africa in the Neoliberal World Order*. Durham, NC: Duke University Press.

Fernandez, James W. 1986. *Persuasions and Performances: The Play of Tropes in Culture*. Bloomington: Indiana University Press.

Flatley, Jonathan. 2001. "Moscow and Melancholia." *Social Text* 19 (1): 75–102.

Forgách, András. 2015. *Élő kötet nem marad* [No live files remain]. Pécs: Jelenkor.

Fowler, Brigid. 2004. "Nation, State, Europe and National Revival in Hungarian Party Politics: The Case of the Millennial Commemorations." *Europe-Asia Studies* 56 (1): 57–83.

Fowler, Brigid. 2006. "Concentrated Orange: Fidesz and the Remaking of the Hungarian Centre-Right, 1994–2002." *Journal of Communist Studies and Transition Politics* 20 (3): 80–114.

Frazon, Zsófia, and Zsolt K. Horváth. 2002. "A megsértett Magyarország: A Terror Háza mint tárgybemutatás, emlékmű és politikai rítus" [The offended Hungary: The House of Terror as presentation of objects, monument, and political rite]. *Regio— Kisebbség, politika, társadalom*. 13 (4): 303–347.

Freud, Sigmund. 1959. "Family Romances." In *The Standard Edition of the Works of Sigmund Freud, Volume 9*, edited and translated by James Strachey, 237–241. London: Hogarth Press.

Freud, Sigmund. 1963. "The Uncanny." In *Studies in Parapsychology*, edited by Philip Rieff, 19–60. New York: Macmillan/Collier Books.

Fritzsche, Peter. 2004. *Stranded in the Present: Modern Time and the Melancholy of History*. Cambridge, MA: Harvard University Press.

Fukuyama, Francis. 1992. *The End of History and the Last Man*. New York: Macmillan/ Free Press.

Gábor, Pál. 2000. "Elszámolni a múlttal soha nem késő" [It's never too late to reckon with the past]. *Magyar Nemzet*, October 24.

Gal, Susan. 1991. "Bartok's Funeral: Representations of Europe in Hungarian Political Rhetoric." *American Ethnologist* 18 (3): 440–458.

Gal, Susan, and Gail Kligman. 2000. *The Politics of Gender after Socialism: A Comparative-Historical Essay*. Princeton, NJ: Princeton University Press.

Galbraith, Marysia. 2003. "'We Just Want to Live Normally': Intersecting Discourses of Public, Private, Poland, and the West." *Journal of the Society for the Anthropology of Europe* 3 (1): 2–13.

Galbraith, Marysia. 2014. *Being and Becoming European in Poland: European Integration and Self-Identity*. New York: Anthem Press.

Gallup. 2002. "A választók nem tartják indokoltnak a miniszterelnök lemondását" [The voters do not think that the resignation of the prime minister is reasonable]. https://web.archive.org/web/20080504081800/http://www.gallup.hu/Gallup /release/ppref020621.htm.

Gallup. 2009. "Zimbabwe, Burundi és Magyarország: Adalék az érzelmi tőke és a remény méréséhez" [Zimbabwe, Burundi, and Hungary: Data for emotional capital and the measurement of hope]. https://web.archive.org/web/20090630062958 /http://gallup.hu/gallup/release/zimbabwe_090605.htm.

Gati, Charles. 2006. *Failed Illusions: Moscow, Washington, Budapest, and the 1956 Hungarian Revolt*. Stanford, CA: Woodrow Wilson Center Press/Stanford University Press.

Gavra. 2002. "Orbán-gyűlés a Szabadság téren: A Jedi visszatér" [Orbán meeting at Liberty Square: Return of the Jedi]. *Magyar Narancs*. May 9.

Gerő, András, ed. 2001. *A XX. század ujjlenyomata* [The fingerprint of the twentieth century]. Budapest: Városháza.

Gerő, András, and Iván Pető. 1997. *Unfinished Socialism: Pictures from the Kádár Era*. Budapest: Central European University Press.

Gervai, András. 2006. "Egy ügynök azonosítása" [Identification of an agent]. *Élet és Irodalom* 50 (4), January 27.

Gervai, András. 2010. *Fedőneve: "Szocializmus"—Művészek, Ügynökök, Titkosszolgák* [Codename: "Socialism"—Artists, Agents, State Security]. Budapest: Jelenkor.

Ghodsee, Kristen. 2004. "Red Nostalgia? Communism, Women's Emancipation, and Economic Transformation in Bulgaria." *L'Homme: Zeitschrift für Feministische Geschichtswissenschaft* 15 (1): 33–46.

Ghodsee, Kristen. 2010. "Minarets after Marx: Islam, Communist Nostalgia, and the Common Good in Postsocialist Bulgaria." *East European Politics and Societies* 24 (4): 520–542.

Ghodsee, Kristen. 2011. *Lost in Transition: Ethnographies of Everyday Life after Communism*. Durham, NC: Duke University Press.

Gille, Zsuzsa. 2007. *From the Cult of Waste to the Trash Heap of History: The Politics of Waste in Socialist and Postsocialist Hungary*. Bloomington: Indiana University Press.

Gille, Zsuzsa. 2010. "Is There a Global Postsocialist Condition?" *Global Society* 24 (1): 9–30.

Gille, Zsuzsa. 2016. *Paprika, Foie Gras, and Red Mud: The Politics of Materiality in the European Union*. Bloomington: Indiana University Press.

Glaeser, Andreas. 2010. *Political Epistemics: The Secret Police, the Opposition, and the End of East German Socialism*. Chicago: University of Chicago Press.

Głowacka-Grajper, Małgorzata. 2018. "Memory in Post-communist Europe: Controversies over Identity, Conflicts, and Nostalgia." *East European Politics and Societies* 32 (4): 924–935.

Goat, Elliott. 2019. "Fresh Evidence of Hungary Vote-Rigging Raises Concerns of Fraud in European Election." *openDemocracy*, May 17. https://www.opendemocracy.net /en/breaking-fresh-evidence-hungary-vote-rigging-raises-concerns-fraud -european-elections.

Gökarıksel, Saygun. 2013. "In the Free Market of Names: Polish Secret Service Files and Authoritarian Populism." *Anthropology of East Europe Review* 31 (2): 30–45.

Gondola.hu. 2002. "Orbán: Ebben az épületben hatalmas erő van, a nemzet ereje!" [Orbán: In this building there is an enormous strength, the power of the nation!]. February 24. https://gondola.hu/cikkek/4416.

Gorbacsov. 2011. "A Meki őrzi Osztyapenkó emlékét" [McDonald's preserves the memory of Osztyapenkó]. June 20. http://fenteslent.blog.hu/2011/06/20/meki _osztyapenko.

Graan, Andrew. 2013. "Transitology Revisited, Or How the Trials of Postsocialism Forecast the Precarity of Neoliberal Capitalism." *Anthropology News*, June 9. http://www.anthropology-news.org/index.php/2013/10/31/transitology-revisited -or-how-the-trials-of-postsocialism-forecast-the-precarity-of-neoliberal -capitalism.

Grant, Bruce. 2001. "New Moscow Monuments, or, States of Innocence." *American Ethnologist* 28 (2): 332–362.

Greenberg, Jessica. 2011. "On the Road to Normal: Negotiating Agency and State Sovereignty in Postsocialist Serbia." *American Anthropologist* 113 (1): 88–100.

Greenberg, Jessica. 2014. *After the Revolution: Youth, Democracy, and the Politics of Disappointment in Serbia*. Stanford, CA: Stanford University Press.

Gruodytė, Edita and Silvija Gervienė. 2015. "Access to Archives in Post-Communist Countries: The Victim's Perspective." *Baltic Journal of European Studies* 5 (2): 147–170.

Gupta, Akhil. 1998. *Postcolonial Developments: Agriculture in the Making of Modern India*. Durham, NC: Duke University Press.

Gyáni, Gábor. 2001. "1956 elfelejtésének régi-új mítosza" [The old and new myth about the forgetting of 1956]. *Élet és Irodalom* 45 (6), February 9.

Gyáni, Gábor. 2006. "Memory and Discourse on the 1956 Hungarian Revolution." *Europe-Asia Studies* 58 (8): 1999–1208.

Gyáni, Gábor. 2012. "The Memory of Trianon as a Political Instrument in Hungary Today." In *Convolutions of Historical Politics*, edited by Alexei Miller and Maria Lipman, 91–115. Budapest: Central European University Press.

Györffy, Miklós. 2000. "Everything and Nothing." *Hungarian Quarterly* 41 (159): 112–117.

Györffy, Miklós. 2002. "Saul and Paul." *Hungarian Quarterly* 43 (166): 130–136.

György, Péter. 2000. *Néma Hagyomány: Kollektiv felejtés és a kései múltértelmezés, 1956 1989-ben (A régmúlttól az örökségig)* [Silent tradition: Collective forgetting and the late interpretation of the past: 1956 in 1989 (From being past to becoming heritage)]. Budapest: Magvető Kiadó.

Gyurcsány, Ferenc. 2006. "A teljes balatonőszödi szöveg" [The entire Balatonőszöd transcript]. *Népszabadság*, September 18.

Hack, Péter. 2003. "A magyar átvilágítási törvény" [The Hungarian Screening Law]. In *Ügynökök és akták: Nemzetközi konferencia az átvilágításról és az állambiztonsági iratok sorsáról* [Agents and files: International conference about transparency and the fate of the state security documents], edited by Gábor Halmai, 69–84. Budapest: Soros Foundation.

Halmos, Ferenc. 1978. *Illő Alázattal* [With appropriate humility]. Budapest: Szépirodalmi Könyvkiadó.

Hamilton, Carrie. 2010. "Activist Memories, Trauma, and the Pleasures of Politics." In *The Future of Memory*, edited by Richard Crownshaw, Jane Kilby, and Antony Rowland, 265–278. New York: Berghahn Books.

Hann, Chris. 2015a. "Why Post-Imperial Trumps Post-Socialist: Crying Back the National Past in Hungary." In *Anthropology and Nostalgia*, edited by Olivia Angé and David Berliner, 96–122. New York: Berghahn Books.

Hann, Chris. 2015b. "Backwardness Revisited: Time, Space, and Civilization in Rural Eastern Europe." *Comparative Studies in Society and History* 57 (4): 881–911.

Haraszti, Miklos. 1987. "The World: A Voice from Budapest, 'So There Remains Only the Old Platform, Reeking of the Old Boots.'" *New York Times*, December 13.

Harper, Krista. 1999. "Citizens or Consumers? Environmentalism and the Public Sphere in Postsocialist Hungary." *Radical History Review* 1999 (74): 96–111.

Havel, Václav. 1991. "Power of the Powerless." In *Open Letters: Selected Writings, 1965–1990*, edited and translated by Paul R. Wilson, 127–214. New York: Vintage.

Herzfeld, Michael. 2004. "Intimating Culture: Local Contexts and International Power." In *Off Stage/On Display: Intimacy and Ethnography in the Age of Public Culture*, edited by Andrew Shyrock, 317–335. Stanford, CA: Stanford University Press.

Hirsch, Marianne. 2012. *The Generation of Postmemory: Writing and Visual Culture after the Holocaust*. New York: Columbia University Press.

Hungary Around the Clock. 2002. "Pokorni Resigns Party Leadership over Father's Past as an Informer." July 4.

Hunt, Lynn. 1992. *The Family Romance of the French Revolution*. Berkeley: University of California.

Hutcheon, Linda. 2000. "Irony, Nostalgia, and the Postmodern." In *Methods for the Study of Literature as Cultural Memory*, Studies in Comparative Literature 30, edited by Raymond Vervliet and Annemarie Estor, 189–207. Amsterdam—Atlanta, GA: Rodopi.

Huyssen, Andreas. 2003. "Diaspora and Nation: Migration into Other Pasts." *New German Critique*, no. 88: 147–164.

Huyssen, Andreas. 2006. "Nostalgia for Ruins." *Grey Room*, no. 23: 6–21.

HVG.hu. 2013. "Orbánék Bambival ünnepelték a Fidesz 25. szülinapját" [Orbán and his colleagues celebrated Fidesz's 25th anniversary with Bambi]. March 29. http://hvg .hu/itthon/20130329_Orbanek_Bambival_unnepeltek_a_Fidesz_25_s.

Index. 2006a. "Sztálin, Petőfi és az ötvenhatos események" [Stalin, Petőfi and the events of fifty-six]. February 23. https://index.hu/belfold/otvenh510.

Index. 2006b. "A nosztalgia szele kapta el a tank vezetőjét" [The driver of the tank was caught up by the wind of nostalgia]. November 19. http://index.hu/politika /belfold/1119hgyrgy.

Index. 2007. "Ellopták Kádár csontjait és felesége urnáját" [Kádár's bones and his wife's urn were stolen]. May 2. http://index.hu/belfold/kadar0502.

Ingram, Judith. 1993. "Hungary Puts Old Symbols out in a Park." *New York Times*, October 31.

Internet Kalauz. 1997. "Vár ránk a síkság" [The field is awaiting us]. 2 (12): 15. archive .org/details/Internet_Kalauz_1997-12/page/n13.

Ivy, Marilyn. 1995. *Discourses of the Vanishing: Modernity, Phantasm, Japan.* Chicago: University of Chicago Press.

Jameson, Fredric. 1991. *Postmodernism, or, the Cultural Logic of Late Capitalism.* Durham, NC: Duke University Press.

Janisch, Attila. 2006. "Kedves Zoltán!" [Dear Zoltán]. *Élet és Irodalom* 50 (5), February 3.

Jensen, Steffen, and Henrik Ronsbo. 2014. "Introduction. Histories of Victimhood: Assemblages, Transactions, and Figures." In *Histories of Victimhood*, edited by Steffen Jensen and Henrik Ronsbo, 1–22. Philadelphia: University of Pennsylvania Press.

Judt, Tony. 2005a. "From the House of the Dead: On Modern European Memory." *New York Review of Books* 52 (15): 12–16.

Judt, Tony. 2005b. *Postwar: A History of Europe since 1945.* New York: Penguin Books.

Kamicheril, Rohan, and Sal Robinson, eds. 2009. *The Wall in My Head: Words and Images from the Fall of the Iron Curtain.* Words Without Borders. Rochester: Open Letter (University of Rochester Press).

Kaufman, Jonathan. 1993. "Pizza's Red, Kitsch Is Too in Budapest." *Boston Globe*, October 11.

Kende, Péter. 1993. "Megmarad-e 1956 nemzeti hagyománynak?" [Can 1956 remain as a national tradition?]. In *Évkönyv II 1993*, 7–14. Budapest: 1956-os Intézet.

Keresztury, Tibor. 2002. "Mi vagyunk azok" [We are those people]. Foreword to *A Nyolcvanas Évek: Irodalmi riportok* [The Eighties: Literary reports], edited by Zoltán Kovács and Gusztáv Megyesi, 5–7. Élet és Irodalom. Budapest: Irodalom Kiadó.

Kézdi-Kovács, Zsolt. 2006. "Jelentek" [I am reporting]. *Élet és Irodalom* 50 (5), February 3.

Kiss, Csilla. 2006. "The Misuses of Manipulation: The Failure of Transitional Justice in Post-Communist Hungary." *Europe-Asia Studies* 58 (6): 925–940.

Klumbytė, Neringa. 2010. "The Soviet Sausage Renaissance." *American Anthropologist* 112 (1): 22–37.

Klumbytė, Neringa. Forthcoming. "Sovereignty, Terror, and Suffering in the Museum of Genocide Victims in Lithuania." In *Museums of Communism: New Memory Sites in Central and Eastern Europe*, edited by Stephen Norris. Bloomington: Indiana University Press.

Knigge, Volkhard. 2002. "Statt eines Nachworts: Abschied der Erinnerung; Anmerkungen zum notwendigen Wandel der Gedenkkultur in Deutschland" [Instead of an afterword: Farewell to memory; Notes on the necessary transformation in the culture of remembrance in Germany]. In *Verbrechen erinnern. Die Auseinandersetzung mit Holocaust und Völkermord* [Remembering crimes: The confrontation with the Holocaust and genocide], edited by Volkhard Knigge and Norbert Frei, 423–440. Munich: Verlag C. H. Beck.

Kőrösi, Zsuzsanna and Adrienne Molnár, eds. 2003. *Carrying a Secret in My Heart: Children of the Victims of the Reprisals after the Hungarian Revolution in 1956, An Oral History.* Translated by Rachel Hideg and János Hideg. Budapest: CEU Press.

Kovács, András. 1994. "Anti-Semitism and Jewish Identity in Postcommunist Hungary." In *Anti-Semitism and the Treatment of the Holocaust in Postcommunist Eastern Europe*, edited by Randolph L. Braham, 125–142. New York: The Rosenthal Institute for Holocaust Studies, Graduate Center/The City University of New York. Boulder, CO: Social Science Monographs. Distributed by Columbia University Press.

Kovács, András, and Aletta Forrás-Biró. 2011. "Jewish Life in Hungary: Achievements, Challenges, and Priorities after the Collapse of Communism." Institute for Jewish Policy Research. http://www.jpr.org.uk/documents/Jewish%20life%20in%20 Hungary%20(English).pdf.

Kovács, András, and Ildikó Barna. 2018. *Zsidók és zsidóság Magyarországon 2017-ben: Egy szociológiai kutatás eredményei* [Jews and Jewishness in 2017 Hungary: Results of sociological research]. Budapest: Szombat.

Kovács, Éva. 2001. "A terek és a szobrok emlékezete (1988–1990): Etűd a magyar rendszerváltó mítoszokról" [The memory of squares and statues (1988–1990): an etude about the Hungarian system-changing mythologies]. *Regio* 12(1): 68–91.

Kovács, Éva. 2003. "Az ironikus és a cinikus" [The ironic and the cynical]. *Élet és Irodalom* 47 (35), August 29.

Kovács, Gábor. 2019. "Annyit is ér? Kiderült, mennyit keres és mennyije van a 100 ezer leggazdagabb magyarnak" [How much are they really worth? It turned out how much the 100,000 richest Hungarians earn and how much they have]. *HVG.hu*, April. https://hvg.hu/gazdasag/20190411_Sokkal_nagyobb_az_egyenlotlenseg _Magyarorszagon_mint_eddig_hittuk.

Kovács, Géza. 2006. "Adjátok vissza" [Give it back]. *Élet és Irodalom* 50 (6), February 10.

Köztársaság. 1992. "A szobrok megmozdulnak" [The statues are moving]. 1 (20), August 28.

Kraenzle, Christina, and Maria Mayr. 2017. "Introduction: The Usable Pasts and Futures of Transnational European Memories." In *The Changing Place of Europe in Global Memory Cultures: Usable Pasts and Futures*, edited by Christina Kraenzle and Maria Mayr, 1–21. New York: Palgrave Macmillan.

Krastev, Ivan, and Stephen Holmes. "Explaining Eastern Europe: Imitation and Its Discontents." *Journal of Democracy* 3: 117–128.

Krasztev, Péter, and Jon Van Til, eds. 2015. *The Hungarian Patient: Social Opposition to an Illiberal Democracy*. Budapest: Central European University Press.

Kürti, László. 2001. "Országimázs Központ: Egy állami intézmény működése" [Country Image Center: The working of a state institution]. In *Magyarország politikai évkönyve 2001* [Political yearbook of Hungary, 2001], edited by Gábor Török, Elemér Hankiss, János Szabó, Attila Ágh, László Lengyel, Pál Tamás, and Béla Pokol, 292–302. Budapest: Demokrácia Kutatások Magyar Központja Közhasznú Alapítvány.

Kurtović, Larisa. 2011. "Yugonostalgia on Wheels: Commemorating Marshal Tito across Post-Yugoslav Borders: Two ethnographic tales from post-war Bosnia-Herzegovina." *Newsletter of the Institute of Slavic, East European, and Eurasian Studies* 28 (1): 2–13; 21–23.

La Bruyère, Florence. 2002. "La Droite Hongroise Ouvre la 'Maison de la Terreur'" [The Hungarian Right opens the "House of Terror"]. *Libération*, February 23.

Lacan, Jacques. 1978. *Four Fundamental Concepts of Psycho-Analysis*. Edited by Jacques-Alain Miller. Translated by Alan Sheridan. New York: Norton.

Lacan, Jacques. 2015. *Transference: The Seminar of Jacques Lacan, Book VIII*. Edited by Jacques-Alain Miller. Translated by Bruce Fink. Cambridge, UK: Polity Press.

Lampland, Martha. 1995. *The Object of Labor: Commodification in Socialist Hungary*. Chicago: University of Chicago Press.

Lánczos, Vera. 2006. "Üzenet az igazság(?) keresőknek!" [Message to the truth(?) seekers]. *Élet és Irodalom* 50 (5), February 3.

Legge, Michele and Michael J. Jordan, "Propaganda: A Pop Sensation?" *Prague Post.* October 22.

Lemon, Alaina. 2000. *Between Two Fires: Gypsy Performance and Romani Memory from Pushkin to Post-Socialism.* Durham, NC: Duke University Press.

Levy, Danial, and Natan Sznaider. 2002. "Memory Unbound: The Holocaust and the Formation of Cosmopolitan Memory." *European Journal of Social Theory* 5 (1): 87–106.

Litván, György. 1996a. "1956-os kutatások és viták a mai Magyarországon" [Research and debates on 1956 in contemporary Hungary]. *Rubicon* 1996 (8–9): 54–55.

Litván, György, ed. 1996b. *The Hungarian Revolution of 1956: Reform, Revolt, and Repression 1953–1963.* English version edited and translated by János M. Bak and Lyman H. Legters. London: Longman.

Litván, György. 1997. "A Forty-Year Perspective on 1956." *Journal of Communist Studies and Transition Politics* 13 (2): 14–25.

Litván, György. 2001. "Az elnémult hagyomány" [The muted tradition]. *Élet és Irodalom* 45 (15), April 13.

Lomnitz, Claudio. 2003. "Times of Crisis: Historicity, Sacrifice, and the Spectacle of Debacle in Mexico City." *Public Culture* 15 (1): 127–148.

Lomnitz, Claudio. 2008. "Narrating the Neoliberal Moment: History, Journalism, Historicity." *Public Culture* 20 (1): 39–56.

Lukács, John. 1988. *Budapest 1900: A Historical Portrait of a City and Its Culture.* New York: Grove Press.

MacLeod, Alexander. 1998. "Budapest Finds Profit in 'Ghastly' Public Art." *Christian Science Monitor.* May 8.

Magyar, Balint. 2016. *Post-Communist Mafia State: The Case of Hungary.* Budapest: Central European University Press.

Magyar Hírlap. 1990. "Kivandorló vörös csillagok" [Emigrating red stars]. February 22.

Magyar Narancs. 1997. "Szövetségbe forrt idióta gyermekkorunk [The unbreakable union of our idiotic childhood]." September 11.

Magyar Nemzet. 1990. "Szoborpark: a megsemmisítőtábor helyén" [Statue Park: in the place of the extermination camp]. April 27.

Magyari, Péter. 2010. "Nálunk inkább az ügynököt védik" [Here they prefer to protect the informer]. *Index.* November 29. http://index.hu/belfold/2010/11/29/nalunk _inkabb_az_ugynokot_vedik.

Mannheim, Karl. 1952. "The Problem of Generations." In *Essays on the Sociology of Knowledge,* edited by Paul Kecskemeti, 276–322. London: Routledge.

McClintock, Anne. 1993. "Family Feuds: Gender, Nationalism and the Family." *Feminist Review,* no. 44: 61–80.

Medián Közvélemény és Piackutató. 1999. "A 20. század értékelése" [Evaluation of the twentieth century]. April 29. https://web.archive.org/web/20181203152042 /http://www.median.hu/object.75f7c814-dc6e-4309-b2d5-43c0a8ab2da0.ivy.

Medvegy, Gábor. 2019. "Medián: rekord magas a magyar EU-tagság támogatottsága" [Medián: support for Hungary's EU membership is at a record high]. *24.hu.* March 1. https://24.hu/kozelet/2019/03/01/median-rekordmagas-a-magyar-eu -tagsag-tamogatottsaga.

Molnár, Adrienne, Zsuzsanna Kőrösi, and Márkus Keller, eds. 2006. *A forradalom emlékezete: Személyes történelem* [The memory of the revolution: Personal history]. Budapest: 1956-os Intézet.

Morris, Rosalind C. 2004. "Intimacy and Corruption in Thailand's Age of Transparency." In *Off Stage On Display: Intimacy and Ethnography in the Age of Public Culture,* edited by Andrew Shryock, 225–243. Stanford, CA: Stanford University Press.

Mravik, László. 1990. "Döntsd a szobrot!! (Ne siránkozz?)" [Topple the statues!! (Don't lament?)]. *Kritika* 19 (5): 9–10.

Újdricza, Péter. 1993. "Politics in Stone: 20 Years of Socialist Realist Architecture."
    Budapest Review of Books 3 (4): 146–152.
Múlt-kor. 2006. "Hiányosak a diákok ismeretei 1956-ról" [Student knowledge of 1956
    is lacking]. https://mult-kor.hu/20060224_hianyosak_a_diakok_ismeretei
    _1956rol.
Munkácsy, Márton. 2006. "Megvezette az állambiztonságot - állítja Szabó István" [Szabó
    István claims that he tricked the state security]. Magyar Hírlap, January 30.
Musil, Robert. 1995. "Monuments." In Posthumous Papers of a Living Author, 61–64.
    London: Penguin Books.
Nadkarni, Maya. 2007. "The Master's Voice: Authenticity, Nostalgia, and the Refusal of
    Irony in Postsocialist Hungary." Social Identities 13 (5): 611–626.
Nadkarni, Maya. 2018. "Warnings from the Future? Central European University and
    the Fate of Europe." Fieldsights, April 25. https://culanth.org/fieldsights/warnings
    -from-the-future-central-european-university-and-the-fate-of-europe.
Nadkarni, Maya, and Olga Shevchenko. 2004. "The Politics of Nostalgia: A Case for
    Comparative Analysis of Post-Socialist Practices." Ab Imperio 2004 (2): 487–519.
Nalepa, Monika. 2010. Skeletons in the Closet: Transitional Justice in Post-Communist
    Europe. Cambridge: Cambridge University Press.
Nemeskürty, István. 1989. "Kinek fájt? 'Kivégzett' szobrok" [Who was hurt? "Executed"
    statues]. Magyarország 26 (30), July 28.
Népszabadság. 1990a. "Lenin-skanzen" [Lenin outdoor park]. April 2.
Népszabadság. 1990b. "Megmenekültünk!" [We escaped!]. April 2.
Népszabadság. 1992. "A múltat végképp eltörölni" [Let us make a clean slate of the past].
    October 16.
Népszabadság. 2006a. "Szabó István: Szembesítés"" [István Szabó: Taking Sides.].
    January 27.
Népszabadság. 2006b. "Pokolra kellett mennem: Szabó István Oscar-díjas filmrendező
    nyilatkozik beszervezésének okairól és körülményeiről" [I had to go to hell:
    Oscar-winning film director István Szabó talks about the reasons and circum-
    stances of his recruitment]. January 29.
Népszabadság. 2006c. "A magyar szellemi élet képviselői Szabó mellett: Újabb aláírók
    csatlakoztak" [Representatives of Hungarian intellectual life in support of Szabó:
    Additional signers joined]. January 30.
Népszabadság. 2006d. "Szabó István: Magamat védtem" [István Szabó: I protected
    myself]. January 31.
Népszabadság. 2007. "Nem azt mondták, hogy hazudtunk minden hullámhosszon: Egy
    ötvenéves mondat sikertörténete pontosításra vár." [They didn't say that we lied
    on every wavelength: The success story of a fifty-year-old sentence awaits
    clarification]. March 1.
Népszava. 1990. "Lebontották a csepeli Lenin-szobrot" [The Csepel Lenin statue was
    demolished]. March 15.
Nyyssönen, Heino. 1999. The Presence of the Past in Politics: "1956" after 1956 in
    Hungary. Jyväsklyä: SoPhi.
Octogon. 2000. "Tárgyas Ragozás" [Objective conjugation]. In "Kis Utazás: A 70–80-as
    évek fesztiválja" [Little Journey: the seventies and eighties festival]. Special issue.
    Octogon Architecture and Design: 3–10.
Olick, Jeffrey. 2003. "Introduction." In States of Memory: Continuities, Conflicts, and
    Transformations in National Retrospection, edited by Jeffrey Olick, 1–16. Durham,
    NC: Duke University Press.
Olick, Jeffrey. 2007. The Politics of Regret: On Collective Memory and Historical Responsi-
    bility. New York: Routledge.

Olick, Jeffrey, Vered Vinitzky-Seroussi, and Daniel Levy. 2011. "Introduction." In *The Collective Memory Reader*, edited by Jeffrey Olick, Vered Vinitzky-Seroussi, and Daniel Levy, 3–62. Oxford: Oxford University Press.

Orbán, Viktor. 2000. "Orbán Viktor ország értékelése a Vigadóban" [State of the Nation address at the Vigadó]. *Népszabadság*, February 4.

Origo. 2006. "Eörsi Mátyás is vallott apja ügynökmúltjáról" [Mátyás Eörsi also admitted his father's past as an informer]. July 10. https://www.origo.hu/itthon /20020710eorsi.html.

Ost, David. 2005. *The Defeat of Solidarity: Anger and Politics in Postcommunist Europe.* Ithaca, NY: Cornell University Press.

Oushakine, Serguei. 2007. "'We're Nostalgic but We're Not Crazy': Retrofitting the Past in Russia." *Russian Review* 66 (3): 451–482.

Oushakine, Serguei. 2009. *The Patriotism of Despair: Nation, War, and Loss in Russia.* Ithaca, NY: Cornell University Press.

Pakier, Małgorzata, and Joanna Wawrzyniak. 2015. "Memory and Change in Eastern Europe: How Special?" In *Memory and Change in Europe: Eastern Perspectives*, edited by Małgorzata Pakier and Joanna Wawrzyniak, 1–19. New York: Berghahn Books.

Paksa, Tibor. 2002. "Nincs bocsánat" [There is no forgiveness (Letter to the editor)]. *Demokrata* 2002 (14).

Pál, Antal. 2006. "Tisztelt Főszerkesztő Úr" [Dear Editor-in-Chief]. *Élet és Irodalom* 50 (5), February 3.

Pap, István Szilárd. 2017. "A Kádár-rendszerről álmodoznak a magyarok" [Hungarians dream of the Kádár system]. *Mérce*, November 3. https://merce.hu/2017/11/03/a -kadar-rendszerrol-almodoznak-a-magyarok/.

Pap, István Szilárd. 2019. "A fejőstehén, amely ránk hozná a migránsokat—így látják a magyarok az EU-t" [The cash cow that would impose migrants upon us: this is how Hungarians see the EU]. *Mérce*. https://merce.hu/2019/04/25/a-fejostehen -amely-rank-hozna-a-migransokat-igy-latjak-a-magyarok-az-eu-t/.

Paxson, Margaret. 2005. *Solovyovo: The Story of Memory in a Russian Village.* Blooming-ton: Indiana University Press.

Pepperell, Nicole. 2009. "Handling Value: Notes on Derrida's Inheritance of Marx." *Derrida Today* 2 (2): 222–233.

Pető, Iván. 2002. "1956-ot taní-tani" [To teach 1956 (Book review of Zoltán Ripp's *1956: Forradalom és szabadságharc Magyarországon* [1956: Revolution and freedom fight in Hungary])]. *Mozgó Világ* 28 (3): 118–121.

Petrović, Tanja. 2007. "The Territory of the Former Yugoslavia in the 'Mental Maps' of Former Yugoslavs: Nostalgia for Space." *Sprawy Narodowościowe. Seria Nova*, no. 31: 263–273.

Petrović, Tanja. 2010. "'When We Were Europe': Socialist Workers in Serbia and Their Nostalgic Narratives—The Case of the Cable Factory Workers in Jagodina." In *Remembering Communism: Genres of Representation*, edited by Maria Todorova, 127–153. New York: Social Science Research Council.

Petrović, Tanja. 2013. "Museums and Workers: Negotiating Industrial Heritage in the Former Yugoslavia." *Narodna umjetnost* 50 (1): 96–120.

Petrović, Tanja. 2014. "Mourning the Lost Modernity: Industrial Labor, Europe, and (Post) Yugoslav Post-socialism." In *Mirroring Europe: Ideas of Europe and Europeanization in Balkan Societies*, edited by Tanja Petrović, 89–113. Leiden: Brill.

Pew Global Attitudes Project. 2009. "Two Decades after the Wall's Fall: End of Commu-nism Cheered but Now with More Reservations." http://assets.pewresearch.org

/wp-content/uploads/sites/2/2009/11/Pew-Global-Attitudes-2009-Pulse-of -Europe-Report-Nov-2-1030am-NOT-EMBARGOED.pdf.

Piot, Charles. 2010. *Nostalgia for the Future: West Africa after the Cold War*. Chicago: University of Chicago Press.

Pittaway, Mark. 2002. "Contemporary History and Hungary's 'House of Terror.'" Post to H-Net Habsburg, February 26. https://lists.h-net.org/cgi-bin/logbrowse.pl?trx =vx&list=habsburg&month=0202&week=d&msg=M73roY2C9wVDc7WepQ /ChQ&user=&pw=1/4From:MarkPittaway.

Pittaway, Mark. 2006. "A Home Front in the Cold War: Hungary, 1948–1989." *History in Focus* 10 (spring). http://www.history.ac.uk/ihr/Focus/cold/articles/pittaway.html.

Plachy, Sylvia. 1993. "Graveyard of the Statues: Communist Heroes in Perspective." *New York Times Magazine*, May 2.

Plankó, Gergő. 2011. "Tíz percre újra '56 volt" [For ten minutes it was '56 again]. *Index*, October 23. http://index.hu/belfold/2011/10/23/tiz_percre_ujra_56_volt/.

Platt, Kevin. 2013. "Russian Empire of Pop: Post-Socialist Nostalgia and Soviet Retro at the 'New Wave' Competition." *Russian Review* 72 (3): 447–469.

Poenaru, Florin. 2017. "The Knowledge of the Securitate: Secret Agents as Anthropologists." *Studia UBB Sociologia* 62 (1): 105–125.

Poós, Zoltán. 2002. *Szivárvány Áruház: Egy korszak kultikus tárgyai* [Rainbow Department Store: Cultic objects of an era]. Budapest: Papirusz.

Pozniak, Kinga. 2014. *Nowa Huta: Generations of Change in a Model Socialist Town*. Pittsburgh: University of Pittsburgh Press.

Pribersky, Andreas. 2009. "The Fight for the National Legacy Becomes a Fight for Political Legitimacy: Hungary 2006 as a (Central) European Example." *Politička misao* 45 (5): 219–234.

Prohászka, László. 1994. *Szoborsorsok* [The fates of statues]. Budapest: Kornétás Kiadó.

Puzsér, Róbert. 2015. "Holokauszt: egy monopólium végnapjai" [Holocaust: The final days of a monopoly]. *Magyar Nemzet*, May 28.

Radnóti, Sándor. 2003. "Mi a Terror Háza?" [What is the House of Terror?]. *Élet és Irodalom* 47 (4), January 24.

Ragályi, Elemér. 2006. "Tisztelt Kovács Zoltán!" [Dear Zoltán Kovács!]. *Élet és Irodalom* 50 (5), February 3.

Rainer M., János 2002. "Regime Change and the Tradition of 1956." In *The Roundtable Talks of 1989: The Genesis of Hungarian Democracy: Analysis and Documents*, edited by András Bozóki, 211–222. Budapest: Central European University Press.

Rainer M., János. 2016. *Az 1956-os magyar forradalom* [The 1956 Hungarian revolution]. Budapest: Osiris Kiadó.

Rausing, Sigrid. 2002. "Re-constructing the 'Normal': Identity and the Consumption of Western Goods in Estonia." In *Markets and Moralities: Ethnographies of Postsocialism*, edited by Ruth Mandel and Caroline Humphrey, 127–142. Oxford: Berg.

Regényi. 2000. "A kommunizmus fekete könyve [The black book of communism]." *Magyar Nemzet*. May 5.

Rényi, András. 2003. "A retorika terrorja: A Terror Háza mint esztétikai probléma" [The terror of rhetoric: The House of Terror as aesthetic problem]. *Élet és Irodalom* 47 (27), July 4.

Réthly, Ákos. 2010. *In the Shadow of Stalin's Boots: Visitors' Guide to the Memento Park*. Translated by Erika J. Füstös and Helen Kovács. Budapest: Premier Press.

Réti, Zsófia. 2017. "Past Traumas and Future Generations: Cultural Memory Transmission in Hungarian Sites of Memory." *Hungarian Historical Review* 6 (2): 377–403.

Rév, István. 1994. "Amnesia: The Revised Framework of Hungarian History." *Budapest Review of Books* 4 (1): 2–6.

Rév, István. 2005. *Retroactive Justice: Prehistory of Post-Communism*. Stanford, CA: Stanford University Press.

Rév, István. 2008. "The Man in the White Raincoat." In *Past for the Eyes: East European Representations of Communism in Cinema and Museums after 1989*, edited by Oksana Sarkisova and Peter Apor, 3–56. Budapest: Central European University Press.

Ries, Nancy. 1997. *Russian Talk: Culture and Conversation during Perestroika*. Ithaca, NY: Cornell University Press.

Rogers, Douglas. 2010. "Postsocialisms Unbound: Connections, Critiques, Comparisons." *Slavic Review* 69 (1): 1–15.

Roitman, Janet. 2013. *Anti-Crisis*. Durham, NC: Duke University Press.

Rosenberg, Daniel, and Susan Harding, eds. 2005. *Histories of the Future*. Durham, NC: Duke University Press.

Sampson, Steven. 2002. "Beyond Transition: Rethinking Elite Configurations in the Balkans." In *Postsocialism: Ideals, Ideologies, and Practices in Eurasia*, edited by Christopher M. Hann, 297–316. London: Routledge.

Santner, Eric. 1992. "History Beyond the Pleasure Principle: Thoughts on the Representation of Trauma." In *Probing the Limits of Representation: Nazism and the "Final Solution,"* edited by Saul Friedlander, 143–154. Cambridge, MA: Harvard University Press

Schielke, Samuli. 2015. *Egypt in the Future Tense: Hope, Frustration, and Ambivalence Before and After 2011*. Bloomington: Indiana University Press.

Schmidt, Mária. 2003. "A Terror Háza első éve" [The first year of the House of Terror]. In *Egyazon mércével: A visszaperelt történelem* [With the same standard—Reclaimed history], edited by Mária Schmidt, 176-207. Budapest: Magyar Egyetemi Kiadó.

Schorske, Carl E. 1978. "Generational Tension and Cultural Change: Reflections on the Case of Vienna." *Daedalus* 107 (4): 111–122.

Scribner, Charity. 2003. *Requiem for Communism*. Cambridge, MA: MIT Press.

Seleny, Anna. 2014. "Revolutionary Road: 1956 and the Fracturing of the Hungarian Historical Memory." In *Twenty Years after Communism: The Politics of Memory and Commemoration*, edited by Michael Bernhard and Jan Kubik, 37–59. Oxford: Oxford University Press.

Seres, László. 2002. "Andrássy út 60" [60 Andrássy Street]. *Élet és Irodalom* 46 (6), February 8.

Shaw, Rosalind. 2013. "Provocation: Futurizing Memory." *Fieldsights*. September 5. https://culanth.org/fieldsights/provocation-futurizing-memory.

Shevchenko, Olga. 2009. *Crisis and the Everyday in Postsocialist Moscow*. Bloomington: Indiana University Press.

Sik, Domonkos. 2012. "The Dual Memory of Holocaust and State Socialism: The Case of Hungary." MYPLACE report deliverable 2.1. http://www.fp7-myplace.eu/documents/Partner%2015%20-%20Hungary_deliverable_2_1_submission.pdf.

Simmel, Georg. 1959. "The Ruin." In *Georg Simmel, 1858–1918; A Collection of Essays, with Translations and a Bibliography*, edited by Kurt H. Wolff and translated by David Kettler, 259–266. Columbus: Ohio State University Press.

Sinkó, Katalin. 1990. "Oh Amnézia úrnő (ne) jöjj el! (Gondolatok a szoboröntögetésről)" [Oh Queen of Amnesia (don't) come! (Thoughts on the toppling of monuments)]. *Magyar Narancs*, May 3.

Sinkó, Katalin. 1992. "Political Rituals: The Raising and Demolition of Monuments." In *Art and Society in the Age of Stalin*, edited by Péter György and Hedvig Turai, 73–86. Budapest: Corvina.

Sollosy, Judith. 2009. "Regardless of the Cost: Reflections on Péter Esterházy's *Revised Edition*." In Kamicheril and Robinson, *Wall in My Head*, 132–135.

Stefka, István. 2002. "Csak az emlékezést hírdetheti a Terror Háza" [The House of Terror can only publicize remembrance]. *Magyar Nemzet*. March 5.

Stewart, Kathleen. 2007. *Ordinary Affects*. Durham, NC: Duke University Press.

Stewart, Susan. 1993. *On Longing: Narratives of the Miniature, the Gigantic, the Souvenir, the Collection*. Durham, NC: Duke University Press.

Stokes, Gale. 1993. *The Walls Came Tumbling Down: The Collapse of Communism in Eastern Europe*. New York: Oxford University Press.

Stoler, Ann Laura. 2013. "'The Rot Remains': From Ruins to Ruination." In *Imperial Debris: On Ruins and Ruination*, edited by Ann Laura Stoler, 1–35. Durham, NC: Duke University Press.

Sümegi, Noémi. 2002. "Szabadon a Terror Házában" [Walking freely in the House of Terror]. *Heti Válasz*, January 18. http://valasz.hu/itthon/szabadon-a-terror-hazaban-2742.

Sunley, Jonathan. 1997. "'Best of Communism' CD Invokes Double Standard." *Budapest Business Journal*, October 13–19.

Szalai, Júlia, and László Gábor. 1997. "My Fifty-Six, Your Fifty-Six, Their Fifty-Six: Teenagers on the Revolution." *Journal of Communist Studies and Transition Politics* 13 (2): 26–50.

Szerbhorváth, György. 2008. "Már a retró sem retró" [Even retro is no longer retro]. *Beszélő* 13 (6). http://beszelo.c3.hu/cikkek/mar-a-retro-sem-retro.

Szikra, Dorottya. 2014. "Democracy and Welfare in Hard Times: The Social Policy of the Orbán Government in Hungary between 2010 and 2014." *Journal of European Social Policy* 24 (5): 486–500.

Szőnyei, Tamás. 2002. "Náci propaganda Magyarországon: Gyilkos könyvek" [Nazi propaganda in Hungary: Murderous books]. *Magyar Narancs*, April 4.

Szörényi, László. 1989. "Leninkert" [Lenin Garden]. *Hitel* 2 (14): 62.

Szucs, Aniko. 2014. "From Shrine to Theme Park: The House of Terror in Budapest, Hungary." In *Death Tourism: Disaster Sites as Recreational Landscape*, edited by Brigitte Sion, 226–244. London: Seagull Books.

Szucs, Aniko. 2016. "Entrapped in the Archive: State Security Documents Recontextualized in the Hungarian Art World." Ph.D. diss., New York University.

Szücs, György. 1994. "Not to Praise, but to Bury: The Budapest Sculpture Park." *Hungarian Quarterly* 35 (135): 100–107.

Szurovecz, Illés. 2019. "A magyar felső osztálynak egyre jobban tetszene egy diktatúra" [The Hungarian upper-class would increasingly prefer a dictatorship]. *Abcúg*, May 22. https://abcug.hu/a-magyar-felsoosztalynak-egyre-jobban-tetszene-egy-diktatura/.

Taussig, Michael. 1999. *Defacement: Public Secrecy and the Labor of the Negative*. Stanford, CA: Stanford University Press.

Ten Dyke, Elizabeth A. 2001. *Dresden: Paradoxes of Memory in History*. London: Routledge.

Tenczer, Gábor. 2017. "A kátrányízű bambi üdítőital titka" [The secret of the tar-flavored Bambi soda]. *Index*. February 9. https://index.hu/tudomany/til/2017/02/09/a_katranyizu_bambi_udito_titka/.

Todorova, Maria, and Zsuzsa Gille, eds. 2010. *Post-Communist Nostalgia*. New York: Berghahn Books.

Tokfalvi, Elek. 2013. "Debreczeni József: a fanatikus, aki rögeszmékkel harcol a rögeszmék ellen" [József Debreczeni: The fanatic who fights obsessions with obsessions]. *HVG*, January 4.

Tóth, András, and István Grajczjár. 2015. "The Rise of the Radical Right in Hungary." In Krasztev and Van Til, *Hungarian Patient,* 133–164.

Tóth, Benedek. 1994. "A Sztálin-szobor ledöntése" [The toppling of the Stalin statue]. *Mozgó Világ* 20 (2): 84–98.

Tóth, István Zoltán. 2001. "A millennium évének megünneplése" [The celebration of the millennial year]. In *Magyarország politikai évkönyve 2001* [Political yearbook of Hungary, 2001], edited by Gábor Török, Elemér Hankiss, János Szabó, Attila Ágh, László Lengyel, Pál Tamás, and Béla Pokol, 756–763. Budapest: Demokrácia Kutatások Magyar Központja Közhasznú Alapítvány.

Tóth, Richi. 2016. "Imádjuk Kádár Jánost, mintha kötelező lenne" [We love János Kádár as if it were obligatory]. *24.hu,* October 28. https://24.hu/kozelet/2016/10/28 /imadjuk-kadar-janost-mintha-kotelezo-lenne/.

Trencsényi, Zoltán. 2001. "Fröccsöntött Frédi, csajos römi: A könyvhét egyik sikere a Szivárvány Áruház" [Plastic Fred Flintstone, girlie playing cards: Rainbow Department Store is one of the successes of book week]. *Népszabadság,* June 16.

Tsing, Anna Lowenhaupt. 2015. *The Mushroom at the End of the World: On the Possibility of Life in Capitalist Ruins.* Princeton, NJ: Princeton University Press.

Uhl, Heidemarie. 2009. "Conflicting Cultures of Memory in Europe: New Borders between East and West?" *Israel Journal of Foreign Affairs* 3 (3): 59–72.

Új Tér-Kép. 1990. "Hová tűnt a sok Lenin?!" [Where did all the Lenins disappear to?!]. March 14.

Ungváry, Krisztián. 2002. "A káosz háza" [The house of chaos]. *Magyar Narancs,* March 7.

Ungváry, Krisztián. 2006. "A beszervezés és az útibeszámoló" [The recruitment and the journey report]. *Élet és Irodalom* 50 (20), May 19.

Ungváry, Krisztián. 2017. "'One Camp, One Banner': How Fidesz Views History." In *Twenty-Five Sides of a Post-Communist Mafia State,* edited by Bálint Magyar and Júlia Vásárhelyi, 389–419. Budapest: Central European University Press.

Ungváry, Zsolt. 2001. "Nosztalgia" [Nostalgia]. *Demokrata* (48), November 29.

USA Today. 1993. "Budapest Is Home for Has-Been Communists." September 7.

Vágvölgyi B., András. 2001. "Milyen június 16-a?" [What kind of June sixteenth?]. *Élet és Irodalom* 45 (25), June 22.

Valuch, Tibor. 2000. "A Cultural and Social History of Hungary, 1948–1990." In *A Cultural History of Hungary in the Nineteenth and Twentieth Centuries,* edited by László Kósa and translated by Tim Wilkinson, 249–349. Budapest: Corvina.

vangog. 2000. "A NAPFÉNY ÍZE, mit is mond?" *Index.hu* message board. http://forum .index.hu/Article/showArticle?t=9012081

Varga, Dóra. 2005. "1956 olykor elsikkad az iskolákban" [1956 sometimes goes missing in schools]. *Népszabadság,* October 22.

Varga, László. 2002. "A kommunizmus áldozatai [The victims of communism]." *Élet és Irodalom* 46 (10), March 8.

Vásárhelyi, Mária. 2003. "Csalóka emlékezet" [Illusory memory]. *Élet és Irodalom* 47 (24), June 13.

Vásárhelyi, Mária. 2010. "Kertész Imre szavai a valóság mérlegén" [The words of Imre Kertész on the balance of reality]. *Élet és Irodalom* 54 (7), February 19.

Vatulescu, Cristina. 2010. *Police Aesthetics: Literature, Film, and the Secret Police in Soviet Times.* Stanford, CA: Stanford University Press.

Velikonja, Mitja. 2009. "Lost in Transition: Nostalgia for Socialism in Post-Socialist Countries." *East European Politics and Societies* 23 (4): 535–551.

Verdery, Katherine. 1996. *What Was Socialism, and What Comes Next?* Princeton, NJ: Princeton University Press.

Verdery, Katherine. 1999. *Political Lives of Dead Bodies: Reburial and Postsocialist Change.* New York: Columbia University Press.

Verdery, Katherine. 2014. *Secrets and Truths: Ethnography in the Archive of Romania's Secret Police.* Budapest: Central European University Press.

Vermeulen, Pieter. 2012. "Memory, Agency, Affect" in "Dispersal and Redemption: The Future Dynamics of Memory Studies—A Roundtable." *Memory Studies* 5 (2): 231–232.

Wanner, Catherine. 1998. *Burden of Dreams: History and Identity in Post-Soviet Ukraine.* University Park, PA: Pennsylvania State University Press.

Waugh, Auberon. 1993. "Jurassic Fashions." *Daily Telegraph*, July 14.

Wedel, Janine. 1986. *The Private Poland.* New York: Facts on File.

Wehner, Tibor. 1990. "Jaj a szobroknak!" [Woe to the statues!]. *Hitel* 3 (10): 48–49.

Werbner, Richard. 1998. "Introduction: Beyond Oblivion: Confronting Memory Crisis." In *Memory and the Postcolony: African Anthropology and the Critique of Power*, edited by Richard Werbner, 1–17. London: Zed Books.

Weschler, Lawrence. 1993. "Slight Modifications." *New Yorker* 69 (12), July 12.

Yampolsky, Mikhail. 1995. "In the Shadow of Monuments: Notes on Iconoclasm and Time." In *Soviet Hieroglyphics: Visual Culture in Late Twentieth-Century Russia*, edited by Nancy Condee, 93–112. Bloomington: Indiana University Press.

Young, James E. 1993. *The Texture of Memory: Holocaust Memorials and Meaning.* New Haven, CT: Yale University Press.

Yurchak, Alexei. 1997. "The Cynical Reason of Late Socialism: Power, Pretense, and the Anekdot." *Public Culture* 9 (2): 161–188.

Yurchak, Alexei. 2005. *Everything Was Forever, Until It Was No More: The Last Soviet Generation.* Princeton, NJ: Princeton University Press.

Zentai, Violetta. 1999. "From Losers and Winners to Victims and Perpetrators." In *Paradigms and Contentions, IWM Junior Visiting Fellows Conferences*, vol. 7, edited by Maria Gomez, Ann Guthmiller, and Stefan Kalt, 1–21. Vienna: Institute for Human Sciences. http://iwm.at/publ-jvc/jc-07-11.pdf.

Živković, Marko. 2011. *Serbian Dreambook: National Imaginary in the Time of Milošević.* Bloomington: Indiana University Press.

Žižek, Slavoj. 1990. "Eastern Europe's Republics of Gilead." *New Left Review* 1 (183) (September/October): 50–62.

Zutyu. 2008. "1990: ledöntötték Münnich Ferenc szobrát" [In 1990, the Ferenc Münnich statue was demolished]. *Index*, March 21. https://index.hu/belfold/tegnapiujsag /2008/03/21/1990_marcius_21_ledontottek_a_munnich_ferenc_szobrot/.

Index

www.ingramcontent.com/pod-product-compliance
Lightning Source LLC
Chambersburg PA
CBHW020242290326
41929CB00045B/1525